ENSOR'S ENDEAVOUR

ENSOR'S ENDEAVOUR

A BIOGRAPHY OF WING COMMANDER MICK ENSOR
DSO & BAR, DFC & BAR, AFC, RNZAF & RAF

VINCENT ORANGE

GRUB STREET · LONDON

Published by
Grub Street
The Basement
10 Chivalry Road
London SW11 1HT

Copyright © 1994 Grub Street, London
Text copyright © Vincent Orange

Orange, Vincent
    Ensor's Endeavour
    I. Title
    358.41332092

A catalogue record is available on request from the British Library

ISBN 0 898697 04 3

Typeset by BMD Graphics, Hemel Hempstead

Printed and bound in Great Britain by
Biddles Ltd, Guildford and King's Lynn

Photo Credits

Most of the photographs in this book come from Mick Ensor's own collection.
However, other credits due are as follows:

Peter and Louise Ensor; Frank Reece; Maurice von Tunzelmann.

Permission was also granted to use photographs from the following publications:

Robin J. Brooks, *Kent's Own: The History of 500 (County of Kent) Squadron, Royal
    Auxiliary Air Force* (Meresborough Books, Gillingham, 1982, p. 80).
Andrew Hendrie, *Seek and Strike: The Lockheed Hudson in World War 2* (Kimber,
    London, 1983).
H L Thompson, *Aircraft against U-Boat* (War History Branch, Dept of Internal
    Affairs, Wellington, 1950, p. 16).
RAF Coastal Command Year Book (RAF Benevolent Fund, RAF Fairford,
    Gloucester, 1992, p. 22).
The *Aeroplane*, 25 October 1957, p. 614.
Lifetime of Service (RAF Benevolent Fund, RAF Fairford, Gloucester, p. 84).

My thanks to them all.

CONTENTS

Foreword by Marshal of the Royal Air Force

SIR DENIS SPOTSWOOD, GCB, CBE, DSO, DFC, FRAeS   6

ACKNOWLEDGEMENTS

OF all the pleasures of authorship, few compare with that of writing this page, partly because it is the *last* page (the rest, for good or ill, are done, thank God), but mostly because it offers an opportunity to thank those who made the book possible. I must first thank Mick Ensor for allowing me unrestricted access to his papers and for bearing so courteously with endless questioning. Tony Spooner suggested that I write Mick's story, when pressure of other duties obliged him to abandon a task that he had well begun, and permitted me to use the material he had collected. Without the vivid, detailed memories of Pat Green this book might have been begun, but it would not have been completed.

I have been greatly helped by several members of the Ensor family. In particular, Louise and Peter (whose letters and cheerful friendship have been an essential encouragement); their daughter Libby and her husband Ben Hutchinson, who made me welcome at Double Hill; Louise's sister Florence (always known as 'Toots', who has since died); Mary Sparrow (Jimmy's daughter) who kindly read part of my manuscript and made valuable suggestions; and Vivienne and Hugh, Mick's daughter-in-law and son.

Margaret Goss and Rusty have helped me to a better understanding of several aspects of Mick's life. Bill Andrews, George Carter, Tom Cockeram, Peter Cundy, Russell Laughland, Douglas Pain, Maurice von Tunzelmann and George Westlake shared with me their memories of service with Mick. Thérèse Angelo (of the RNZAF Museum, Wigram), Arthur Arculus, William Bell, John Crawford, Jill Durney, David Duxbury, Terry Gardiner, Rodger Haworth, Errol Martyn, Ian Wellsted and Heather Dalton White have saved me from blunders and/or filled in gaps, as have Sebastian Cox (Air Historical Branch,

Ministry of Defence, London), Yvonne Kinkaid (Center for Air Force History, Bolling AFB, Washington DC), Carolyn Carr and Carolyn Taylor (Librarians, HQ New Zealand Defence Force, Wellington) and Stephanie Tyler-Wright (Office of the Chief of that Force). I am especially grateful to John Chrisp for his excellent painting of a dramatic incident in Mick's career and to Sir Denis Spotswood for agreeing to contribute a foreword.

I value more than I can say the financial support and moral encouragement I receive from the University of Canterbury, my colleagues in the History Department (not least the secretaries) and everyone who bears with me in the Library and in the Photographic Department. The ladies and gentlemen mentioned above are collectively responsible for much that is worthwhile in this book. The mistakes and misjudgements are my very own. Nothing that I write would ever emerge from the grip of electronic machinery without the skill and devoted care of my beloved wife, Ann Margaret Orange.

I dedicate this book to the memory of four good men and true who did not return home from their endeavours: Neville Atkinson, John MacGillivray, Roderick McCracken and Cyril Prior.

Vincent Orange
Christchurch,
February 1994

FOREWORD

I AM pleased to be asked to write a foreword to this book. The author must have faced a formidable challenge in tracing details of events and impressions of more than fifty years ago—and then to carry forward the relevant ones to the less happy story that followed.

I was fortunate, in 1942, to have Mick Ensor in my Squadron. He had earlier gained a well deserved reputation as an Aircraft Captain, not least in bringing back his severely damaged aircraft from an operation over (and almost in) the North Sea.

Whilst we were together in that year I recall, amongst many things, that we had an internal Squadron Training Programme by which each member of an aircraft crew learnt something of each other's role. Mick and his crew paid great attention to this programme and I believe that it was this that stood him in such good stead on a remarkable sortie in the Mediterranean (and possibly during his other successes) which are described in this book.

There can be few who had a better operational record during World War II than did the very young Mick Ensor. This stemmed not only from his natural ability, but from his gallantry and cool approach towards operational flying. The resultant decorations of two DSOs and two DFCs, all whilst he was in his early twenties, must nearly be unique.

Regrettably, for me, our paths scarcely crossed after 1942 and I have found it very sad that he was unable to settle down to Service life after the War, during which he had made such a great contribution.

I readily commend this well-researched biography which will be read with great interest for its fascinating record of outstanding war service and its sympathetic treatment of the later years, tinged nevertheless with admiration for the way they were tackled.

MARSHAL OF THE ROYAL AIR FORCE
SIR DENIS SPOTSWOOD, GCB, CBE, DSO, DFC, FRAeS

CHAPTER I

SELF-RELIANT COUNTRY BOY
JANUARY 1922 TO DECEMBER 1938

MICK ENSOR is very much a Canterbury man. On both sides, his family goes back to the early days of European settlement. The connection with New Zealand began with Edmund Smith Ensor (1808-60), grandson of a Deputy Lieutenant of Norfolk county in England who lived in some style at Rollesby Hall, about five miles north of Great Yarmouth and a similar distance from the sea. As rector of the nearby village, Edmund presided over local affairs with stern benevolence. In 1836, he married a Norfolk lady of his own rank, Ellen Pointer Thompson (1809-50) of Witchingham Hall, and they had nine children in rapid succession. Their third child was Edmund Henry (1840-84) who arrived at Lyttelton, the port of Christchurch, aboard the *William Miles* in 1860 with his brother Charles (1841-1901). Their father having recently died, the brothers had been sent overseas (with a small inheritance) to seek their fortunes under the guidance of another prosperous Norfolk clergyman, Octavius Mathias (1805-1864), who had reached Lyttelton in 1851 and was currently archdeacon of Akaroa in Banks Peninsula.[1]

The Ensor brothers, joined in 1862 by a third brother—Alfred (1843-1922)—made a partnership with archdeacon Mathias to buy a sheep station in the Burke's Pass area, west of Fairlie in South Canterbury. They named it Rollesby in memory of their Norfolk home. Charles managed it skilfully during a decade of generally low prices until 1872, when he and the archdeacon's executors sold it for

---

[1] Information about family background from family members. See also Robert Pinney, *Early South Canterbury Runs* (Reed, Wellington, 1971) pp. 208-210; L D G Acland, *The Early Canterbury Runs* (Whitcoulls, Christchurch, 1975) pp. 85-6 & 316; Peter Ensor's unpublished memoir, 'Many Good Years, Some Not So Good: A History of Double Hill Station', completed in 1990, it covers events up to 1971.

more than it was worth and bought a better property for less than it was worth (according to envious contemporaries) at Mount Grey. One of the oldest stations in North Canterbury, it covered good, rolling country between the north bank of the Ashley river and the south branch of the Kowhai and stretched inland from the sea to the foot of Mount Grey. In the same year, 1872, Charles married Edith (1846-1919), daughter of Valentine Leach of Devizes in Wiltshire, at St. John's Church in Latimer Square, Christchurch. By 1881 he was able to buy out the Mathias interest in Mount Grey. It proved not to be a 'well balanced' property, having too few nicely sheltered eastern faces, but Charles made excellent use of it. He earned a high reputation as an expert judge of sheep in general and the Merino breed in particular.

The fifth child of Charles and Edith was Mick's father: Hugh Charles, born in 1880. In 1907, Hugh married Kathleen Mary McCracken. She was the daughter of James McCracken, member of an old-established Melbourne family who founded a very successful brewery, permitting them to become prosperous landowners. James bought Hayland, a station near Rangiora in North Canterbury, in 1885 and Kathleen was born there four years later, but largely educated in Australia. By the time of her marriage, when she was eighteen and Hugh twenty-seven, Hayland had already become a most impressive estate, thanks to Melbourne beer and Canterbury sheep, and was the natural setting for the district's annual harvest festivals.[2]

Hugh and Kathleen spent most of their life together at Rakahuri, a 3,000-acre sheep farm about ten miles west of Rangiora, which Hugh had purchased in 1903. The original wooden homestead burned down in 1917, but the Ensors had prospered so well that they were able to re-build and re-furnish on a splendid scale.[3] An architectural wonder for its time and place, the style of the new thirty-room homestead has been variously described as "French Renaissance Modern" and "Grand Old Home of the Southern United States". Kathleen had visited the United States and the design was inspired by her memories of that visit. Apparently the local builders failed to match her vision and she expressed her displeasure forcefully. In time, however, she became reconciled to what was, and still is, a very fine achievement.

---

[2] Alexander Henderson (ed.), *Henderson's Australian Families: A Chronological and Biographical Record* (Hamer, Melbourne, 1941) pp. 289-95.
[3] Tessa Copland, 'A Canterbury Tale' in *NZ Home & Building*, December 1988/January 1989, pp. 108-113; David Killick, 'A Taste of Southern Grandeur' in the *Press*, Christchurch, 27 October 1993; G C Sweely, 'An Architectural History of the Early Ashley County' (Research Paper, School of Fine Arts, University of Canterbury, Christchurch, 1988) includes many pictures of Rakahuri and Hayland.

Unfortunately, Rakahuri passed out of the Ensor family in September 1944, some fifteen months after Hugh's death. Now re-modelled and re-named the Okuku Country Lodge, it is much in demand for wedding receptions, business conferences and tourist parties anxious to sample rural life in North Canterbury.

In 1916, Hugh had bought a huge sheep station on the south bank of the great Rakaia river in Mid-Canterbury above the Gorge. Known as Double Hill, it is overlooked by the magnificent Southern Alps and lies about fifty miles south-west of Rakahuri as the crow flies. "This is a grand station," wrote one historian (Peter Newton), "but it runs up to well over 7,000 feet and is *the* shingle country of Canterbury." Hugh and Kathleen lived there between March 1930 and December 1937, returning to Rakahuri only after Hugh suffered a heart attack. According to his son Peter, "Pop was a quiet man who never raised his voice in anger whatever the provocation may have been, but he had a quiet determination and generally got his own way in most things." A good-natured, humorous man, Hugh loved horses, all sports and was easy to live with. He was nevertheless a firm manager of men and well able to keep musterers and shearing gangs under control. A notable sheep-breeder, like his father before him, Hugh was keen to produce an animal both hardy enough to survive on high windswept hills and yet strong enough to produce a first-class fleece. The 'Ensor Corriedale' (an English Leicester-Merino ewe cross) could also be taken off the hills and quickly fattened on good lowland country either for the local butcher or the export market.[4]

Kathleen bore five children in six and a half years. First came James in January 1908 and by June 1914 Anne, Peter, Duncan and Roderick had arrived. She remained nevertheless an elegant women with a keen dress sense and was an excellent hostess on all occasions, formal and informal. After resting on her laurels for seven and a half years, Kathleen did her duty for the last time when another son was born on 5 January 1922. Christened Maechel Anthony, the unique spelling of his first name is said to be because his father disliked the Irish, and yet the boy has usually been known throughout his life as Mick.

He was evidently an afterthought and very much an 'autumn leaf'; virtually an only child not merely in his own family, but also in the entire district, for the Ensors had few near neighbours. Mick's closest friend was his cousin Roderick (Roddy), son of John Davies

---

[4] D N Hawkins, *Beyond the Waimakariri: A Regional History* (Whitcomb & Tombs, Christchurch, 1957) pp. 119 & 317-8; Peter Newton, *Big Country of the South Island: North of the Rangitata* (Reed, Wellington, 1973) pp. 215-6.

McCracken, his mother's elder brother. That family lived nearby at
Hayland and Roddy, who was three years older, would become a vital
influence in Mick's early life. In March 1930, when Mick was eight,
falling sheep prices obliged his father to re-organise the family farming
business. The onset of the Depression hit the Ensors hard and quickly
because the upkeep of a grand home, plus the expense of an
appropriate lifestyle, depended on high prices. Jimmy was left to
manage Rakahuri and Anne stayed there too; Duncan and Rod were
still at boarding school; so that left only Peter and Mick to accompany
their parents in an even more isolated life at Double Hill. For years
Mick saw little of Roddy or any other boys. As for girls, they simply
didn't exist.

"The old house", recorded Peter, "was of sod walls and snow-grass
thatching, later covered by corrugated iron and some weather board
covering on the walls and matched lining on some of the inside walls.
A long, low verandah, one chain [sixty-six feet] in length faced north
with five rooms along it, with a big kitchen and cook's room on the
east side, the sitting room on the north and west side going into a small
kitchen and bathroom, but no connecting passage to the other room.
It was all very dark with only some small windows and no glass doors.
Again on the west side there was another verandah containing a
laundry and big storeroom. These had been of a later construction,
not cob and thatch." It may have been primitive and there was no
money to spare for major improvements, but Kathleen Ensor saw no
reason to lower her standards. A gong sounded each evening to
signal dinner and holding a silver candelabra aloft, she led her family
out of the cosy kitchen and into the frigid, though more graceful,
dining room.

Road access to the homestead was difficult and long remained so.
Stormy weather, coupled with sudden rises in the Rakaia (a most
temperamental, unpredictable river) caused slips or washouts and
many creeks were still unbridged. At that time, there was no electric
power, no telephone and only a battery-operated wireless: it was
switched on briefly for weather forecasts, announcements of farming
importance and never for mere entertainment. As for schools,
libraries, sports grounds, shops, dance halls or cinemas, these were all
far out of reach. Although his parents loved him dearly, Mick *needed*
to be self-reliant and practical at a very early age.

A disproportionate number of New Zealanders in both world wars
made great names for themselves and Mick has plenty in common with
such other famous airmen as Keith Park, 'Mary' Coningham and
Johnny Checketts. Like the best All Blacks, they were country boys

at heart and used to fixing things—fences, tractors or buildings—by themselves. Horses and guns were part of their lives and all four were (or still are) dependable friends to those whom they respected, but ready to be blunt to those whom they did not. When not working, Mick learned—like Park, Coningham and Checketts—to hunt and to shoot. All four men had a distinct advantage over most young Britons when war came in their familiarity with weapons (which they could use accurately) as well as in their understanding of how engines worked and their ability to repair them when they didn't.[5]

In addition, Mick's eyesight was naturally sharp, but equally important was the fact that he used it purposefully. "I was good at spotting deer", he recalls. "My brothers always said that if I couldn't find a deer, there weren't any about." When schoolfriends came to stay, Mick was always surprised to learn how hard it was for them to catch even a glimpse of animals that were glaringly obvious to him. A few years later, he found himself able to spot U-boats or aircraft sooner than most other men. He had acquired an affinity with the outdoors, learning (in his own words) "to read both country and clouds and generally have a feel for wide open spaces." As a Coastal Command pilot, required to carry out patrols lasting for up to thirteen hours over the featureless sea, this background would prove a great advantage.[6]

Mick was brought up in a very happy, hard-working family both at Rakahuri and Double Hill. As a child, he felt particularly close to his brother Duncan, even though Duncan was more than nine years older. For example, Mick once laid out an elaborate network of neatly flattened roads in a clay pit and carved his own fleet of trucks, buses and cars out of old pieces of wood to trundle round them. Duncan, much impressed by this show of energy and imagination, willingly helped to bake tiny bricks for the retaining walls and bridges of his little brother's transport system.

In some ways, recalls Lou Ensor (Peter's wife), Mick was very strictly raised, "but I do know that he generally achieved whatever he set out to do.... He was in his element at Double Hill during the slump years his parents spent there.... A boy with quaint sayings which were made much of by the family, but his mother frowned upon

---

[5] Vincent Orange, *Sir Keith Park* (Methuen, London, 1984); *The Road to Biggin Hill* (Mallinson Rendel, Wellington, 1987); *Coningham* (Center for Air Force History, Washington DC, 1992).

[6] Quotations from Mick, family members and friends in this and subsequent chapters are from correspondence, conversation or tape recordings made by, or made available to, the author.

anybody who disagreed with his statements." It amused her when he brought schoolfriends home for the holidays and then went off shooting by himself, leaving her to entertain "the hapless youths". Lou believes Mick's mother was responsible for his determination to get what he wanted, a determination which would stand him in good stead during the war years, though Mick—Lou emphasises—has never played the gallant war-hero. Quite the reverse, in fact: most people who believe they know Mick have only the vaguest knowledge of his outstanding record during and after the Second World War. As he grew older, his friendship with Peter developed because they shared a love of aeroplanes, but all Mick's brothers (and his sister) were ready to chide him if he stretched their indulgence too far.

Peter Ensor recalls that at the age of about eight Mick talked his mother into attaching a pair of goose wings to one of his jerseys. Trying to fly with those kept him happily occupied for some time and he already had sufficient practical sense to attempt all his take-offs from level ground and never from a hill top. Later, Mick made an aeroplane that he would launch successfully from high ground behind the homestead at Double Hill. One day, a cow took exception to his activities and attacked him. A man heard the cow bellowing and rushed up just in time to grab her by the tail, diverting her attention from this small boy who was in some danger. Though pale and shaken, all Mick would say later was: "the cow turned hostile."

During the early thirties, Mick was taught at home by his mother, helped by a correspondence programme. She was a kind but strict ruler of her large family. Even so, her youngest child often got his own way. His constant and faithful companions were two dogs, 'Big Nig' and 'Little Nig', from whom he could hardly bear to be parted, despite their fleas and incessant scratching. One day, a family outing was arranged and everyone except Mick was eager to leave the dogs behind. Within a few miles, however, his ardent pleas persuaded his father to compromise: he would turn the car back to pick up *one* of the dogs if Mick would thereafter hold his peace, which he did. Whenever he could escape from school work, he would be making model aeroplanes or out shooting in the company of his dogs. He was taught to ride at an early age, encouraged by his parents who were both excellent riders, and from then on 'Tommy' became an essential part of his life.

But Mick did not escape farm work. At lambing time (August and September), Mick had his own territory to patrol every day, looking for ewes in difficulty and lending them a hand, regardless of the weather: and heavy snowfalls, drenching rain or freezing winds often harass farmers at that season in the South Island's High Country. The territory assigned to young Mick expanded every year and before long he was out all day, entirely alone, except for Tommy and Big Nig, taking with him some sandwiches, a billy-can and a packet of tea. He had learned where to find snug shelter, clean water and how to make safe fires. "I had a lot of freedom", he recalled, "and did a lot of riding." And shooting, for rabbits and deer in that district were a "major plague" and Mick did his best to keep them down. At shearing time (in contrast to lambing time) hot, dry gales were a likely hazard and Mick's task was no longer solitary but communal: hard labour in support of professional gangs who were paid by results and therefore had a rough way with idle or incompetent helpers. "I must have been fit", reflected Mick, "because I was neither big nor strong, and yet after working a hard eight hours with the shearers in gruelling conditions I would often grab some food and take myself off to stalk deer."

"I honoured my father and mother", he said, looking back on his early years. "Father was a good organiser and when he wanted something done, it got done. My years at Double Hill were certainly formative: very few children can have had such independence and so many adventures." His brothers, however, found him one job to do that was very much to their taste if not to his. Once a week, one of them had to drive into Methven (the nearest village or 'township', to use the New Zealand name) to pick up supplies and mail, always taking Mick along for the ride —and also to open and close eighteen gates on the way out and eighteen on the way back. Mick claims eighteen, Peter allows fifteen and always laughs at this recollection of brotherly exploitation: "I doubt if he got down and up as often as he thinks he did and I'm sure the exercise didn't break his back." Transport on the station was usually by horse-drawn waggon and Mick greatly enjoyed being allowed to handle the reins behind a team of six horses and, while still young enough to sit on his father's lap, to steer one of the district's few motor-lorries. Anything mechanical interested him, so much so that Mr Pulley, the appropriately-named driver of a traction engine, nicknamed him 'Mr Why'. It was a well-earned title and Mick bore it proudly.

Mick's mother had a keen interest in flying and a Mr Hurrell, who lived in Rangiora and owned an Avro 504K, would sometimes take her up with him. One of Mick's earliest memories is of a tiny biplane buzzing overhead at Rakahuri, presumably with his mother gazing down at her apprehensive family and impressive home. She may also have flown with Captain Euan Dickson of the Canterbury Aviation

Company. Her interest certainly encouraged that of two of her sons: Peter and Mick. They both remember the arrival of the *Southern Cross* (a Fokker trimotor monoplane, commanded by the great Australian pilot Charles Kingsford Smith) at Wigram airfield in Christchurch on 11 September 1928 to complete the first successful aerial crossing of the Tasman Sea.

The whole family had come to town to see this wonderful flying machine and Mick (in his seventh year) enjoyed a perfect view, perched on the shoulders of his tall—and obliging—brother Peter (who was then eighteen). The Ensors had access to the hotel where Kingsford Smith stayed and they all attended the reception held for him and his fellow-heroes. Sitting on a staircase, Mick saw the great men at close range and was enthralled. A few years later, in 1933, when Kingsford Smith returned to Christchurch, Mick's brother Duncan took him out to the aeroplane and they went for a joyride, Mick's first flight: "it made a lasting impression", he recalls, speaking not only for himself but also for thousands of young New Zealanders who dreamed of emulating the immortal 'Smithy'. From his earliest days, Mick had "a never-ending interest in things that fly—why they fly and how they fly." He made himself many model aircraft, progressing to models that flew and operating them from his own little airfields about a mile apart: "I had a real, burning interest in them; I loved them."

In 1935, at the age of thirteen, Mick was sent to school for the first time: to St. Andrew's College in Christchurch as a boarder. Naturally, he was at first homesick (not helped by a dormitory window that looked out towards the familiar Southern Alps) and took a long time to feel comfortable with so many other boys. Cousin Roddy had left school and was working on the family farm, so Mick rarely saw him. Unlike his brother Peter, a splendid athlete who became head prefect at St. Andrew's, Mick's school career was (in his own words) "outstandingly unspectacular". Eating his meals under a board proclaiming Peter's record did nothing for Mick's self-esteem. Although most of the boys were 'townies', not even the farmers' sons had been brought up in such isolation as Mick during his Double Hill years. His parents returned to Rakahuri in December 1937, but Double Hill remained in the family and Mick now regarded it as home, spending as much time there as he could. Apart from hunting and shooting, his interests were strongly practical, especially mechanical, and he did not shine at any sports.

Boarding school, he thought, fitted him very well for service life. "I was never anti-authority, despite the usual escapades. Boarding school experience is good as long as it is fair—which it was, most of the time. Therefore, I was able to accept people who had authority over me quite cheerfully and without question—and when you first join the service as a recruit, that's virtually everybody. Compared to the strict discipline at St. Andrew's, the subsequent indoctrination which I received as a raw recruit in the RNZAF was easily assimilated. I took it in my stride." Mick also learned how to *give* as well as *take* orders, a skill that would soon prove essential when he became a captain of aircraft, responsible for the lives of other men.

The Rector of St. Andrew's set up a hobbies room which became almost a second home for Mick. By this time, as well as building aeroplanes, he had his own .303 rifle and in the hobbies room re-shaped the stock and shortened the barrel in order to shoot deer more accurately during school holidays. It was with money earned by selling deer skins that Mick bought from the United States a model aeroplane kit including a real engine. He assembled the machine and flew it successfully at Harewood aerodrome.

On 20 January 1938, Mick wrote to his mother at Rakahuri from Double Hill. He was then just turned sixteen. "I went out to Cookie's when they mustered", he told her, "and shot seven deer, but I only got the skins of five. These holidays so far I have shot nineteen and got twelve skins, but these are nearly all very light." During the past week, he had been to Home Gulley. "The heat was terrible all the time and the day we arrived out there the butter was just like cream, it had to be poured onto the bread. I rode Wayward round that trip, the first day she could hardly go, the second she was a bit better, and on the last day she tried to bolt coming down the Top Flat." Since then, he continued, he had been across the Rakaia river to Manuka Point. "I only shot three deer, but saw a lot of new country. On Sunday, I went up to the top Manuka Point hut, up the Mathias. The country is very rough and steep up there, but I wish I could camp there for a few days. Jenkins was up there for three weeks a little while ago and brought out 100 skins, about £50 worth. I am going to sell my skins to the Government. Frank's tame paradise duck has got five young ones and he gave me one. I brought it over today. They have been able to fly about a fortnight. I gave it to Lou so it will form a sort of belated Christmas present.... Please tell Jimmy I won 12 shillings at roulette the other night—and kept it."

Mick left school at the end of 1938 and though eager to join the RNZAF was still too young—not yet seventeen—to be considered for pilot training. When he could afford it, Mick would take a flight with the Canterbury Aero Club. On one occasion, he was taken up in a

Tiger Moth by a famous pilot, Bert Mercer. With his cousin, Roddy McCracken, Mick took and passed a course in navigation and mathematics organised by the air force. He and Roddy were rarely apart until April 1941. Being three years older and therefore vastly more worldly wise, Roddy set the pace for Mick to follow, on the ground and later in the air. Mick greatly envied his other friends, among them Malcolm MacFarlane, who were already learning to fly. Malcolm (who later earned a DFC as a bomber pilot with 75 Squadron) would sometimes fly over the Ensors' farm in a Vickers Vildebeest biplane and waggle his wings.[7] "I would stand there, staring dreamily, but I just had to wait my turn."

---

[7] H L Thompson, *New Zealanders with the Royal Air Force* (War History Branch, Department of Internal Affairs, Wellington, 1953), vol. i, pp. 189 & 192.

CHAPTER II

A SMOOTH, NATURAL PILOT
JUNE 1939 TO FEBRUARY 1941

MICK ENSOR left school at the end of 1938 and applied for a short-service commission in the RNZAF on 30 June 1939, when he was seventeen and a half. "As I live in the country", he wrote, "I get very little opportunity for sport other than shooting, of which I do a considerable amount. I have a fair knowledge of internal combustion engines and aircraft construction. I have built three petrol-driven model aircraft. I took a two-year course of practical electricity at school. I have made four flights as a passenger, totalling forty minutes' flying." Despite these excellent qualifications, the RNZAF chose to do without this eager young man for another year. Mick had passed no public examinations while at St. Andrew's (which helps to explain the lack of enthusiasm for his service), but he was currently studying algebra and trigonometry by correspondence with Gilbey's Commercial College in Christchurch and this evidence of determination to improve his potential usefulness no doubt weighed favourably with the authorities.[1]

Mick began his service career at the age of eighteen and nearly eight months as a Leading Aircraftman at the Ground Training School, Weraroa (near Levin, about fifty-eight miles north of Wellington) on 28 July 1940. He wrote to his mother from there in early August. Then and later, his letters were only rarely addressed to both his parents, but there was no rift between them. Mick was simply obeying his father literally, who told him when he left home for his first visit to the North Island: "Be sure and write to your mother every week." Although Hugh Ensor shared his wife's concern for their youngest son, he was a reserved man, not in the habit of revealing emotions—

---

[1] Information from service record, family papers and interviews.

and Mick was certainly in the habit of obeying him. "We are having a very good life up here", he reported, "the food is very good and plenty of it. We get up at 6 o'clock in the morning and either do PT or sweep out our barracks. Usually one morning PT and the next on the broom. We have about one hour's drill per day. All the rest of the day is taken up with lectures. About one hour a day is taken up with general studies, where we see films on flying and navigation, airmanship, etc. Morse code is causing me a bit of trouble, but otherwise I am getting on pretty well."

Last week, Mick went on, "we learnt all about the different poison gases" and on Monday "we are going to learn the Browning gun". It was, he said, the only example in New Zealand of the new model that fires 1,000 rounds per minute. The fact that this information may have distressed his mother, at a time when German armed forces were triumphant everywhere in Europe, seems not to have occurred to him. As we shall see, Mick often mentions death or injury with apparent unconcern. It may well be, of course, that his mother, no shrinking violet herself, much preferred her son to spare her the pretence that he had left home on some kind of working holiday. "We can get morning tea if we want it," he assured her. "Stout and beer are sixpence a pint at the canteen and I am getting very fat.... After work yesterday, I ran in a four-mile cross-country (I wasn't last) and we had a very good concert and dance in the mess last night. Went to bed at 2 o'clock." With two friends, he had walked on the nearby hills that morning and ended his letter with surprising words for a Canterbury man: "I have never seen anything so beautiful as the country about here. Everything is green and even the hens are so fat they can hardly walk. It is all very prosperous-looking country."

From Weraroa, Mick returned to the South Island, to Taieri (south of Dunedin) on 26 August 1940 for elementary flying training in single-engined de Havilland Tiger Moth biplanes. Practically every British or Commonwealth pilot trained during the Second World War began his career in this much-loved machine. It was easy to fly, but not too easy to fly well; it would respond quickly to the controls and, not least, it was simple to build or repair and cheap to maintain. "On a fine summer's day," as one Moth-lover wrote, "there is still today [in 1982] no better way of encapsulating the quintessential qualities of flight than in an open cockpit biplane. You are of the air rather than in it, enveloped by the battering slipstream, which the small windscreens in the Tiger Moth appear to deflect straight into your face, especially in the rear cockpit." Take-off was no problem;

accurate flying was; "and achieving a daisy-cutting three-pointer is an elusive goal that can make your whole day."[2]

"I was delighted to get into aeroplanes", Mick recalls, "and in everything about them. I was told I was over-confident by the Chief Instructor, but I was trying very hard to do the best I could. The business of learning to fly is a bit like someone who knows all about cars, how to build one, etc., but if he's never been taught to drive one he's liable to come unstuck because the conditioned reflexes haven't been tuned to the job. So, I knew a lot of theory, but the actual business of physically flying a Tiger Moth is a question of going through all the exercises, manoeuvres, that sort of thing, until you can do them without thinking—and that is virtually what the process of learning to fly is."

He wrote to his mother from Taieri on 5 September. "We have been having a lot of fun down here this week", he began. Roddy McCracken, his cousin, had gone solo in record time and Mick had achieved that feat on the previous day. "I had done 6 hours 50 minutes and Rod went up in 5 hours 40 minutes. The average time down here is about 11 hours.... I had to spend one and a half hours practicing landing and taking off by myself this morning. It is bad enough when you have nothing else to think about, but when there are twenty other planes all doing the same thing it becomes pretty tiring." That afternoon, Mick added, "my instructor told me I could take a spare plane and go down the valley to practice turns. I scooted down at two thousand feet just under the clouds for about seven miles and found Rod doing steep turns and whatnot with his instructor (each plane has a large number on it so we can tell who is who). I have been up five times today. All our nerves are perfectly all right, these machines are very safe and we have good parachutes, in any case we don't get time to think about what might happen." His first service flight was made as a pupil of Pilot Officer Douglas Greig[3] in Tiger Moth No. 718 on 26 August 1940. It lasted for fifteen enchanted minutes. On 4 September, having flown with Greig on nine of the past ten days, he made his first solo in No. 703, his usual machine. Before that ever-memorable occasion, lasting ten minutes, he had been taken up for half an hour by Flying Officer Frederick Adams, CO of B Flight.[4]

"Dear Mother and Pop", wrote Mick on 22 September 1940 from Wain's Hotel, Princes Street, Dunedin. "Rod and I come in here on

---

[2] John Fricker, 'Tiger Tails', *Air International* (August 1982), pp. 74-5.
[3] Retired in 1945 as Squadron Leader with AFC, US Air Medal. Two Pacific tours as fighter pilot, 1942-3.
[4] Ended the war as a Flight Lieutenant, m.i.d. No wartime service overseas.

Sundays," he told them, "it is a very good place and they look after us well.... Our flying is going very well, a few unfortunates have been weeded out, but most of us will make the grade all right. I have done about fourteen hours solo now. Last week we were doing a lot of instrument and low flying. Low flying with the instructor is great fun, we go flat out at below a hundred feet, dodging trees, going through gaps in plantations, hopping over houses and chasing bulls across paddocks, etc., but the best fun I have had is trying to follow the Taieri River and keep below the level of the willow trees. It winds round all over the place and we have to do steep turns from one side to the other all the way. There is one hairpin bend beside a little town that I haven't been able to get round yet. Instrument flying is not so much fun, we have the cockpit completely covered in and have to fly compass courses and on a rough day it is very hard to keep straight."

They had had "a lot of fun", he went on, during a recent gale: "it blew at 60 mph at 3,000 feet and on the lee side of the hills it was practically impossible to climb and Rod was on the windward side of them and shut off his engine to glide, but instead of coming down he got in an up-draught and actually gained height. At one stage, I battled for half an hour to get over one hill at about 3,000 feet and suddenly got caught in the up-draught and went up to 8,000 feet in under four minutes. It blew great guns from the sou'west yesterday: it took me twenty-three minutes to fly ten miles to Taieri mouth against the wind and I could stay dead still over the one spot by throttling down to 50 mph." Mick did sometimes enjoy life outside the cockpit: at Cargill's Castle, for example, which had "a very good little dance floor and band. There are large open fires all round the room in sort of alcoves where one can keep all the liquor necessary for a good party." In those days, as an unurbanised teenager who knew hardly any women of his own age, Mick was happier (or at least more comfortable) with his new mates and a few beers. Levin, Taieri, the comparatively huge city of Dunedin and above all learning to fly in company with a group of like-minded young men offered sufficient excitement for such a solitary lad. He even regretted, for a little while, leaving Dunedin.

Mick had passed his final flying test, which was, he told his mother, "pretty simple, all I got was ten minutes instrument, some steep turns and a loop, a few spins and three forced landings. All my dual instruction was finished today, Mr Lewis[5] took me down the valley a

---

[5] Flight Lieutenant Colin Lewis, released by the RNZAF in November 1942 to fly with Air Travel (NZ), was the pilot of a De Havilland Dragon that crashed during a Greymouth-Nelson flight on 30 June 1944. Bert Mercer, manager of the airline, died in the crash and Lewis was badly injured.

few miles and let me have a shot at every form of aerobatics he could think of. All I have to do now is about two more hours solo. It gets a bit boring at times, just tootling around doing a few loops and rolls and whatnot every now and again. It is not bad on a nice fine day, but when it is wet and raining and you can't get up high enough to do aerobatics it is just damn cold and miserable. We have also nearly finished our machine-gun firing, which is a good job done."

By the end of September, Mick had more than fifteen hours in the second cockpit to his credit (with Greig, Lewis and, occasionally, Flight Lieutenant Alfred Burbidge, the Chief Flying Instructor)[6] and nearly twenty hours as solo pilot. He had practiced take-offs and landings (normal and forced), sideslips, steep and climbing turns, spins, low flying, aerobatics, cross-country, action in the event of fire, re-starting the engine in flight and instrument flying. During October, he spent much more time on aerobatics. Mick's last flight at Taieri, on 21 October, brought his total of dual flying to over twenty-five hours, plus twenty-five hours solo. He had flown in nine different Tiger Moths. At that time, his longest dual flight had lasted one hour and forty-five minutes, his longest solo ninety minutes; he had not yet flown at night nor carried a passenger. He had completed the first four exercises of the Link Trainer syllabus and been assessed as "above average". Squadron Leader Gerry Stedman, CO of Taieri and one of New Zealand's most experienced airmen, assessed LAC Ensor as an "above average" pilot, but only "average" for navigation and instrument flying: "no obvious faults", he added, though "inclined to be a little over-confident."

The next stage in training began at Wigram, near Christchurch, on 30 October 1940. "Our futures were largely determined by the type of training we got there", he said later. About half the novice pilots (including Mick) were assigned to the twin-engined Airspeed Oxford. Although it was "a tricky aeroplane" to handle properly, in his opinion, Mick has always been grateful (as we shall see) that he was made to master it early in his flying career. The rest of the novices were assigned to the Fairey Gordon, "a huge single-engined biplane" which was easier to fly. Mick was paired with Roddy McCracken, each spending half his time in the pilot's seat and half at the navigator's table, and they had an excellent instructor, Flight Lieutenant Richard Ayling.

Then twenty-four, Ayling was an RAF officer on loan to the

---

[6] Ended the war as a Squadron Leader. Chief Flying Instructor of Otago Aero Club before the war, Engineer Officer in Pacific theatre in 1945.

RNZAF who returned to England in 1943 and ended his distinguished career as an Air Vice-Marshal (CB, CBE, MBIM) in 1969. "I admired him greatly," said Mick. "He was the first real *flying* officer I ever knew and looked just like an officer and gentleman should. He set us all an example, but better even than that he was a good teacher, patient and understanding. Not a man to stand for any nonsense, though: he knew his place and made sure we knew ours. Only now, looking back, do I realise what a dull time he must have had here, teaching novices at the other side of the world in wartime, but he never showed his feelings. Or if he did, I didn't notice. Every flight with him was a pleasure."

Mick's first flight at Wigram was with Ayling in an Oxford (No. 1206) for forty-five minutes on 30 October 1940. His first solo came a week later, on 7 November in No. 256, and ended very badly indeed. He made a poor landing, bouncing all over the place, and on finally coming to a halt, somewhat shaken, he looked up to see Ayling running towards him. "Now I'm for it," thought Mick. "He's going to ground me." Mick sat there, anxiously sweating, until Ayling arrived. "Well, you're still alive," the great man said, staring coldly at the young pilot. Then, after what seemed a very long pause, he smiled and said: "I think that's enough for today, don't you?" and walked away. Mick has rarely felt more relieved.

He usually flew with Ayling, though sometimes with Flying Officer Laurie Page and once with the Chief Flying Instructor, Squadron Leader Malcolm Calder.[7] Having mastered take-offs, straight and level flying and landings, he practiced flying on one engine, action in the event of fire as well as turns, stalls, climbs, glides, cross-country flying and forced landings. By the end of December, Mick had had twenty-eight hours dual instruction and more than twenty-five hours solo in the Oxford, including—on 10 December—his first taste of night flying, making six landings with Ayling and then three on his own. Two of his flights, both solos, had lasted exactly two hours. In addition to Ayling, he flew with Flying Officer Albert Agar[8] on one occasion, practiced "bad weather" and "operational" low flying (once each) and carried his first passenger—AC1 Castons—for twenty minutes on 16 December. He flew sixteen different Oxfords at No. 1 Flying Training School and his assessment, on leaving that school on 17 December, was "above average" as pilot and navigator, though only "average" for instrument flying.

---

[7] Page ended the war as a Flight Lieutenant. Served in Fiji, 1944. Calder, who served with the RAF 1931-9, then transferred to the RNZAF and became Chief of the Air Staff, 1958-62.
[8] Retired in 1970 as an Air Commodore: CBE, AFC.

LAC Ensor then joined the Advanced Training Squadron, also at Wigram, and from 27 December flew regularly with LAC McCracken. They took turns, as pilot and navigator, in making several cross-country flights and practiced formation flying, low-level bombing and the use of a camera gun. Mick also flew with many other pilots, both instructors and pupils, as pilot or navigator in twenty more Oxfords. He had his last Oxford flight on 6 February 1941 and next day enjoyed only his second flight in a Gordon, acting as spotter for LAC Irvine, practicing dive-bombing. Although Mick's first solo landing nearly ended in disaster, in general he had no real trouble with Oxfords. Roddy was also doing well. Nevertheless, Mick still recalls a day when his cousin really frightened him by turning *towards* a hill, shortly after take-off, at a height of no more than 200 feet and only just clearing it. They used to fly low over the farms they knew: it was fun, it was showing-off and it was essential practice too, although Mick never deliberately flew directly over a mob of sheep or a team of horses.

Awarded his wings at Wigram on 16 January 1941, Mick was one of a group of twenty-five new pilots: thirteen would be killed during the war, five became prisoners and most of the rest, including Mick, suffered injury or wounds. Of three other men who began their Wigram training with Mick, two re-mustered as navigators: one was killed, the other captured.[9] Mick left Wigram on 8 February with a commission and (in round numbers) 215 hours of flying experience in his log book: 164 as a pilot (dual and solo, in single- and twin-engined aircraft) and fifty-one as a passenger. He was described as a pupil "who might make a good officer when he adopts a more assertive manner." As for his flying ability, he was considered "a smooth, natural pilot, with nice hands and sound judgement and has attained a standard of flying well above the average. Instrument flying and navigation give him no trouble." In general, "Although very young [he had just passed his nineteenth birthday], Ensor is a keen and determined worker, and possesses plenty of initiative and personality to warrant a commission. He is of good appearance and address and is interested in flying to an unusual degree." In Mick's opinion, the standard of training at both Taieri and Wigram was good and pupils certainly got plenty of time in the air. Looking back, however, he regrets the fact that so little time was spent on instrument or bad weather or night flying: all three of which were

---

[9] Fates of Course 4A members checked by aviation historians Errol W Martyn and David Duxbury.

essential parts of operational flying in Britain.

In late February, Mick bade farewell to his parents at Rakahuri. He would never see his father again, for he died of a heart attack in June 1943, aged sixty-three, while trying to start a pump engine in a shed behind the house. Mick's mother told him that his father's dogs hung about that shed for days afterwards, refusing to leave. Nor would Mick ever live at Rakahuri again, for by the time he returned to New Zealand, both house and farm had been sold.

CHAPTER III

A FORTUNATE DIAGNOSIS
FEBRUARY TO JULY 1941

PILOT OFFICER Ensor sailed from Auckland with many other New Zealanders as well as Australians on 27 February 1941. He was nearly two months past his nineteenth birthday on leaving his homeland for the first time. These young warriors travelled across the Pacific to Vancouver in British Columbia via Suva in Fiji aboard a luxuriously-appointed Union Steamship Company liner, the *Awatea* (13,482 tons). Mick shared a cabin with a Dunedin man, Frank Reece, who kept a diary which has survived.[1] They agreed that the food was not too bad, "but not like home or even like Wigram." More disturbing was an instruction that from now on they must cease "fraternizing" with the NCOs, even those with whom they had trained. "Seems hard to do this," recorded Frank, "and will cause some ill opinions, but mostly we all understand the situation."

While still at sea, on 15 March, Mick wrote to his parents. "We expect to reach Vancouver tonight", he said, "and I am sending this letter back with the ship.... The night before last, the Australians and New Zealanders got together and put on a very good concert of one-act plays, music and singing. One or two Maori gunners have very good voices and they, with about a dozen other chaps with guitars, sang some Maori songs which got about the best applause of the lot." He enclosed with this letter a sketch he had made of the *Awatea's* escort, as seen through his porthole. That escort was the *Prince Rupert*,

---

[1] Loaned to me by Frank himself and much used in the present chapter. Requisitioned by the British Ministry of Transport in September 1941 for use as a troop transport, the *Awatea* was stripped of its comfortable fittings, converted into an infantry landing ship and sunk during the Allied landings in North Africa in November 1942 (John Crawford, *Atlantic Kiwis: New Zealand and the Battle of the Atlantic* NZ Defence Force, Wellington, 1993) p. 24.

a small Canadian steamer converted into a gunboat, which accompanied the *Awatea* from Fiji to Canada. Mick was handy with a pencil (and later with a paint brush) and the accuracy of his sketch is neatly confirmed by a photograph taken from a similar angle by Frank Reece.

Landing first in Victoria, British Columbia, during the morning of 16 March, the New Zealanders (together with a couple of hundred Australian airmen who had sailed with them) were amazed to be invited to march through the streets of the port. Their amazement turned to delight when they found that brass bands had assembled to march with them, front and rear, and numerous people lined the streets to cheer "the Anzacs". Confetti and flowers were thrown and some girls kissed the men as they passed by. Actually, they dashed up to the column, bestowed a hasty peck on the cheek of a willing face and dashed back. None singled out either Mick or Frank, though they smiled as invitingly as they could. Re-embarking after this exhilarating interlude, everyone finally left the *Awatea* that evening, at Vancouver. Fleets of buses carried them to the railway station and their train departed almost at once. They crossed Canada in style during the next few days, swept along by a huge and magnificent steam locomotive—No. 6027—which they photographed whenever it stopped to take on water and fuel. Shortly before the war, as they were frequently told, this locomotive had been selected to pull the train of His Majesty King George VI when he visited Canada.

Plenty of snow fell throughout the journey and they were granted only the briefest glimpses of Edmonton, Winnipeg and Ottawa. All the untrained personnel were dropped off at various places and the survivors finally reached a Royal Canadian Air Force base at Debert, near New Glasgow in Nova Scotia, late on 21 March: "the last place on earth", was Frank Reece's initial impression. It had been snowing all day and was bitterly cold. No-one was expecting them and when they were picked up, after hanging about the station for an hour, they found the base very crowded. Although a friendly reception and effective central heating did something to improve their spirits, Mick agreed with Frank: "all the boys wish they were back in New Zealand."

While waiting for a ship to England, they had nothing to do, but numerous people in New Glasgow were only too eager to entertain them. "Rod and I", wrote Mick to his mother on 28 March, "are with a Mr and Mrs Frank Sutherland. Mr Sutherland is one of the leading lights of the town and his daughter Kaye takes us everywhere in the car and is giving us a royal time. We have all been made honorary members of the club and all the sporting outfits such as the curling club. We have done a bit of ice skating, but up here they use the skating rink for curling.... It is something like bowls, but is played with sort of flat stones on ice. The club members think nothing of going 200 miles to play a curling match." Mick finished the letter on 2 April. "The people gave us a wonderful send-off when we left, they even closed Woolworths so the girls could go down and kiss all the RNZAF goodbye! Mr Sutherland would not hear of us going in the train, so he and Kaye drove us over here in the car. He even wanted to give us $50 each, but of course we couldn't accept it even though we were broke."

But Mick did not leave Canada, not yet. On 4 April, a case of scarlet fever was identified at Debert and everyone was tested to see if they were liable to catch it. Mick, Frank Reece and Reg Baker were among a lucky handful to test positive. Consequently, they were sent to bed and left behind when the rest of their companions sailed for England. Those men were all assigned to Bomber Command and many of them (including Mick's cousin and dear friend, Roddy McCracken) were dead before Christmas. Others were wounded or imprisoned. He only saw Roddy once more before he was shot down and killed in August while flying a Bomber Command Blenheim over the Netherlands.

Meanwhile, Mick was found not to have scarlet fever after all and on 15 April he wrote home from Debert. "It is just over a week since Rod and co. left here", he told them, "and Reg Baker, Frank Reece and myself are the only NZ officers left. Frank and I are going now, but Reg has to wait and he will join us in about a week after we land, I hope." Reg, in fact, was assigned to Fighter Command and became an outstanding combat pilot and squadron commander before losing his life while flying a De Havilland Mosquito over Germany in February 1945. After Mick left, Grace Sutherland wrote to his mother on 27 April to say how much she had enjoyed the visit of "Maechel" and Roddy. "I think they enjoyed themselves, they were so interested in learning our Canadian ways and no doubt some of our peculiarities amused them." Grace thought Maechel "the dearest boy, he is so young and full of spirit and so interested in his work. Good Friday we motored to Halifax, just one hundred miles from here, we showed them the points of interest and the harbor was full of ships. Maechel was so anxious to get started, he loves his work. I am sorry to say we have no sons, just one daughter, so we are only too pleased to do any little thing we can for somebody's boy, who is brave enough to go over and fight for us. We tried to cook the things they liked. One night at dinner Maechel said: 'Mrs Sutherland, I could eat broiled steak and peaches every day.'"

Halifax harbour was indeed full of ships, freighters and escort vessels of all kinds, a breathtaking sight. Among them were the British battleship *Ramillies*: Mick would next see her more than two years later, when hard operations had quite eliminated the boyishness which so charmed Grace Sutherland. He also saw his first submarine (a British one) and his first Hudson aircraft (trussed up in canvas, as deck cargo aboard a freighter). Submarines and Hudsons would soon become essential parts of his life. Mick sailed from Halifax on 16 April aboard HMS *California* (Captain Pope), an armed merchant cruiser (16,792 tons):[2] "slow and as old as the hills," wrote Frank Reece. She was a great disappointment after the comfort enjoyed aboard the *Awatea*. The New Zealanders now learned that their virtual peacetime days were behind them. They were lectured on discipline, lifeboat drill and assigned fire-fighting positions. It was no doubt just as well that they did not realise how dangerous an Atlantic crossing had become: no fewer than 174 ships had been sunk during the first three months of 1941 and forty-five more were destroyed during that month of April. Mick's crossing was an exceptionally fortunate one.[3]

The *California* formed part of the escort for a convoy of forty-six ships. Usually she sailed somewhere in the middle, except for sudden forays to look for a suspected U-boat or to assist a straggling freighter. Impressed by this show of aggression, Mick asked an officer about the performance of the guns and was told that since the deck mountings were insecure, no practice shooting with live ammunition had yet been attempted. "Not to worry," the officer added cheerfully, "if Jerry shows his ugly head, we'll give him what-for." Mick smiled and walked away, realising, for the first time in his life, that there are indeed times when "ignorance is bliss." One night they heard "Lord Haw Haw" (William Joyce, a Briton who served Hitler) announce over German radio the sinking of the *California*. This news delighted everyone aboard and some sailors told Mick that this was the seventh time they had gone down without even getting their feet wet.

At 9.15 am on 27 April, after ten days of boredom punctuated only by frequent lifeboat drills, fire-fighting practices and evening cinema shows, the *California* left the convoy and steamed at maximum speed for Iceland, accompanied by a single destroyer. She anchored next day in the narrow Hvalfjordhur, near Reykjavik, close to HMS *Hood*. Mick had never seen so impressive a man-made sight and was

---

[2] She would be set on fire and destroyed by German aircraft west of Oporto, Portugal, in July 1943: J Rohwer & G Hummelchen, *Chronology of the War at Sea* (Greenhill Books, London, 1992) pp. 7 & 222.
[3] John Terraine, *Business in Great Waters: The U-Boat Wars, 1916-1945* (Leo Cooper, London, 1989), p. 767.

astounded to learn, less than a month later, that such a mighty battle-ship could be utterly destroyed within a few minutes. Some 900 men immediately transferred to a small ferry, the *Royal Ulsterman* (3,000 tons), which in peacetime plied between Glasgow and Belfast. Mick and Frank were the only New Zealanders aboard and once again shared a tiny cabin. Though overcrowded, the ferry maintained an excellent speed and safely reached Greenock in the Firth of Clyde on 1 May, anchoring about 10 am. En route, as they passed the southern end of the Outer Hebrides (islands with which Mick would become very familiar) they were alarmed and saddened to see several ships lying wrecked along the coasts.

Mick and Frank were by now shrewd travellers and managed to bag a compartment to themselves on a special train heading towards London. After more than two months at sea, with only a brief interval in a wintry Nova Scotia, the New Zealanders were greatly refreshed by the sight of lush green grass and rolling, snow-free countryside. Their long journey finally ended at RAF Uxbridge, west of London, at 6 am on 2 May 1941. Exactly ten weeks had passed since Mick left Rakahuri. Uxbridge was a first-class station, run with a style not then common in New Zealand. For example, on arriving in the Mess, Mick asked a waiter if they might have some tea. The waiter nodded gravely, murmuring: "China or Ceylon, Sir?" Later, Mick and Frank agreed that their bumbling responses to this question had done nothing for their status as officers and gentlemen in the eyes of the servants.

During the following week, they were allowed to visit the capital and take in a host of indelible impressions: the sight of Spitfires and Hurricanes hurtling overhead, as well as a glimpse of a huge, brand-new four-engined Short Stirling bomber; the sight also of widespread destruction of houses, shops and public buildings. Mick tried on his first gas mask, filled in his first identity card, stood in his first queue for a meal; sampled his first glass of weak, wartime British beer; experienced his first air raid; stumbled about in the blackout for the first time; enjoyed his first journey by underground railway and was struck dumb by his first sight of hundreds of men, women and children crowding onto the platforms of tube stations in the late afternoon to take shelter from the expected German bombers.

Mick was luckier than many of his fellow-countrymen in that he had relatives waiting to greet him in and around London: his sister-in-law Lou (Peter's wife) had one sister (Dorothy) living in Amersham with her husband Bob Strang, and another sister (Clare) living in Henley-on-Thames with her husband John Cridlan. Mick also had a godmother on hand: Nancy, Lady Campbell, wife of Sir Charles Campbell. They had left a beautiful home and sheep station called Locheil (near Hanmer in North Canterbury) to retire to the Isle of Wight. And not least there was Betty Trewin, an old family friend, who lived in London. Throughout the war, these men and women were only too pleased to offer Mick their friendship and hospitality.

Having been assigned to Coastal Command, a decision that probably saved his life as well as giving him the opportunity to excel, Mick went to Andover in Hampshire on 10 May for operational training. Andover had been the prewar home of the RAF Staff College and so the Mess was very comfortable (even more so than Uxbridge) and catering remained in the hands of an expert pre-war civilian staff. There were good pubs in the nearby town and surrounding countryside and the Southern Railway carried one into Waterloo quite quickly, if the line was not blocked as a result of air raids or required for a diversion. No sooner had Mick and his fellow-trainees settled in for their first night than German aircraft arrived. "One flew right over this building," recorded Frank Reece in his diary, "at about 200 feet. Never let any bombs go. I shivered in my shoes or rather pyjamas." Others did drop bombs, however, causing casualties and shattering every window in the lecture rooms. These were only slowly replaced and Mick, never an enthusiast for lecture rooms at the best of times, vividly recalls how cold and noisy they were. His own room had been damaged, in his absence, costing him most of his clothing. Shortly after the raid, it was decided to move these potentially valuable pilots to a place of greater safety: Thruxton Manor, a country house about four miles away. "Although it is a lovely old place", Mick told his mother on 24 May, "it is rather over-crowded and I think I would rather have kept my nice little room at the 'drome", raids or no raids.

The school had been established to provide crews for two Army Co-operation squadrons and when Mick first learned that he was to go there, he thought he had been assigned to fly Westland Lysanders. "You should have seen his face," laughed Frank, "he thought he was going to spend the rest of the war trundling about in Lizzies, picking up messages or doing artillery spotting for the Army!" However, Mick was spared what he would then have regarded as a fate worse than death because the school was about to undergo a change of role. It was now to provide crews for an Auxiliary Air Force unit, No. 500 (County of Kent) Squadron, which had recently converted from Avro Ansons to Bristol Blenheims and had been in Coastal Command for some time. The two Army Co-operation squadrons, having very little army to co-operate with since the evacuation from Dunkirk, were assigned to that command. So, not surprisingly, the school was re-named No. 6 Operational Training Unit, Coastal Command, in June 1941. During Mick's time at Andover, there were still some army officers about: men who had transferred to the RAF for pilot training and were no doubt surprised to find themselves being prepared for work with the Navy instead of the Army.

The aircraft used at Andover was the twin-engined Blenheim (mostly the Mark IV long-nosed model). It was, Mick thought, a kindly aircraft and the only real mechanical difference from the Oxford was the two-pitch propellers. All ground running and take-off had to be made in *fine* pitch; so, too, the approach and landing. Otherwise, *coarse* pitch was used and Mick found engine behaviour similar to that in the Oxford. He needed less than three hours dual instruction before going solo, in a totally strange countryside, after not flying for fourteen weeks. As well as skill, Mick had another quality essential to the successful airman in wartime: one day, for instance, he managed to fly unscathed through a balloon barrage, a feat which caused him to reflect: "I've had a lot of good luck in my life!"

Visibility that was considered adequate in England was such, said Mick, that in New Zealand "we wouldn't have flown in it." Another problem was that determined efforts had been made to disguise Andover from enemy bombers by painting continuations of hedgerows across landing areas. While these may not have deceived experienced German airmen, they certainly fooled many British novices. The drill was to find the local village and set a short course from there. Also, it took Mick a little while to get used to the midday sun appearing in the south rather than the north and the behaviour of the magnetic compass was completely reversed.

What in retrospect surprised Mick was the fact that most of the flying was done over *land*, even though most of the flying in prospect for Coastal Command pilots would be done over the *sea*. And although he was to be provided with an 'observer' (a title indicating how lightly the RAF still regarded navigation), Mick would have welcomed serious instruction in that difficult art, on the principle that pilots commanded aircraft and should therefore be able to guide as well as fly them. Mick would have to learn about finding his way over the sea later, 'on the job'. For these reasons, when Mick arrived at his first squadron, he was not considered ready for serious employment.

Meanwhile, he enjoyed flying the Blenheim, his first operational aircraft (even if an obsolete one) and acquiring his first crew: two men, Sergeant Bertram Paige (observer) and Sergeant Horace Roe (wireless operator/air gunner). Bertie Paige was a Canadian whose previous navigating experience had been gained mainly in clear weather and like Mick he found England's cloudy skies a severe trial at first. His accent sounded like "broad Yankee" to Mick's ears, while Horace, a farmer's son from Suffolk, sounded (Mick thought) like George Formby, a famous Lancashire comedian. Clearly, his New Zealand ear was tuned far from either the North American or British wavelengths. Until mid-July, they worked steadily through the training programme, with occasional diversions to 'beat up' tanks on Salisbury Plain and trains on the main line to London: great fun for young lads pleased with their growing ability to handle fast aircraft at very low levels.

Among Mick's fellow pupils at Andover was Howard Morley Saville Green (always known as 'Pat'). They served together several times during and after the war, becoming good friends, but lost touch in the mid-1960s. In fact, Pat thought Mick had died until October 1987, when he received a letter from Tony Spooner, an exceptional Coastal Command pilot and later a successful author, asking for information about Mick. "It will be a great joy to get in touch with him again", Pat replied, "having always held Mick in the highest personal and professional regard."[4]

"We were delighted with the Blenheim," Pat recalled, "but there was one snag—I recorded at the time, 'the cockpit layout appals me'! A modern student of ergonomics would find it an interesting study. On a bulkhead behind and below one's left ear were a couple of push/pull knobs; one was the cut-out for the engines, the other was the variable pitch control for the propellers. One's left hand reached back to use the latter soon after take-off to change the propeller pitch—and similarly before landing. The possibility of stopping the engines instead did exist, despite a different shaped knob, but I never heard of it happening, so we must have been well drilled! Another hazard was the positioning of the levers for raising and lowering the flaps and undercarriage. These were awkwardly placed, below the right-hand edge of one's seat and most Blenheim pilots kept the nail on the right thumb very well trimmed after painful experiences while fumbling for and operating the levers."

Mick wrote home on 4 June, from the Officers' Mess, with a bluntness that his parents already expected, though whether they relished it is another matter. "Well, nothing very interesting has happened since I last wrote," he said, "except that one of my friends managed

---

[4] Pat Green's memories have been most helpful in this and subsequent chapters.

to crash and kill himself yesterday, but we are getting quite used to that now. We are still living very well although we don't get much money to go on leave with because the Government takes back £1 a week and mess bills run up to about £2 a week after paying for washing, etc. I also have to buy a new uniform (so I will have two) but it so happens that I have a lot of back pay due so will be able to manage all right." Roddy McCracken, he added, was stationed some 200 miles away, but they were trying to keep in touch.

Mick had no news of his eldest brother Jimmy, who had left New Zealand for Britain as a Second Lieutenant with the 23rd Battalion, New Zealand Expeditionary Force, in May 1940. All Mick knew was that the battalion was then somewhere in the Mediterranean. In fact, Jimmy served throughout the ill-fated Greek campaign in command of a pioneer platoon and was one of the last to get away from Crete. His efforts there earned him a Mention in Despatches for helping to organise a road block to delay German troops while wounded men were got away. Jimmy was later promoted to the rank of Captain and served as 5th Brigade transport officer in Egypt and Tunisia before returning to New Zealand, just in time for Christmas 1943. Jimmy would be on hand to welcome his little brother when *he* returned home four years later with a chestful of medals and, not least, a wife and child.[5]

On 2 July, Mick wrote from Andover to his brother Duncan, who was at that time trying to get into the RNZAF. It pays, he sagely advised a man more than nine years older than himself, "to get a commission if you are going to be sent out here, of course a pilot officer is broke all the time, but we have a better life than the sergeant pilots. I think heavy bombers are the best things to go for, this job on Blenheims is dangerous and thankless". Young and green as he was, Mick already realised the Blenheim's limitations as a war machine and believed his prospects of transferring to the Lockheed Hudson, a much superior aircraft, were quite good. This was partly because Bertie Paige's long-distance navigation was above average and partly because Horace Roe was "rather too broad to fit in a Blenheim turret". The fighter pilots, Mick continued, "don't see much future in life either. They put all the scatterbrained sods on Spitfires and Hurricanes and my God they have a wild time while they are alive. Of course Jerry never shoots them down; they just crash through their own crazy flying, it seems to me."

---

[5] Angus Ross, *23 Battalion* (War History Branch, Department of Internal Affairs, Wellington, 1959) pp. 10, 30, 70, 74 & 145.

"If you do come over here in the Air Force," he told Duncan, "you will find flying totally different to NZ: visibility is usually four to six miles and there are bloody balloons sticking up everywhere. On my first three long trips I got thoroughly lost and had to land at another aerodrome for lack of fuel. However, it is not bad when one gets used to it, but these planes go at such a hell of a speed." Whatever the Blenheim's other limitations, it certainly left the Oxford standing and Mick was learning to do everything much more quickly. After fully two months in England, he felt sufficiently at home to advise his brother that "beer in this country is not too good now and the cigarettes are frightful, that is all I have to complain about just now."

Mick's first flight at Andover had been in a Blenheim I (L1717) with Flying Officer Musgrave on 26 May 1941. Two days later, after three flights with Musgrave lasting almost three hours in total, he made his first solo in L1445. Altogether, he flew eight different Blenheim Is in a single week and thereafter flew sixteen different Blenheim IVs. During June and July, Mick flew nearly every day, often two or three times a day, and several of his flights lasted for more than three hours. The longest—in a Blenheim IV (5382)—on 2 July lasted for three hours and fifty minutes. Mick had his last flight at Andover on 14 July. He spent about 110 hours in the air there, almost all of them as a first pilot, but he had only a single hour of "night experience" (and even that was with another pilot) to bring his night flying to a grand total of six hours, dual and solo combined. Overall, on leaving Andover, Mick had a total of nearly 244 hours in his log book, made up of fifty-odd hours in Tiger Moths at Taieri, the rest in Oxfords or Blenheims. Would it be enough to equip Mick to cope with operational flying—seeking out enemy targets while avoiding both flak and fighters?

CHAPTER IV

DEATH AND DECORATIONS
JULY 1941 TO FEBRUARY 1942

MICK ENSOR joined his first operational unit—No. 500 (County of Kent) Squadron—at Bircham Newton in Norfolk on 27 July 1941.[1] Some eighty years earlier, his grandfather had left that county to advance his fortunes in New Zealand and now Mick had returned, like so many other colonial boys in two world wars, to help defend a land which they still regarded, in some mystical sense, as "home". Bircham Newton lay in west Norfolk, about forty miles (as the seagull flies) in a direct line from his grandfather's old home at Rollesby in east Norfolk, near Great Yarmouth. The airfield lay ten miles north-east of King's Lynn, six from the east coast of The Wash and belonged to 16 Group, Coastal Command. Even though there were no sealed runways (such refinements had yet to be built and aircraft took off and landed on grass), Mick was relieved to observe that Bircham Newton was much easier to find from the air than Andover had been. At least it was in clear summer weather: he did not yet know about the extensive fogs rolling in from the sea and settling over the Norfolk lowlands for many days in autumn and winter. Bircham Newton, recalled Pat Green, "was a well-established station, going back to the earliest days . . . close to Sandringham, near the sea and rather a bleak spot. It also had a very undulating and bumpy grass airfield." The squadron had moved there only recently, from Detling in Kent. Like Andover, Bircham Newton was at that time well supplied with a staff trained in peacetime and Mick smilingly remarks that "it was as well that I had been properly brought up and knew which knife and fork to use."

---

[1] Michael J F Bowyer, *Action Stations 1: Wartime Military Airfields of East Anglia, 1939-1945* (Patrick Stephens, Cambridge, 1979) pp. 60-68.

At Bircham Newton, Mick was to fly the Bristol Blenheim, the type on which he had trained, with his Andover crew: Bertie Paige and Horace Roe. Mick had just spent a week's leave with John MacGillivray, a friend made at Andover who was also to join 500 Squadron. John's father was a notable breeder of stud cattle at Calrossie, near Tain in Ross-shire, Scotland. "I think it is the best farming country I have ever seen", Mick told his father, "they have New Zealand white clover in their pastures and on that particular piece of ground it does even better than at Glenrock. I had a wonderful time and the old captain [John's father] lent us his car and we motored all over the place and met a lot of very interesting people." After this delightful interval, the two young pilots made their way by train to Bircham Newton. From then until the end of the war, Mick would amply prove the truth in Coastal Command's grim motto, *Constant Endeavour*.

"We chaps from Andover", wrote Pat, were "viewed with some suspicion" when they arrived at Bircham Newton. "Dependent upon non-pilot observer-navigators, we were at first sight rather second-class citizens, what with those brass letters VR instead of an A on our lapels and here and there a colonial accent." The letter A identified 500 Squadron as an Auxiliary Air Force unit, a select company in the peacetime service which had few social contacts with *regular* officers, let alone wartime volunteers. Some auxiliaries who survived from happier days were reluctant to accept newcomers, either socially or professionally, but Mick and his fellow Andover graduates did their best to ignore petty slights. More important, they reckoned that they were better able to handle Blenheims than most of the old hands because 500 Squadron had only recently converted to that aircraft from Avro Ansons, an easier aircraft to fly. On the other hand, the auxiliaries were much more experienced in navigation.

As Mick settled into the squadron, he gradually became aware that it seemed rather "headless" under a new CO, Wing Commander G. T. Gilbert, an Australian. "Days drifted by," recalled Mick, "without us being told what we were supposed to do or how to do it. Grumbling began, none too quietly either, and the atmosphere became very poor." Evidence of low morale was the readiness of some crews to find fault with their aircraft and so avoid hazardous operations. Mick never found Gilbert an inspiring leader (he rarely flew, even for practice) nor an attractive personality and throughout the war years spared him little sympathy. However, when reflecting in later years on the tasks assigned to 500 Squadron in 1941 and the equipment provided to carry out those tasks, his feelings towards

Gilbert became more charitable. "Let's face it," he says, "the Blenheim was not a machine to go to war in; not in winter, not across water and least of all not against Germans. Gilbert knew this better than most of us and certainly better than some of us youngsters who were stupid enough in those days to give practically anything a go." Mick emphasises the fact that Gilbert was by no means solely responsible for what he calls the squadron's "subdued" attitude. Gilbert only took command in July 1941 and Mick noticed that some of his senior officers were conspicuously absent whenever danger beckoned. Days of rain or low cloud, he remembered, were bitterly referred to as "Sergeant Pilots' Weather" because men of that rank found themselves ordered to fly in it more often than their numbers or experience warranted.

"In those early days," Mick recalled, "taking off two hours before dawn (very cold in winter) and going across to the Dutch coast, just single aeroplanes—my feelings on such a morning were far from charitable and I was always glad to get back." Before take-off, there was always plenty to do "and even in Blenheims, once you got into the cockpit, any apprehensions disappeared in the interest of what was always to me the pleasure of taking off and flying again. On return, there's no doubt that one felt a sense of relief at having got the thing safely down in one piece. Then you had to turn in a report—that usually took an hour or so—and what you did next depended on whether the bar was open or not." These Blenheims, Mick added, "had only one machine-gun firing forward. Navigation and communication equipment was virtually zero. There was nothing to help direction finding, just normal airmanship rules. The whole carry-on would have done credit to any agricultural pilot." At that time, most of Coastal Command (like the rest of the RAF) was still without professional navigators. Some pilots were trained and experienced in that skill, but many were not. "My own star recognition", admitted Mick, "was terrible—I was used to southern skies—but in any case you didn't see much of the stars in low-level flying."

The squadron had four main tasks. The first task, searching for dinghies carrying survivors of Bomber Command aircraft, required on some days as many as nine Blenheims to go out on searches that only too often proved fruitless. Depending on the area and the weather, these searches were flown in loose formation, for mutual protection, though sometimes an escort of powerful, twin-engined Bristol Beaufighters was provided. The second task, standing by at night for operations against E-boats coming from the Dutch coast to attack convoys, required shore Direction Finding stations to take bearings on W/T (Wireless Telegraphy, i.e. Morse code) transmissions from the aircraft. The resultant fixes permitted aircraft to be directed to the E-boats' estimated position where, with luck, parachute flares would reveal the boats and permit attacks to be made with four 250-lb bombs. "It may have worked sometimes," thought Pat Green, "although not in my memory." Strikes against enemy convoys, the third task, were equally rare. On numerous occasions, either they could not find the ships (having no radar equipment) or the weather was too bad to permit prolonged, low-level searching. Fourthly, there were spasmodic attempts to attack German airfields in Holland. "Not altogether unusually," wrote Green, "we found ourselves into something that we knew nothing about." Moreover, the Blenheim had neither the speed nor the armament for such dangerous tasks and in consequence the only success it *could* enjoy was to avoid being destroyed itself.

Mick's first flight at Bircham Newton was on 28 July: twenty minutes as second pilot in a Blenheim IV (MK-LF). During August, he made half a dozen further local flights before his first operation in a Blenheim IV (MK-D). On 12 August, he began a letter to his mother, telling her that Roddy McCracken was based at a nearby airfield. "I flew over to see him yesterday, he is looking very fit and doing very well." In his ignorance, Mick thought Roddy "rather lucky in that he doesn't have to do any night flying whereas ours is more than half night work, when we get going again properly". They never met again, because within a few days, on 19 August, Roddy was killed on operations with 114 Squadron. He was twenty-two years old. Frank Reece flew over to West Raynham (about seven miles south-east of Bircham Newton) to see 'Cracker' on 2 September and learned the sad news. The Germans, he was told, had announced his death and burial with full military honours. When Grace Sutherland in New Glasgow, Nova Scotia, learned of the tragedy, she offered her con-dolences to his parents through Mick's mother: "Life", wrote Grace, "seemed to be one big adventure to Roddy." Mick agreed. "He was a wonderful chap; a terrific chap who would never shirk *anything*. Right from the start he had been a bold, almost an over-bold, pilot. I missed him greatly. With a chap like that on Blenheims, there clearly wasn't much future for him."

Mick returned from his first operation on 15 August 1941 and the account he sent his parents was characteristically brief. "Today I and my crew have been highly commended by our CO for a job over the North Sea", he wrote. "Three of us went out, one turned back through bad weather, the other (my room mate, by the way) was shot down and we, like asses, finished our job while flying through shocking rain at fifty feet over the sea a few miles off the Dutch coast. It took us four and a half hours, but we got back quite OK." Mick had begun a search patrol with Mike Gummer and Chris Elgar (one of two brothers who had been in 500 Squadron for a long time). The east coast convoy route was marked by buoys and the bigger ones had been fitted out as havens for ditched aircrew (or the survivors of sunken ships) and here and there special floats were moored. Periodically, they were inspected, to see if any were occupied. The three Blenheims found a dinghy and while Elgar circled it, the other two went off to look for a launch thought to be in the area. Bad weather forced Gummer to go home, but Mick returned to the dinghy. There was no sign of Elgar—only a large patch of oil spreading over the sea and Mick supposed that he must have been shot down. At four and a half hours, it was the longest flight of his career, so far.

The squadron also carried out some night flying training from a small grass 'satellite' field at Langham, fourteen miles to the north-east, on the north coast of Norfolk. Crews usually travelled to and fro in a splendid vintage Bentley motor-car belonging to Flight Lieutenant Duff Mitchell, who was in charge of training, and stayed overnight in a fine old requisitioned country house, Langham Hall. On one dark night, whoever laid out the flare path of goose-neck flares pointed it straight at the only house for miles around. Pat Green had just taken off when one propeller and one undercarriage leg hit the chimney of that house. Somehow, he got safely down again after "a very sweaty circuit" and went next morning to apologise to the lady owner, who had been asleep in bed until her chimney got in the way of his Blenheim. Even though pieces of chimney had actually burst through the ceiling and scattered around the bed, she welcomed him warmly, saying with a smile: "I thought it was the Last Trump and am glad to learn it wasn't." Later, perhaps because of Pat's mishap, a better satellite field at Docking (only a couple of miles north of Bircham Newton) became their overnight base for operational sorties. It was larger, with some huts and even a control tower, but fog was often a problem. One particularly dense night inspired from Flight Lieutenant 'Boozie' Pain a remark often repeated in later years: "If the level-crossing gates at Docking had been closed, I couldn't have got back to the airfield."

After his alarming debut, Mick did not fly on operations again for nearly a month, until 11 September, when he and his crew carried out their second operation in a Blenheim IV (MK-V), an uneventful anti-shipping patrol lasting two hours and forty minutes. On the 15th, several crews flew south to Harrowbeer, on the edge of Yelverton village, about five miles inland from Plymouth. "I have been down on the south coast for a while," Mick told his mother on 22 September, "doing night raids on ports and day sweeps now and again. It has been rather good fun because we are all living in a hotel and we park our planes almost in the centre of the town, about fifty yards from our hotel. I came back here [to Bircham Newton] the day before yesterday to get my machine repaired and so am having a bit of a spell.... We had great celebrations the other night because one of our chaps sank a ship single-handed about 300 miles out to sea. When he came back, he had at least fifty bullet holes in his aircraft. There was a piece in the papers about it. The other night when we went out, I was the only one who found the target. It was only by good luck as it was a very black night and we just flew round where we thought it was until they started shooting at us. We knew we must be pretty close by then and by a bit of luck the moon started to come up and we could see the docks away below us. My navigator dropped his bombs very well and I think we must have done quite a lot of damage, although that is not for us to say." On the night of 17-18 September, recorded Pat Green in his diary, "Six crews went over to St. Eval for a night strike, but only two got off from there; Brown and Ensor. The others u/s. Brown didn't find his target, but Ensor did and bombed it. A bloody fine show."

Mick and Pat formed part of a detachment based at Harrowbeer from 15 September to 6 October 1941: "a very odd period," thought Pat. "We not only darted around in our Blenheims over the Channel and the Bay of Biscay (just a bit fruitlessly) but also made some night attacks on such places as St. Nazaire. Quite absurd!" On arriving at Harrowbeer, Pat recorded in his diary: "No Officers' Mess ready. No quarters ready. Shambles. After the AOC [of 19 Group] came out from Plymouth, we moved into a hotel in the village." It was, in fact, a temperance hotel, but no objection was raised when some crates of beer were carried in. In any case, there was a good pub across the road and an even better one less than a couple of miles away. The secondary runway ran slightly downhill and finished a few yards short of the main road, separated from it by a few strands of wire, and pointing more or less straight down the village street. There were several dispersal pans for aircraft off the end of the runway and since the hotel was only some fifty yards away, some of the intrepid young aviators were rather inclined to show off by clumping to and fro in flying kit. They were able to get away with this because, as Frank Reece recorded, few villagers had seen either aircraft or airmen at close range before and all were mightily impressed by their exotic visitors.

Several night raids were attempted on Biscay ports. "We did our best", wrote Pat, "at a task for which we'd had no training and at which we were totally inexperienced. That made our losses even sadder." Among the saddest losses was that of Frank Reece, shot down during the night of 29-30 September. It would be years before the New Zealanders learned that Frank was not dead. He had, in fact, managed to bring his damaged Blenheim down on a Breton beach and actually evaded capture for nearly five months, with French assistance, before his luck ran out. Frank then spent the rest of the war as a prisoner in Germany. "We lost Frank Reece the other night," Mick told his parents on 3 October, "we don't know what happened, but think he was caught by AA fire from the ground. The trouble about this job", he added in his usual blunt way, "is that one seldom does know what has happened to these chaps."

Considering the small amount of damage that 250-lb bombs could do, these raids were pointless. While daylight sorties were mounted from Harrowbeer, night raids required the Blenheims to fly over to St. Eval (thirty-five miles due west, on the north coast of Cornwall) for briefing and then to return there for debriefing, a meal and a sleep. Mick had been glad to get away from Bircham Newton for a welcome "breath of fresh air" at Harrowbeer, although there were times when he thought the staff officers at 19 Group HQ as mad as those at 16 Group. Like Pat, he thought there had been a most noticeable change for the better in the general atmosphere while at Harrowbeer although it must be said that there did sometimes seem to be a surprisingly high number of unserviceable Blenheims at St. Eval prior to take-off. Perhaps it was that half-hour flight from Harrowbeer?

Mick's third operation (in MK-T) was flown from St. Eval. It was a night-strike on St. Nazaire, a port on the south coast of Brittany where the Germans were building a massive U-boat base. A round trip of some 600 miles lasting four hours, it was Mick's second longest flight and almost doubled his slender experience in darkness, for he had only five hours to his credit before take-off that night. According to Mick's log book, they dropped four 250-lb bombs "on target area". Without an efficient bomb-sight, nothing more accurate was to be expected and without more (and much heavier) bombs, no significant damage was possible.

The briefing, Mick recalled, seemed almost designed to depress: "a whole team of experts went on and on about what to do if we were shot down, what survival gear was provided, how to use it and how to evade capture. All very necessary, of course, but these fellows looked and sounded so miserable. Nobody said anything cheerful, anything encouraging or positive. No wonder one or two of the weaker brethren found something wrong with their aircraft!" The drill for night raids was to leave Cornwall at low level, keep clear of Ushant Island (off the tip of the Breton Peninsula), turn in towards St. Nazaire and start climbing hard, when twenty minutes from the French coast, to something like 15,000 feet. Mick flew a Blenheim without oxygen equipment. Ironically, none of the briefing experts had said a word about the dangerous consequences of high flying without oxygen, so that by the time Mick got near St. Nazaire, neither he nor his crew were quite 'with it' and were grateful to the German gunners for both waking them up and indicating the location of a likely target. Returning home, one could choose a route overland for much of the way or head back out to sea. Both were risky, as indeed was every moment of these raids.

The pilots were told that small ships, pretending to be fishing boats, were helping U-boats to find their way home to the Biscay ports. However, since the whole area was littered with French tunnymen and Spanish trawlers, neither of which were to be attacked, the pilots were left wondering how to identify a legitimate target. The consensus was that they should attack anything with wireless aerials, if not flying a Spanish flag. Mick and his companions looked at numerous small ships, but hardly any were even attacked, much less sunk. One or two flashed "V" in morse code, either in response to the use by the BBC of "dit dit dit dah" before broadcasts to France, or as a deception. A few sorties were flown in search of suspected mine-sweepers around the Channel Islands, but lack of cloud cover prevented the highly vulnerable Blenheims from spending too long in such a dangerous area.

Mick wrote to his parents on 3 October from Davaar, Bembridge, in the Isle of Wight. This was the home of his godmother: Nancy, Lady Campbell. Mick was enjoying a week's leave with the Campbells, after "a rather hectic fortnight, during which time we have been doing night strikes and shipping sweeps from an aerodrome near Plymouth." Mick liked that part of England much better than Norfolk, which was "far too flat and sort of bleak-looking and I expect it will be very cold in the winter, if we are still there." Except for a sergeant pilot in a different flight, Mick was now the only New Zealander left in 500 Squadron. They shared their newspapers from home, though all were sadly out-of-date by the time they reached England. But Mick was far from unhappy. "So far", he told his parents, "I have had incredible luck and have not even had a bullet hole in my plane, although we have had to go through some pretty heavy AA fire at times. It gives me great pleasure to drop a few bombs on some of Mr Hitler's toys now and again, but each of us feel that the little we do is insignificant when compared with the tremendous efforts of Bomber Command."

By November 1941, when Mick had nine operational sorties in Blenheims to his credit, the squadron was re-equipping with the much superior Lockheed Hudson, to everyone's undisguised delight. This famous aircraft proved to be a lifesaver in 1938 both for the RAF (in desperate need of an efficient bomber-reconnaissance machine with a realistic range) and for the Lockheed Corporation (in equally desperate need of a large contract). Nearly 3,000 were built, of which more than half went to Britain, and they served almost everywhere from Iceland to Fiji. The Hudson holds many proud records. It was Lockheed's first warplane, the first American aircraft to serve with the RAF, the first to shoot down a German aircraft in the Second World War, the first to force the surrender of a U-boat, the first to be fitted with ASV (Air-to-Surface) radar and the first to sink a U-boat with rocket projectiles. It also accounted for the first U-boats sunk by the US Navy, the US Army Air Force and the Royal Canadian Air Force. The Hudson was one of those rare examples of a successful warplane evolved from a civilian airliner, in this case the L-14 Super Electra.[2]

For all its merits, the Hudson "must have been one of the most formidably 'manual' aeroplanes ever built", in the opinion of Tony Taylor, a noted wartime test-pilot. "From the moment of preparing to start the engines to that when the idle-cut-off levers were operated on the apron of the destination aerodrome, any pilot of this mildly alarming technological achievement found himself in need of more arms, fingers and eyes than are normally available." Pilots of its civilian predecessor were given a minimum of fifteen hours of dual instruction by British Airways before flying it solo. This was more than twice as long as Mick received, though Taylor admitted that "apart from the manual and mental dexterity needed in an exciting battle with science—the Hudson was comfortable and docile enough. The great thing was not to try too hard to make it do what it didn't want to do—such as a three-point landing": it much preferred to bowl along for a

[2] 'The Handy Hudson: Lockheed's First Warplane', *Air International* (November 1985 pp. 240-263 (no author named); Andrew Hendrie, *Seek and Strike: The Lockheed Hudson in World War II* (Kimber, London, 1983) p. 247; Bill Gunston, *The Encyclopedia of the World's Combat Aircraft* (Salamander Books, London, 1976) p. 129; W R Matthews, *Air Enthusiast* (July 1972) p. 45.

great distance on the main wheels before settling in its own time onto the tailwheel.[3]

The Hudsons used by 500 Squadron came in two versions, the Mark III (with Wright Cyclone R-1820 engines) and the Mark V (with Pratt & Whitney Twin Wasp R-1830 engines). The main difference was that the Mark III had a far better single-engined performance, a fact that would shortly help to save the lives of Mick and his crew. Re-training in that month included the use of airborne radar (for the first time) and crews were increased to four with the addition of a second wireless operator/air gunner who had received rudimentary instruction in the new, highly-secret gadget. Sergeant Cyril Prior joined Mick, Bertram and Horace. These early radars, though little use for finding targets in daylight and no use in darkness, did at least give crews valuable training in electronic methods and would eventually be replaced by effective sets. Better still, they proved excellent as navigation aids, giving good early warning of land ahead. "The little screen fascinated us," said Mick. "Just like television in later days—and often making about as much sense." Having a second 'wop/ag' aboard meant that both the rear turret and the wireless set could be manned simultaneously (to Mick's great relief) and the turret itself was much superior to that equipping the unlamented Blenheim (to the relief of both wop/ags, Horace and Cyril). An efficient Boulton & Paul turret, it came with two machine-guns instead of one and could be readily traversed.

Several experienced Hudson pilots arrived in the squadron, notably Squadron Leader Jim Romanes and two Flight Lieutenants, Ian Patterson (a New Zealander) and John Ensor. Remarkably, given their very rare surname, the two Ensors were not related. They looked rather alike though, and both were convinced that a connection could be found somewhere in the past if anyone had nothing better to do than seek it. John was usually known as 'Tubby', a nickname that would not then have suited Mick, but (he wryly admits): "I might fairly have earned it later." These pilots passed on their expertise to the other pilots, making it clear that the new aircraft was perfectly safe. This assurance was necessary because rumours were rife at the time, following a spate of accidents elsewhere, that Hudson pilots were awarded a 'Survivor's Medal'. In fact, at least eight of 500 Squadron's Hudsons crashed during the conversion period, killing or injuring thirty men. Mick had seven hours of dual instruction before

---

[3] H A Taylor, 'Flying the Harassing Hudson', *Air Enthusiast* (December 1972) pp. 292-4.

flying solo in a Hudson V (MK-F) on 23 November; he first flew with his crew on the 25th in another Mark V machine, MK-G. He personally found no difficulty whatever with the Hudson, provided he remembered to lock the tailwheel straight, prior to take-off.

This aircraft gave him his first experience of constant-speed, feathering propellers, manual mixture control override, exhaust gas analysers and several other refinements not found in the Blenheim. "I was lucky", he wrote, "in that I had a reasonable working knowledge of and interest in engines, including carburation and ignition systems. This background was a great help in absorbing service lectures, and when it came to the Hudson systems, I bullied the technical people considerably until I was satisfied that I knew all that I needed to know." There speaks the voice of Keith Park, 'Mary' Coningham and Johnny Checketts: three other New Zealand airmen who "bullied the technical people" of their day in order to give themselves the best possible chance of staying alive, as well as carrying out operations successfully. "If your basic training has been good," Mick added, "and in an aircraft that makes you work for your living, there is not a lot of difference between flying one type and another. However, power-plants *do* vary and the differences must be mastered in order to survive."

On 16 January 1942, Mick lost a very close friend, John MacGillivray. John was also a farmer's son and a man with whom he had shared a room; a man whose home in Scotland he had visited—and a man whose fiancee (Margaret Douglas) would thereafter play an important part in Mick's life. John died about 7.50 pm when his Hudson crashed shortly after take-off at Bircham Newton. Ian Patterson, Mick's flight commander, asked him if he wanted to see the wreck. Mick refused, saying he was too upset, and later Ian gave him the twisted remains of what had been John's cigarette-case. "I cried", said Mick, "for the first time since leaving school." Forty-five years later, he asked Pat Green: "Did you fly Oxfords or Ansons before Blenheims?" When Pat answered: "Oxfords", Mick replied: "That is why you are alive and John MacGillivray is dead."

John's death hurt Mick deeply (and would never be forgotten), not only because he had been such a close friend, but even more because he believed that the accident would not have happened if John had been trained on the demanding Oxford and not on the easy Anson. As John's best friend, Mick had the task of accompanying his body on the long journey north to Calrossie, meeting his parents, telling them something of how their son had died and all the time aware of the resentment, however deeply buried, that bereaved parents must often feel: "Why are *you* alive and our son dead?" Only just past his twentieth birthday, Mick had already found that several of the young men with whom he felt at ease, casually chatting one day were dead the next. During the next three years, this gut-wrenching experience would be repeated time and time again. Outwardly, Mick showed less and less concern for the misfortunes of others, maintaining a composure as necessary (if he were to continue doing his duty) as it was admired, both by his seniors and by those whose very lives depended upon his calm good judgement. It would be Mick Ensor who had the luck, skill and (eventually) the experience to earn the reputation that might have been either Roddy McCracken's or John MacGillivray's or any one of the dozens of other men killed before their time who served as bravely as Mick. By the end of the war, he would be described in the New Zealand press with good reason as "probably the most outstanding New Zealander" in Coastal Command.

A few nights after this heart-breaking accident, Mick won his first decoration, the Distinguished Flying Cross. It was earned during his eleventh operation (but only his second in the Hudson) on the night of 29-30 January 1942. For some reason that seemed compelling to his masters, this inexperienced pilot was ordered to go alone, entirely unescorted in dreadful weather conditions, eastward to the Heligoland Bight. He was then to turn north, fly parallel to the Danish coast, cross the entrance to the Skagerrak and reach a point barely twenty miles from the Norwegian coast before turning for home. At the time of take-off, Mick had a grand total of twelve hours' experience at night as a first pilot; this flight (lasting just over five hours) was the longest of his career to date; and he was all of twenty years old. On that night, recalled Pat Green, "Mick and I were the only people airborne from our squadron. In fact, we were told subsequently (don't know how accurately) that we were, because of the weather, the only people airborne from the RAF! We were flying a search called a 'Nomad', an accurate name because one did roam around from place to place, seeking not pasture but ships. My patch was from Texel to Norderney and Mick's continued on to the Bight."

Off Heligoland, shortly before 4 am on a black, blustery morning, Mick sighted three supply ships of about 900 tons each, ploughing their way through icy waters. He attacked at mast-height. The turret-gunner (Horace Roe) reported a direct hit on the stern of one vessel and thought other hits possible. Even near misses would represent a considerable tribute to Mick's powers of judging height, distance and speed because the Hudson was not equipped with a bomb-sight. While taking violent evasion action to avoid fire from the vessels, there came a sudden "grinding crash" (as Mick reported later) "and the aircraft bounced up a good many feet; we had hit a rock that none of us had seen." In fact, as he later realised, there were no rocks in that area: Mick had actually struck the sea. The airscrew of the starboard engine was bent right back over the cowling and the motor, not surprisingly, was screaming angrily. Mick shut it down and flew with only one engine. He then had time to notice that several instruments were not working, all the lights had gone out, the gun-turret was unserviceable and so too were the wireless and the radar set. One of the petrol-tanks was holed, but for the moment that was the least of his problems. Climbing gingerly to about 1,000 feet, he set a course for home by gyro-compass.

It was only when Mick pinpointed himself over a town in Holland that he realised the compass was 180 degrees out. The Germans started to send up flak and he was forced to fly further inland and get down to hedge-hopping level. The Canadian navigator, Bertie Paige, scrambled down into the nose and told Mick when to lift it to avoid trees, houses, factories and (not least) flak batteries and searchlight positions. An undamaged Hudson, flying on one engine with the airscrew of the other neatly feathered, required almost full power from the live engine to avoid a fatal stall. In Mick's situation, unable to feather the dead engine's airscrew, he needed to seek even more power from the live engine and risk it overheating and seizing up. Apart from the risk of that ultimate disaster, Mick was well aware that the hard-working engine was trailing a long bright torch from its exhaust as a handy visual aid for ground gunners or night fighters.

"The flak was fairly intense," recalled Mick, "it was as though somebody was spraying red sparks at us from a gigantic hosepipe. That went on for about half an hour and once we narrowly missed hitting a wireless station." Eventually, he got out to sea again, but could not be sure of his speed or direction. As fuel was consumed, the Hudson became noticeably lighter and Mick was able to ease the strain on his lovingly-cossetted port engine. It took two and a half hours to get back to England on one engine, everyone aboard growing more grateful by the minute for the decision to send them on this flight in a Mark III aircraft, which had a superior single-engine performance to the Mark V.

Mick decided to encourage its steady rhythm by singing hymns and everyone joined in heartily: most passionately and appropriately, they later agreed, in a sparkling rendition of "Onward Christian Soldiers". Then came a sudden, blinding snowstorm. Silent now, they peered anxiously ahead: fearing the effect of icing on the wings, uncertain of their height above the sea and dreading the discovery of high ground ahead. The storm passed as suddenly as it had arrived and scudding clouds even allowed a little moonlight to appear. Mick knew that fuel must be very low and shouted aloud in joyful relief on sighting land, covered in snow though it was. He decided boldly—and perhaps unwisely—not to climb high enough to permit everyone to bale out safely. Half a century later, he is amazed at the confidence his young self had. "Today," he says, "with masses of experience, I would never attempt to land a Hudson without an airspeed indicator, flaps or landing lights in a field at night on only one engine; wouldn't dream of it; stupid thing to do." But then, having come so far, he never hesitated. He would attempt a belly-landing. The Hudson always came down quickly, even with the restraint of its big flaps; this one would land quicker than ever—safely or otherwise.

In an attempt to illuminate the frozen land below and so permit the choice of a long flat stretch of open ground, Bertie jettisoned the top hatch and fired off several Very lights in quick succession. They spotted a promising landing area almost at once. Mick reduced power, slowed the Hudson to what he hoped was an appropriate approach speed and flew a cautious circuit at an estimated height of 300 feet. As Bertie fired the last of his lights, Mick manoeuvred into what seemed the correct line of approach and hoped for the best. Without flaps, he had to keep the Hudson's nose well up and so immediately lost sight of the ground. These moments were as dangerous as any over enemy territory, but now Mick could only keep his wings level and await the crunch. Although it came long after he expected and the noise was appalling, the Hudson withstood the shock much better than he feared. It bounced and slithered to a halt surprisingly quickly. Then and later, Mick had good reason to be thankful for the sturdy construction of American aircraft.

After a brief deafening silence, everyone unflinched. No-one was hurt except Bertie, who banged his head and suffered a black eye and a broken tooth. He would be consoled by the award of a Distinguished Flying Medal and recalled to Canada, where he was commissioned. Meanwhile, Mick ordered everyone to get out as quickly as possible, in case of fire. He walked slowly round the aircraft, checking the damage and looking for fuel leaks, his ears ringing and his heart pounding. Suddenly he lurched forward and threw up. While he was regaining his composure, Horace noticed a windmill and laughed briefly: "Just as well we didn't find it the hard way!" No-one had seen it from the air. Surely they couldn't be in Holland? A ditch ran alongside their landing field and Mick ordered everyone into it. They huddled together, shivering with cold and shock, unwilling to believe that they might soon be on the run from the Germans.

Dawn was breaking in the east and a few minutes later a farm worker appeared, "whistling in English", Mick thought, and soon he was speaking in English. Norfolk English anyway, for thanks to Bertie's brilliant navigation, based mainly on an unreliable magnetic compass, they had landed on the north-east coast of that county, near Winterton-on-Sea. They were only forty-five miles from Great Bircham. More interesting, from Mick's point of view, is the curious fact that the Hudson came to rest barely five miles from Rollesby, the village his grandfather left to make a new life in New Zealand.

The grateful airmen thawed out in a wonderfully warm kitchen and once full of hot tea everyone felt totally restored. Mick was able to telephone Bircham Newton with good news, for once, about a missing crew. When daylight came, they strolled back to the Hudson and only then did they see the tall poles studded irregularly around the field since the summer of 1940 to discourage German troop-carrying aircraft. Mick had luckily missed them all. There were also high-tension wires stretched across the field and the Hudson must have scraped over them in its last descent. When they learned later that no more than ten gallons of petrol remained in the fuel tanks, Cyril Prior summed up their collective opinion: "The devil doesn't want us lot yet, that's for sure." Mick took several photographs, in heartfelt tribute to a well-built, carefully-maintained (and brilliantly-flown) Hudson, but all were stolen from his locker at the end of the war.

An anonymous, undated newspaper clipping has been stuck in Mick's log book on the appropriate page. Headed WRECK FLEW HOME, it briefly summarises this exceptional feat without identifying the pilot. Before long, however, Mick's name would be widely known in Coastal Command and throughout New Zealand. On 6 February, he received the first of several congratulatory signals from on high. The Air Officer Commanding, reads this one, "warmly congratulates P/O M A Ensor and Sgt. B Paige on the awards made to them by His Majesty the King in respect of their recent meritorious achievements." The citation for Mick's award mentions "the coolness and skill he displayed in bringing his aircraft and crew safely back to England when, after a successful attack on a convoy off Sylt, the aircraft hit a rock [sic] and one engine and all instruments were put out of action." Bertie's citation commends him for his skill in "navigating this same aircraft back under very bad weather conditions and his initiative in assisting the pilot to make a landing with the aid of Very lights when

all other means of illumination had failed." As well as his own decoration, Mick was elevated in February to the dizzy heights of Flying
Officer, though that promotion would have come to him anyway,
on completing an unsullied year as a Pilot Officer. "Everyone was
surprised to see us when we got back to the station," he wrote, because
"after our wireless set packed up they hadn't heard from us and
thought we'd gone for a Burton."

Mr J P Mawson, Rector of St. Andrew's College, Christchurch,
wrote to Mick's parents on 25 February 1942 to express his delight at
the award of a DFC. Mawson himself had earned the Military Cross
during the Great War and informed the Ensors that Mick was the
first old boy to be decorated in this war. "It was duly announced to
the School", Mawson continued, "and I hope to have it recognised
with the time-honoured half-holiday when a suitable opportunity
occurs.... It brought back very vividly the days when he used to have
that five-foot bomber of his parked in my study. He must have put up
a very good show indeed and this is indicated by the fact that the award
was apparently 'immediate'. This occurs only when the performance
is of outstanding merit." A few weeks before this "very good show",
Mick had advised his parents not to bother looking in the papers to
see if he had been decorated because in Coastal Command "we very
seldom get the chance to do anything worth a decoration. The only
medal we want is the victory medal!"

CHAPTER V

THE PRUDENT LIMIT OF ENDURANCE
MARCH TO NOVEMBER 1942

BY 24 March 1942, 500 Squadron had moved from the Norfolk coast to Stornoway on the island of Lewis in the Outer Hebrides, off the north-west coast of Scotland. Some crews had spent a few days on Atlantic duty at Limavady, near Londonderry in Northern Ireland, before re-joining their friends. These moves gave added point to this Kentish squadron's Latin motto, which may be translated as "wherever duty calls us". It was now in 15 Group, which had its headquarters in Liverpool alongside those of the Navy's C-in-C Western Approaches. The squadron moved north in order to help patrol a U-boat passage route from German bases round the north of the Shetland Islands and then south-westward between the Shetlands and the Faeroe Islands. Most of 500 Squadron's patrols would be flown between those island groups.[1]

Knowledge of the squadron's poor state of morale had reached Sir Philip Joubert de la Ferté, head of Coastal Command, and in April he personally instructed a most able young officer, Denis Spotswood, to take charge and revive it.[2] Spotswood gradually did so, and then went on to higher commands, eventually reaching the very top of the service as Chief of the Air Staff in 1971. His effect on the squadron, in Mick Ensor's opinion, was quite remarkable. In particular, Spotswood kept himself well informed about policy and opinion at Group HQ and passed on as much as he could of that information both to air and ground crews. Everyone then had a clear idea of the squadron's place in the war effort and Spotswood had the gift of making any man he was talking

---

[1] *The RAF in Maritime War* (unpublished Air Ministry narrative) vol. iii, p. 79.
[2] Air Commodore Henry Probert, *High Commanders of the Royal Air Force* (HMSO, London, 1991) p. 71.

to, whether junior pilot, aircraft hand or filing clerk, feel that his efforts *mattered*. Spotswood was highly visible and widely respected for his obvious concern to get the best out of everyone. Mick observed him closely and years later, when he was himself a squadron commander, he deliberately chose 'Spots' as a model for his own conduct.

Although 500 Squadron had been trained in army co-operation, its actual employment had been on anti-shipping duty in the North Sea. Consequently, as Mick later recalled, "we had only a sketchy knowledge of the U-boat war, but we did get some good lectures from HQ. I must have had an interest in U-boats from an early age because my favourite book was *Raiders of the Deep* by Lowell Thomas. Set in the First World War, it then seemed a very good book." Mick had an equal interest in surface raiders, inspired by the visit of Count Felix von Luckner to St. Andrew's in April 1938. The Count had earned great fame in New Zealand during the First World War, as a daring and chivalrous opponent in the Pacific and then, after his capture, for a most ingenious (though brief) escape from an island in the Hauraki Gulf near Auckland.[3] "I thought the world of him", said Mick. "He was everything I wanted to be: brave, chivalrous, clever, handsome— and rich! I liked to imagine myself as a bold corsair and never dreamt that I'd ever hunt German seamen. I don't suppose many U-boat captains were as attractive as von Luckner, but most of them were just as brave and clever." Of more immediate value, perhaps, was Mick's friendship with Flight Lieutenant Wickham Martin of the Blenheim Meteorological Flight at St. Eval, who was finding U-boats from *high* altitudes at a time when orthodox opinion decreed that they be sought at low levels. Mick listened carefully to everything 'Wickers' had to say.

The standard U-boat used throughout the war by the Kriegsmarine was the type VIIC, a sturdy vessel of some 770 tons surfaced (870 submerged) with a very long range of nearly 10,000 miles at a surfaced cruising speed of ten knots (driven by two powerful, reliable diesel engines) and a sufficiently high maximum speed (seventeen knots) to overtake most merchant ships. It had a surprisingly good turning circle under water, considering its long, narrow shape, and a safe diving depth much greater than its designers expected. Twelve torpedoes were carried, as a rule, and a crew of forty-four. A submerged U-boat, however, could move only very slowly. Driven by electric motors, it could manage no more than seven knots and then only for a brief

---

[3] Robin Bromby, *German Raiders of the South Seas* (Doubleday, Sydney & Auckland, 1985) pp. 168-199.

period in an emergency. Its maximum range submerged was a mere 130 miles and even that distance required a top speed of two knots. The U-boat was not, in fact, a true *submarine* at all. It was not an "artificial fish" (in John Terraine's phrase) capable of travelling indefinitely as fast submerged as surfaced. And it was almost blind. Even on the surface, a U-boat sat so low in the water that visibility in the calmest conditions extended for only a few miles. Attacks were therefore made surfaced at night and most of a U-boat's travelling was also made surfaced, in order to permit re-charging of electric batteries.

At this stage of the war, most operational U-boats were crewed by carefully-trained men, experienced in combat. Their captains were shrewd and aggressive. Still confident of victory, morale throughout the U-boat service was consequently high and it then seemed that only a shortage of boats might prevent the Germans from sinking merchant ships quicker than the Allies could build them. Allied naval and air commanders, as well as thousands of merchant seamen, were acutely aware that these formidable opponents had ample reason for their confidence. Not until the end of 1941 was a U-boat sunk solely by air attack and a second unaided success did not follow until the middle of 1942. During 1941, more than two million tons of Allied shipping were sunk for a loss of only thirty-five U-boats: an average of 62,000 tons per boat lost represented, ultimately, victory at sea for Germany.[4]

Several good, experienced air crew followed Spotswood to 500 Squadron and so, "stirred and spurred into action", in Pat Green's words, it became a happy, efficient squadron. Two principal tasks were assigned: to escort convoys during the last stages of their approach to Britain and to prevent U-boats from attacking them. These were new tasks obviously of prime value to the war effort. Unfortunately, U-boats using this "Northern Transit Area" were outward-bound on their first cruise. Having inexperienced crews and being in no particular hurry, they naturally remained safely submerged for most daylight hours and travelled rapidly on the surface in darkness. Patrolling in darkness was a waste of time and fuel for these Hudsons, without either an effective radar or a powerful searchlight, and they had little chance of spotting a U-boat in daylight.[5]

Briefing for such patrols was of its nature quite different from the

---

[4] Robert C Stern, *Type VII U-Boats* (Arms & Armour Press, London, 1991); Gunter Hessler, *The U-Boat War in the Atlantic, 1939-1945* (HMSO, London, 1990); Air Ministry, *Operational Research in the RAF*, p. 76; *The RAF in Maritime War*, vol. v, p. 289; John Terraine, *Business in Great Waters: The U-Boat Wars, 1916-1945* (Leo Cooper, London, 1989) pp. xv-xvi.
[5] *The RAF in Maritime War*, vol. iii, p. 79.

detailed instruction given to Bomber Command crews. It could only be couched in the most general terms, with much emphasis on the need for pilots to operate at "the prudent limit of endurance". As a general rule, wrote Pat, "nothing much happened—occasionally a whale or a shark caused momentary excitement and, of course, Mick caused some excitement! However, we did begin to feel that we were part of a well-led team that knew what it was supposed to be doing." Although the work was unspectacular, it was important enough for the Admiralty to resist the use of Coastal Command aircraft in the massive raids mounted by Bomber Command from the end of May 1942 onwards. But in anticipation of taking part in such raids, recalled Pat, "the beautiful duck-egg blue undersides of some of our Hudsons had a revolting dark brownish-black dope splashed over them."

"Stornoway", Green emphasised, "was damp! Even in the summer. The whole place seemed to lie on a sort of peat bog" and taxying felt like travelling across a water-mattress. Everything, not only the aircraft, was widely dispersed. The squadron offices were a mile or more from the Mess and the crews slept half a mile or so from where they ate. They slept in Nissen huts that were damp and dark, with ablutions some twenty yards away: not very convenient, on a wet and windy morning. Getting around such a dispersed station on a bleak day was a trying business. But there were spells of lovely weather and Green remembered some very enjoyable bicycle tours: "I took a picnic and rode for miles in peace and solitude. Strange islands, the Outer Hebrides. I'm sure if there is anywhere where one might see the 'little people' it is there. Very ancient land and, I often thought, a strange atmosphere", owing something to the moaning wind, unfamiliar bird calls and distant bagpipes. Contact with the locals was virtually restricted to the sellers of Harris tweed and kippers, though a few nurses were found—by the lucky or diligent—to exist. "The Wee Frees", added Pat, "were certainly a force to be reckoned with. In fact, when the airfield first opened and a small detachment of Hudsons from Wick came over to use it, after the first Sunday (when, of course, some sorties were flown) a crowd marched out from the town, so we were told, to protest about the Sabbath being desecrated and old ladies, it was said, threatened the aeroplanes with their umbrellas! Perhaps apocryphal, but we believed it at the time."

The airmen got to know other parts of northern Scotland when bad weather closed Stornoway: principally, Wick in the far north-east and Sumburgh at the southern tip of the Shetlands. "I felt perfectly at home in all these desolate places," Mick recalls. "Compared with the Rakaia Gorge, they were thoroughly urbanised. People everywhere and even formed roads. Wind and rain didn't bother me, I'd seen worse at home." It was bad weather that contributed to the squadron's only fatal loss at Stornoway, when a Hudson flew into a cloud-covered hilltop while returning from a sortie. Pat thought the captain saw the ground at the very last moment and pulled back hard on the stick because the Hudson struck just short of the summit, bounced over and disintegrated on the downward slope. Another loss had its amusing side. "The pilot allowed a swing on taking off to get out of control", recalled Pat, "swung off the runway, wrote off the undercarriage and caught fire. The crew were out and running like rabbits in no time and, as Spotswood drew near in his car, off went the four depth charges—the most phenomenal explosion. It was said that one engine sailed over the top of Spotswood's car as he skidded to a stop! We then saw a sight to become familiar later, on a bigger scale: a mushroom cloud. It was an astonishing sight at the time."

Stornoway became a re-fuelling stop for Lockheed P-38 Lightning fighters en route to England from the United States. Led by a Boeing B-17 Flying Fortress, they flew via Greenland and Iceland to Stornoway and then on to bases in the south of England. The Americans, at that time practically unknown allies, amused and sometimes irritated the more staid Britons. Pat remembered them invading the Mess in full flying gear, "wearing their caps (gad, sir!) and armed to the teeth with revolvers and knives. Poor chaps, they didn't really know where they were or what was happening. They reported the Stornoway herring fleet as an enemy convoy on one occasion, so gossip had it."

Mick became very interested in the problems of finding and sinking U-boats. Because of its shape, a U-boat left an enormous wake when travelling on the surface, quite unlike that of a conventional vessel of similar weight travelling at a similar speed. It could be seen for miles. Looking down from 6,000 feet is only a vertical distance of about a mile and this, said Mick, "is nothing if you know the size of the object you are looking for. By contrast, a U-boat's vision is strictly limited. The platform is moving constantly and unevenly and the lookout man is normally using field-glasses. It is difficult for him to scan upwards for long and a high-flying aeroplane is not readily visible and can disappear in a moment. Getting close enough to a U-boat to damage it has a lot in common with stalking a deer. Once we had efficient radar sets and powerful searchlights for use in darkness, I reckon it was easier."

By April 1942, Mick had a new navigator—Flying Officer Neville Atkinson—to replace the Canadian, Bertie Paige. Good teamwork, Mick emphasises, was vital to the success any crew enjoyed. Everyone on board a Hudson had his own duties apart from keeping a lookout for targets and in any case no-one could see more than a segment of sea. A comprehensive lookout was only possible if a crew had discussed the difficulties before take-off, working out a means of keeping most of the sea in sight most of the time and, not least, helping each other to keep alert. Mick made everyone's task harder (Neville's most of all) by his determination to be an *active* hunter.

As in his Double Hill days, when looking for deer or rabbits, he was never prepared merely to wait for something to happen. A lazy hunter remains a hungry hunter because wild animals rarely make his life easy and Mick never supposed U-boats would either. He had no patience with crews who simply trundled round assigned circuits, becoming bored stiff at the lack of incident. *Constant Endeavour* was for the true hunter as apt a motto as for Coastal Command: unlimited reserves of alert patience were essential and Mick got this idea across to his crew. Consequently, his patrols were always eventful even when no target appeared because he spent the whole time dodging in and out of cloud, making frequent changes of altitude and speed. "There was game out there," he said, "and I felt that if we worked hard enough and kept out of sight as much as possible, we could find it without the beast getting wind of us too soon." These positive, aggressive methods gave him his best chance of surprising a boat and also kept boredom at bay. Neville soon showed himself a first-class navigator, well able to follow a devious route without getting lost. Although he shared Mick's enthusiasm for the chase and became an excellent lookout, he never forgot his PLE (Prudent Limit of Endurance). Mick trusted him absolutely and did not press for "one more look" when Neville announced "Home James Time".

On 26 April, Denis Spotswood and Ian Patterson (Mick's Flight Commander) being away for the day, Mick and Neville decided to "borrow" the squadron car and make a short tour of the island. A couple of nurses agreed to go with them. "It was all very innocent," Mick smiles. "Neville was very married and I knew virtually nothing about women in those days. We were really interested in the scenery and keener still on finding some kippers. Stornoway kippers were marvellous, best in the world." The end of a perfect day, replete with exquisite views and food, was marred by the unwelcome sight of Spotswood and Patterson. They had returned unexpectedly to find the car gone and promised "suitable punishment" next day. Mick was therefore glad to get away before dawn in a Hudson III (MK-Q) on his twenty-fifth operation. As luck and skill would have it, he was able to report an achievement on his return that put car thievery out of everyone's mind. Mick had attacked his first U-boat. It was also the first boat seen, let alone attacked, by 500 Squadron. Neville spotted it, travelling on the surface north of Stornoway, but the depth charges overshot because, Mick admitted, "my attack speed was at least 100 knots too fast."

Pilots dropped several of these devices (shaped like small oil drums with light-metal tail fairings added) at specified intervals, each one so fused as to explode at a specified time or depth. They could destroy a U-boat without actually hitting it because each explosion created around it a "lethal sphere" within which pressure would cause fatal damage. But it took years of trial and error by a positive galaxy of scientists and technicians to find the optimum intervals, time and depth for dropping and exploding these weapons. They also had to find substances that would generate a truly lethal explosion. Then came the problems air crews faced in actually finding U-boats and making accurate attacks during the very short time it took a boat to dive and change course.[6] In his log book, Mick wrote: "Large ocean-going sub sighted and attacked with machine-gun fire and four 250-lb depth charges. Claim damage." Unfortunately, Mick's claim is mistaken. U-boat records are remarkably complete and no boat reported significant damage on or about that day in that sea area.[7] "We really didn't know what we doing," Mick reflected later, "except that we were doing it wrong. The boat hadn't spotted us because it didn't even begin to dive until after the depth charges dropped. Everyone made a great fuss of us at de-briefing, but we knew we could have done a lot better."

A week later, Mick sent his parents a cablegram, telling them that he was on leave, having a wizard time, and had been promoted to the rank of Flying Officer. That promotion took effect from 8 February, when he was one month past his twentieth birthday. He wrote again to his parents on 30 May, telling them that he was "stationed in the Isle of Lewis now, you will find it on the NW side of Scotland, rather nice now in the summer but God knows what it will be like in the winter." His parents were at first delighted to learn that Mick had "a good chance" of returning to New Zealand within the next ten months or so. However, he went on to say that he was reluctant to leave his crew because "we are all very much attached to each other now." On

---

[6] Air Ministry, *The Origins and Development of Operational Research in the Royal Air Force* (HMSO, London, 1963), pp. 76-8.
[7] Gunter Hessler, *The U-Boat War in the Atlantic, 1939-1945* (HMSO, London, 1990) contains charts enabling the reader to trace the record and deployment of every boat.

reflection, therefore, neither Hugh nor Kathleen Ensor can have had any high expectation of seeing their youngest son again before the war ended. In fact, long before those ten months had passed, the crew broke up in tragic circumstances, but Mick never again mentioned the prospect of returning home.

He went on to describe "the best leave I have ever had"—seventeen days in London—"and it cost me nearly £40 so I am now living a pretty sober life for a while." He had intended staying with various friends, "but on my second day in London I met Allan Williamson, John Doleman and Ken Crankshaw who I was at school with and of course we all decided to stay together for a few days. Well, the few days sort of flashed past in a whirl of parties and we discovered that at the end of ten days we were four sadder but wiser men with no leave left to go and visit people at all." His present job, he ended, "is very interesting and I don't get that awful feeling that 'Well, if we get away with this trip we will all be damned lucky' sort of thing, and I must say that the seven months on the other lot was pretty solid. I had a minor victory of my own a while ago, but unfortunately can't say anything about it yet." This "minor victory" was his attack on the U-boat on 27 April: he may not have damaged it, but at least he found it, caused it to crash dive and presumably gave everyone aboard a thorough shaking.

Wing Commander Spotswood flew as second pilot with Mick on 22 May and assessed him on 10 June "above the average" as a general reconnaissance pilot. During June, as well as much flying to practice bombing and machine-gun firing, Mick carried out five more operations, bringing his total up to thirty-five. All were uneventful anti-submarine sweeps. Staff officers at Coastal Command HQ were keen to talk to men who had actually sighted U-boats and so Mick flew down to Northwood, about twenty miles north of central London, with Spotswood for a couple of days at the end of June. Mick was most impressed by his warm reception. He had tea with Sir Philip Joubert de la Ferté, head of the command, and soon found himself "nattering away" to "a real old world gent" about the problems of hunting U-boats. The great man listened patiently, interrupting only to ask sensible questions. It was during this visit that Mick also met several experts with whom he would work closely for six months in 1943. Mick was flattered by their attention—"in those days, I had no very high opinion of myself"—and also greatly encouraged by this clear evidence that the squadron's efforts were thought to be important by the very topmost brass. The idea of making his career in this service, should he survive the war, now took shape in his mind.

After his failure on 27 April, Mick had realised that intelligent use of cloud and/or height was the key to success in hunting U-boats. This technique meant one had to *approach* the target as fast as possible, but *arrive* there with speed reduced to about 160 knots and at no more than fifty feet above the sea. It took a great deal of practice and was "very unkind to the engines." The Hudson was not easily manoeuvred at low speed and Mick had to work hard to keep it straight and level, without skidding or slipping, at the critical moment when the depth charges were released. He learned that no last-minute change in the angle of attack was feasible: if his line was not ideal, it would have to do because seconds were vital. Although Mick and his crew were very tired at the end of every flight, a vigorous and occasionally tuneful rendering of "The Happy Hudson Ballad" put everyone in a good mood for landing. The words went something like this:

They say there's a Hudson just leaving Norway,
Bound for old Blighty's shore.
Heavily laden with terrified men,
Terribly scared and prone on the floor.

The cloud was ll/l0ths, down on the deck,
And trying so hard to be more.
There's many a Heinkel been pumping in lead,
And many a Messerschmitt too.

They've shot off our bollocks,
They've stuffed our hydraulics,
But [long pause]
they made a jolly landfall in the Firth of jolly Forth,
So cheer up, my lads, bless 'em all.

Then, on 6 July, while Mick was flying Hudson MK-S, Neville Atkinson spotted another surfaced U-boat north of Stornoway and Mick made a much better attack than he had in April. Horace Roe said the depth charges straddled the boat, but no oil or wreckage came up. They aimed plenty of machine-gun fire at the conning tower before it disappeared. "Don't suppose it did much good", Mick remarked, "but it can't have pleased the Germans either. They must have got a fright and we cheered ourselves up immensely. Had a grand singalong on the way home that day."

On 24 August 1942, Mick made what he himself proudly called "a copybook attack" in Hudson MK-A, also north of Stornoway. It was his fiftieth operation. This time, he himself sighted the boat from 5,000 feet. "Made low-level attack with four depth charges while U-boat was submerging," he recorded in his log book. "Direct hit with No. 2 ahead of conning tower. Ninety feet of stern rose to an angle of 50 degrees and then sank. Very large oil patch seen five minutes later." Four photographs are stuck in the log book here, showing the U-boat before submerging, while submerging, the position of the depth charge explosions across its wake, and the oil patch seen from 1,500 feet. Mick's words and pictures certainly seem conclusive, of serious damage at least. Sadly, he was again mistaken about the degree of damage caused because no U-boat reported any kind of trouble on that date in that area. When attacked by aircraft, U-boats often dived at a very steep angle and released a quantity of oil. Some also ejected clothing, rubbish, bits of wood—indeed, anything that would float— through torpedo tubes in an attempt to persuade an attacker that he had been successful. Once submerged, a U-boat was usually safe from further attack by a single aircraft because it could neither fly slowly enough nor hang about long enough to pinpoint and plaster the danger area—assuming, of course, that it had anything left to drop.[8]

At that time, unfortunately, the squadron was still using obsolete Amatol depth charges—not nearly as lethal as the Torpex charges used later (a mixture of TNT and powdered aluminium), which would certainly have sunk this boat, in Mick's opinion. As well as a more powerful explosive, a triggering device was needed that would ensure detonation at a shallow depth. His endeavours, however, were not going unnoticed. Two days later, he received a signal from Sir Philip Joubert de la Ferté himself, via his Group Commander. "Please convey my congratulations to captain and aircrew of A/500", said Sir Philip, "on their attack on a U-boat on 24/8. This is the third very promising attack made by A/500 and reflects a high standard of training, tactical appreciation and keenness on the part of all concerned. Splendid work." Mick was delighted to learn that Sir Philip remembered him and was noticing his efforts. The sharp eyesight and growing experience of Mick and his crew at least saved him from blasting away at oil slicks, whales and basking sharks.

The squadron left Stornoway for St. Eval, on the north coast of Cornwall, at the end of August 1942. Stornoway had not been the most popular of postings, given its extreme isolation, its wet, chilly

---

[8] Letter, Rodger B Haworth to Orange, 16 November 1993. David J Smith, *Action Stations 7: Military Airfields of Scotland, the North-East and Northern Ireland* (Patrick Stephens, Cambridge, 1983) p. 188 is mistaken in saying that Mick's attack blew off the boat's bow and that he was awarded the DFC for this exploit.

and windy weather even in summer, the incomprehensible Gaelic language of its people and (above all) the brief drinking hours they permitted and their fierce objection to the playing of football on Sundays. Not every member of 500 Squadron felt the same passion as did a majority of islanders for long, compulsory church services every Sabbath. However, as a reward for several well-executed attacks on U-boats during five months of hard work over Atlantic waters north of the Outer Hebrides, Mick would be awarded a Bar to his DFC in October.

But first, in September 1942, he had the honour of a summons to Buckingham Palace. It was the proudest moment of his life to that time and there have been few to match it since. Mick felt it deeply, especially for those he loved far away in Rakahuri and Double Hill. His mother would say little, his father less, but their joy would be profound. Mick invited his godmother, Lady Campbell, to accompany him and she described the occasion in a letter to his parents. "The show took place in one of the long corridors," she wrote, "and we all sat on chairs in rows, those who were receiving medals, etc., were in another room and had to be sorted out so as to come in order. While we were waiting, there was a band playing, which was lovely, all old tunes and very softly, it went on all the time the Investiture was taking place." Eventually, it was the turn of "your baby, who looked very smart and tidy, his hair was smooth and shiny and he was very solemn till it was all over and then he was one beam. The King spoke a few words to him, asking him how long he had been in this country, but Mick said he spoke so quietly that he could hardly hear him.... Almost the first thing he said as we came away was: 'I do wish mother could have been there.'"

Jimmy Ensor, fighting against Rommel in North Africa, learned of his brother's exploits only via their mother in New Zealand because efforts to communicate direct all failed. Jimmy actually heard the BBC mention Mick's name one February morning, but reception in the Desert was so poor that he caught only the fact of his decoration. That evening, when an account of Mick's Heligoland adventure was broadcast, reception had improved—but duty prevented Jimmy from listening. Being *told* about it later was a poor substitute. For nearly three years, from early in 1941 until late in 1943, Jimmy regularly expressed delight in whatever good news his mother transmitted about Mick and sympathised with her disappointment in the limited range of subjects raised in his letters. "I can quite understand", wrote Jimmy, "how he couldn't talk about anything but flying. It happens to us all out here and one always has to be on guard against it." Being almost fourteen years older than Mick no doubt helped Jimmy to write about something other than soldiering in his letters home.

Henry Dowling, a senior master, wrote to Mick's parents on 12 November from St. Andrew's College to offer his congratulations on the award of a second DFC. "When we heard that he was our first old boy to win a military decoration, we at St. Andrew's, who had watched him building and flying his perfect little model aircraft, were delighted but not surprised. Now, by his latest achievement, he has joined an even more select company of distinguished pilots." Within days of the writing of this letter, Mick would earn a third decoration, more prestigious even than his two DFCs, for one of the war's most remarkable feats of airmanship.

Left: Mick's mother, Kathleen. A powerful influence upon Mick until her death in 1979, aged 90. New Zealand-born daughter of James McCracken, member of an old-established Melbourne family who founded a successful brewery, permitting them to become landowners both in Australia and New Zealand.

Middle: Mick's father, Hugh. An example to Mick of honest man-management both before and after his death in 1943 at the age of 63. Seen here with his sons Duncan (left) and Mick in 1938. New Zealand-born son of Charles Ensor, member of an old-established Norfolk family who settled in Canterbury, Hugh earned a high reputation as a sheep-breeder.

Bottom: Rakahuri, near Rangiora in North Canterbury, where Mick was born. Designed and built about 1920 to his mother's specifications, this fine house was sold in 1944 and is now known as the Okuku Country Lodge.

Top: Mick in 1924, under dual instruction from his nurse on the drive at Rakahuri. In the foreground sits his Godmother: Nancy, Lady Campbell.

Above: Double Hill in the late thirties, when Mick lived there. A huge sheep station on the south bank of the Rakaia river in Mid-Canterbury, it was bought by Mick's father in 1916 and remains in the Ensor family.

Right: Mick aged six with a model of the *Southern Cross,* a Fokker trimotor monoplane in which Charles Kingsford Smith made the first successful aerial crossing of the Tasman Sea in September 1928. Mick saw the great man at close range and his enthusiasm for aviation has not waned from that day to this.

Top left: Mick at Double Hill in 1938, mounted on 'Tommy' with 'Big Nig' rolling on the ground at his feet. 'Little Nig', his other dog, won't be far away. It was here that Mick learned to be self-reliant and practical, a cunning hunter and an accurate shot: essential foundations for his later success as a Coastal Command pilot.

Top right: A happy trainee, leaning to fly at Taieri, near Dunedin. Mick went solo in a Tiger Moth on 4 September 1940 after only 6 hours and 50 minutes of dual instruction.

Above: Six young men out for a stroll. Awarded their wings at Wigram (near Christchurch) on 16 January 1941, they are (left to right) Mick Ensor, Roddy McCracken, Bruce Ingram, Maurice von Tunzelmann, Alan Harris and Desmond Bradley. Only Mick and Maurice survived the war.

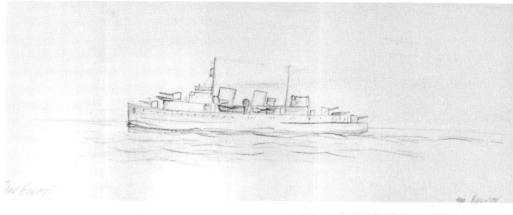

Top: Mick with his parents and friends at Rakahuri in late February 1941, shortly before he went overseas. His father sits in the shade behind him, his mother at his left. Mick would never see his father again.

Above: Mick's sketch (made from the liner-now-troopship *Awatea* in March 1941) of the *Prince Rupert*, a small Canadian gunboat that escorted the *Awatea* from Suva in Fiji to Vancouver in British Columbia. The accuracy of his sketch may be judged from the photograph, taken through the same porthole by Frank Reece, with whom he shared a cabin on this voyage across the Pacific.

Top: Four New Zealand Pilot Officers, one from each of the four main centres, relax from the strain of learning to fly the Bristol Blenhein at Andover, Hampshire, in June 1941. They are (left to right) Frank Reece of Dunedin, Mick Ensor of Christchurch, James Murray of Wellington and Albert Hawkins of Auckland.

Above left: Sergeant Bertram Paige at Andover, July 1941. Bertie, a Canadian navigator, was a member of Mick's first operational crew, flying Blenheims and Hudsons. Awarded the DFM for his contribution to Mick's first great flying achievement in January 1942, Bertie then returned to Canada where he was commissioned.

Above right: Sergeant Horace Roe at Andover, July 1941. A wireless operator/air gunner from Suffolk, Horace was the other member of Mick's first crew. He would be awarded the DFM for his contribution to Mick's second great flying achievement in November 1942 and was also commissioned.

Left: Pilot Officer Pat Green, photographed in the grounds of Thruxton Manor, near Andover, in August 1941 by Frank Reece. Pat and Mick often served together during and after the war, becoming great friends; Frank, unfortunately, would spend most of the war as a German prisoner.

Middle: Pilot Officer John MacGillivray and Mick on the Cam near Cambridge in August 1941. A few months later, in January 1942, John was killed in a flying accident at Bircham Newton, Norfolk. "I cried", said Mick, "for the first time since leaving school".

Bottom: The Hudsons of John MacGillivray and Pat Green, as seen from Mick's Hudson III (MK-P) on 15 January 1942, the day of his first operational flight in that aircraft. John was killed about 7.30 pm on the following evening.

Top: Margaret Douglas, John MacGillivray's fiancee, photographed by Mick at her home, Hindhope, near Jedburgh in Scotland in April 1943. Margaret and he became good friends, but she eventually married another New Zealander, Bill Goss, and settled in Christchurch.

Above: Mick at Margaret's home in April 1943. Mick loved the Jedburgh district, which reminded him of Canterbury: it was also "about the only place where one can get a real feed of mutton these days, the whisky hasn't run out either!"

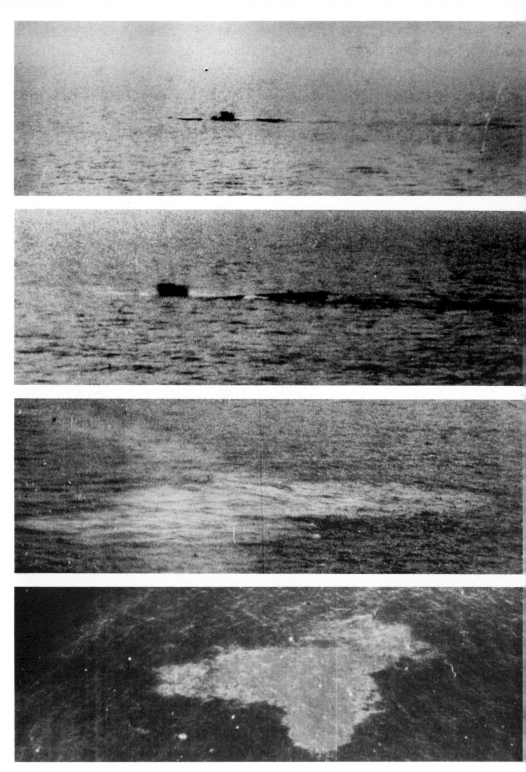

Mick's attack upon a U-boat on 24 August 1942. These four photographs are stuck in his log book, showing the boat before submerging, while submerging, the position of the depth charge explosions across its wake and a subsequent oil patch seen from 1,500 feet. The boat actually escaped without significant damage because scientists, technicians, and airmen had yet to determine the ideal method of dropping and exploding these weapons - and substances that would generate a truly lethal explosion were not then in general use.

CHAPTER VI

A TRAGIC TRIUMPH
AUGUST TO DECEMBER 1942

MICK ENSOR returned with 500 Squadron to St. Eval, six miles north-east of Newquay on the north coast of Cornwall, in late August. That station was "perhaps unique", wrote Roy Nesbit (once a pilot, later an historian) "in that, when work began on the Coastal Command aerodrome in 1938, a church which had stood on a mound in the site since Norman times was incorporated within the station boundaries."[1] Its tower had been painted white in the 18th Century to serve as a landmark for mariners sailing along a rocky coast. For different reasons, the aircraft which now came to share the saint's home were also painted white: tests had shown that aircraft were harder to spot from the surface of the sea if they were painted white. Carefully restored in 1889, St. Eval's tower would help many an airman home during the station's lifetime, from October 1939 until March 1959. In the Second World War, it became one of the largest and best-known of all Coastal Command stations, whereas St. Eval himself (a 6th Century Cornish bishop) is among the least-known in the Catholic Church's long list of saints. His church now contains a memorial stained glass window, together with a plaque, squadron badges and a book of remembrance recording the names of all those who lost their lives while serving there and, incidentally, perpetuating his own name.

After two weeks at St. Eval, the squadron moved on to Gosport, opposite the Isle of Wight, to prepare for service overseas in support of Operation Torch, the Anglo-American invasion of North-west

---

[1] Roy Nesbit, *Aeroplane Monthly*, November 1990, p. 699; Chris Ashworth, *Action Stations 5: Military Airfields of the South-West* (Patrick Stephens, Cambridge, 1982) pp. 163-170.

Africa. That operation, beginning on the morning of 8 November 1942, caught the German Supreme Command completely by surprise. Once it realised what was happening, Atlantic U-boats were ordered to go immediately to the invasion area and those already in the Mediterranean, Italian as well as German, hurried westward.[2]

On 30 October, Mick air-tested "a good Hudson", MK-S, in which he would carry out another eight operations before being forced to bale out of it over the Mediterranean. Early in November, with its Hudsons now painted white, the squadron flew to Gibraltar. Mick was thrilled to see the famous Rock for the first time and astounded at the sight of so many aircraft of all sorts both on the ground and trying to get down safely. Clearly, something big was about to begin, but he had not the slightest idea what it was. Nor did he much care, after eight hours in the air since leaving Cornwall and now finding the sky full of aircraft, all aiming at a single runway.

"We landed in the late afternoon," wrote Pat Green, "and by the time we had unloaded our kit, put it aboard a truck, found beds in the Nissen huts and had some food, it was getting dark. The Wingco [Denis Spotswood] had summoned us all to the Crew Room for briefing and as we came out of the Mess a searchlight came on from the Rock and shone straight down on us. We sat on a balustrade and gazed in amazement—24 hours ago, we had been in blacked-out England! From half a dozen 'rabbit holes' on the Rock face search-lights came on, floodlighting the aerodrome." The briefing that evening was short and general because everyone was tired, but next day Spotswood was able to tell them that a major operation would start that night and from dawn next day the squadron would be on standby. He emphasised that this information was still highly secret and must not be discussed even among themselves. Later that evening, Green recalled, he and Mick joined Spotswood in the Mess "and there was a rather awkward silence while we waited for our drinks. Only one thing to discuss and that forbidden! So we grinned at one another over our glasses and drank in silence."

They crossed the strait to lands ruled by Vichy France under German supervision. Looking back, Mick realises that the organis-ation necessary to shift massive armed forces from the United States and Britain to North Africa was simply taken for granted and yet 500 Squadron's ground crews materialised at Tafaraoui (near Oran, in Algeria) on the very day required. To everyone's delighted surprise, a convoy of lorries loaded with the squadron's ground crews drove

---

[2] *The RAF in Maritime War*, vol. iii, pp. 504-6.

onto the airfield. The air crews had not seen them for nearly two months, since leaving St. Eval in September. They had come out by sea and after landing had a bad day or two in Oran at the hands of Vichy supporters. There was also ample petrol available at Tafaraoui, even if it came in small and flimsy tins that made re-fuelling an endless task. Denis Spotswood quickly set up a HQ on the mezzanine floor of a hangar with a handful of Signals and Ops Room staff who had established a W/T link with Gibraltar and the squadron was open for business.

No-one knew where the French were and some fairly light-hearted concern was expressed about the prospect of field-gun fire. In fact, the French had gone inland to a Foreign Legion base and the airmen were left undisturbed on their first night, except for the incessant barking of dogs. They sat around on the floor of a hangar, dining out of tins. Next morning, everyone moved into quarters vacated by the French. Attractive to look at from the outside, with creamy-white walls and tiled roofs, they were fully populated inside by a huge army of bugs and insects, all avid biters. On the second night, some Algerians came to barter tiny eggs for cigarettes through the perimeter fence and the leading barterer on the squadron side was a New Zealander, Flight Lieutenant Peter Holmes, who had worked for a while before the war on the Ensor property at Double Hill. Like his brother Jimmy, Mick often wondered where the eggs came from, since neither ever saw a hen in North Africa.

Tafaraoui would later earn an evil reputation as a mudflat, but during 500 Squadron's short stay it was very dusty. It had been agreed that one member of each crew, as a rather token guard, would sleep in his aircraft, which turned out to be a bitterly cold chore, rarely repeated. From Tafaraoui, the squadron moved to Maison Blanche (near Algiers) before coming to rest farther inland from that city at Blida on 19 November. It was kept intensely busy escorting convoys, carrying out sweeps or searches and ferrying people and stores.

One mystery prior to leaving England was the fact that everyone was issued with khaki battledress: no explanation, just instructions to sew on RAF badges of rank. At that time, since no-one knew where the squadron was going, khaki battledress certainly provoked lively speculation. They were also issued with revolvers: "Great fun they were too," says Mick. "We used to blast away on the range, whenever we got the chance, playing Cowboys and Indians or G-men and Chicago gangsters. Not very mature, I'm afraid." When the air crews at last reached Gibraltar and were briefed about the invasion, they were told to wear khaki on moving to North Africa because the invasion was supposed to be an entirely American affair and khaki looked more American than RAF blue. The French had no love for the British and would prefer to be liberated by 'Americans'. Later, an alternative explanation surfaced: they would look less like German airmen in American eyes. After a few days, to everyone's relief, the khaki uniforms were withdrawn. Thick, rough and close-fitting, they were less than ideal for the North African climate, quite apart from the squadron's pride in its familiar RAF blue.

Mick worked hard in November, flying on eight operations within the space of eleven days from the 5th to the 15th, all in the same Hudson (MK-S, 'S for Sammy') with his usual crew: Flying Officer Neville Atkinson (navigator), Flight Sergeant Horace Roe and Sergeant Cyril Prior (air gunners and wireless/radar operators). During those days, there were at any one time between fifteen and twenty U-boats in the western Mediterranean and about the same number of Italian submarines off the Algerian coast, just to the eastward of the main German patrol area. The Italians lost one boat in that period, while the Germans lost five.[3]

On 7 November, during an anti-submarine sweep from Gibraltar, Mick sighted but failed to get near a U-boat before it submerged. Next day, he flew to Oran and from there helped to cover the landing of troops on that day and the next. On the 11th, he flew from Gibraltar to Tafaraoui, and carried out a convoy escort. During another anti-submarine sweep on 12 November he attacked a twin-engined Italian bomber: a Fiat B.R.20 Cicogna, larger and heavier than the Hudson. He saw hits, followed by smoke, on the starboard engine and fuselage, but "it was too fast for us to bring down", he later admitted ruefully. While returning home, Mick saw a liner aground and on fire off Bougie, about 110 miles east of Algiers. On landing, he learned with a shock that she was the *Awatea*, the New Zealand ship in which he had sailed from Auckland to Vancouver, British Columbia, a lifetime ago. Already damaged by mines, she was finished off by an Italian submarine, German bombers and torpedo aircraft.[4]

On the afternoon of 13 November, Mick attacked a U-boat northeast of Oran with four 250-lb depth charges just after it submerged.

---

[3] R M Coppock (Naval Historical Branch, Ministry of Defence, London) to H W Thomson (former member of 233 Squadron) of Blenheim, New Zealand, 20 July 1987. See also *The RAF in Maritime War*, vol. iii, pp. 508-514.

[4] Jurgen Rohwer & Gerhard Hummelchen, *Chronology of the War at Sea, 1939-1945* (Greenhill Books, London, 1992) pp. 174-5; Sydney D Waters, *Union Line: A Short History of the Union Steam Ship Company of New Zealand Ltd., 1875-1951* (CSW, Wellington, 1952) pp. 101-5.

"Damaged U-boat surfaced", he wrote in his log book, "and manned machine-gun on conning tower. We shot them up with our guns until out of ammunition, leaving several of gun crew dead and wounded. U-boat last seen down at the bows and making little headway." This was U458 (a Type VIIC, commanded by Kapitänleutnant Kurt Diggins), which in fact managed the very fine feat of struggling home to La Spezia, on the north-west coast of Italy: a journey of at least 800 miles. German records do not mention any crew fatalities, but the fortunes of Mediterranean boats are in general poorly documented. "It submerged on sighting me", Mick wrote later, "and I released depth charges ahead of the swirl. To our astonishment, it re-surfaced, though with no way on and manned its guns. We just shot them up a bit and radioed for help. Low on fuel and not feeling very intrepid, we returned to Oran." Under Diggins' command, U458 had sunk at least two merchant ships in the Atlantic during 1942. The boat was back in action by February, but its luck finally ran out in August 1943 when British and Greek destroyers sank it south of Sicily. Diggins, however, was among the small minority of captains who did not die with their boats. He was captured and survived the war.[5]

Two days later, on 15 November 1942, Mick began his sixty-sixth operation in 500 Squadron, an operation which ended in the deaths of two members of his crew, the loss of his aircraft and his departure from the squadron. It also saw the destruction of U259 (a Type VIIC, commanded by Kapitänleutnant Klaus Köpke) and all forty-eight members of its crew, four more than the usual complement. Köpke had only just arrived in the Mediterranean from the Atlantic, on the night of 8-9 November, in response to the sudden crisis caused by the Allied landings. This is how both the U-boat and the aircraft met their fates, in Mick's own words.[6]

"We're flying an anti-submarine sweep north of Algiers at 7,000 feet when the crew report a surfaced U-boat some distance to the north of us. The sky is clear and the sea calm. I'm fairly confident that we won't be spotted by the boat, thanks to our high altitude and white under-surface: sea-birds use height and camouflage and they're better

---

[5] Rowher & Hummelchen, *Chronology*, pp. 149, 174 & 226; letters, Rodger B Haworth to Orange, 24 October 1993 & 16 November 1993; Norman L R Franks, *Search Find and Kill: Coastal Command's U-boat Successes* (Aston Publications, Bourne End, Bucks., 1990) p. 144.

[6] The comment in Rohwer & Hummelchen, *Chronology*, p. 174 that U259 shot down the attacking aircraft is mistaken and Alfred Price, *Aircraft versus Submarine: The Evolution of the Anti-Submarine, 1912 to 1980* (Kimber, London, 1980), p. 102 is also mistaken in writing that Ensor took part in the attack on U595 on 14 November. See also Franks, *Search Find and Kill*, pp. 146-7.

hunters than we are. Even so, I immediately swing the Hudson around and down in the direction indicated, whereupon the boat comes into my line of vision about fifteen miles away, fully surfaced and leaving a huge white wake. Time is vital because it can dive out of my reach within forty seconds of sighting me and at my maximum speed of four and a half miles a minute it will take from three to four minutes to get within range.

"The muted rumble of the one-time passenger liner soon becomes a loud roar as speed increases during a steep dive to sea-level. I'm not watching the airspeed indicator or any other instruments, but I know my speed is very great, so close the throttles and wind on forward trim to ease pressure on the control wheel. I never take my eyes off the target while we're diving towards a point on the sea some two miles short of it and have the hunter's calm certainty that this time I cannot miss. At sea-level now. The target still seems completely unaware of us. I know that for a successful depth charge attack, I must fly over it slowly. With only two miles to go, I must therefore lose nearly half my flying speed and make a deliberate attack from as stable a platform as possible.

"So I put the propellers into fine pitch and open the bomb-doors: together these make effective but noisy airbrakes. I feel that I alone am attacking the U-boat, I just happen to be surrounded by an aeroplane. Now's the time for total concentration. My brain has to absorb a hundred and one variable factors of speeds, angles and height. I see that my speed is down to 150 knots and judge my height at about fifty feet. I'm relaxed and satisfied that I'm going to track over the U-boat's foredeck. I take a deep breath and, as with a sporting rifle, wait for my reflexes—trained by practice—to make me press the release button and let go four 250-lb Torpex high-explosive depth charges in a row spaced fifty feet apart. They should all explode on reaching a depth of twenty-five feet and if one does so within twenty feet of the U-boat, that will certainly be enough to sink it. By that time, the aeroplane will have flown on, out of range of the explosion.

"I press the button and a second or so later something goes badly wrong. There's a great *whoomph* and a feeling of being compressed. To me even now, it seems that I was in a slow-motion horror movie. For a moment, I've no outside vision—but my instinct is to pull the nose up. The control wheel falls back uselessly into my lap—which is covered with bits of perspex from the shattered cockpit windows. A memory of someone who'd controlled an aeroplane by the trim-lever alone flashes into my mind, so I go for the trim-lever. It too is useless. Where blasphemy ends and prayer begins I don't know, but a wave of sheer terror floods over me and I call on Jesus Christ for help.

"By then, I can see the sparkling blue sea flashing under the nose and there's only one thing left that can possibly save us from a fatal high-speed crash: I ram the throttles fully open. There's a little movement in the aileron controls and with that I hold the wings level. The engines respond, thank God, and slowly the Hudson's nose comes up and I can feel that we're starting to climb away from immediate peril. I don't want too much nose-up though; that'll lead to loss of speed and a fatal stall. I don't remember any airspeed indicator readings, the instruments may have been out of action. I manage to stabilise the situation somewhat by finding the best throttle setting and then feel the effect of Neville and Cyril moving.

"I realise that if I use the crew as moving ballast I'll have better control and manage to convey this idea to them. It isn't easy because of the tremendous noise in the flight-deck area: the cockpit windows have been blown in and the engines are running at maximum revolutions just outside. Fortunately, I can talk to Horace Roe (in the rear turret) on the intercom. I ask: 'What can you see, Horace?' 'Sub's blown up', he replies, 'bits everywhere and I saw a gun in the air.' That at least is marvellous news, I think, and makes our effort worthwhile whatever happens now. Then I ask: 'What's wrong with the tailplane?' and he tells me: 'The elevators and one rudder have gone, other rudder is just hanging on and there's a bloody great hole under my feet!' I tell him to come forward to help me balance the aeroplane, watch my hand signals and organise the other two accordingly.

"At least we're flying, but in the wrong direction—away from land. Now that I've time for a better look-round, I can see that about six feet of each wingtip are bent up, bending the outer portions of the ailerons with them and greatly restricting their movement. However, we've got ourselves balanced now and so I can reduce engine speed and power a little because the temperatures are well over the high limit. Opening the cowling gills has a bad effect on the flying characteristics of these Hudsons, but I inch them open as much as I dare. We start a slow climbing turn to the south, making for the North African coast. The human elevator substitute is working well and not too much movement is needed. The splendid discipline of those men is beyond praise; not once do they query my instructions or fail to respond immediately. I have plenty to do and am therefore not frightened, but their situation must be terrifying.

"My thoughts turn to the next move. Although we seem safe enough at 3,000 feet with land clearly visible ahead, the only way to get down will be by parachute; there can be no question of landing the Hudson in its battered condition. Temperature gauges are still hard against the *high* stop, so there's no guarantee that the engines will keep going for much longer. Fortunately, I'm wearing a seat-type parachute, but the crew have to put on harnesses and then attach their parachutes to hooks on the chest. I tell them to do this, but because they have to go to various stowage areas I lose my 'moving ballast'. To make matters worse, Neville has to go down into the nose for his and all the time he's there we're losing height. Horace reports that although Cyril Prior's parachute has been partly opened in the explosion, they both think it'll be OK. By the time all this is sorted out, we're down to about 1,000 feet, so back we go to the old drill and start to climb again.

"We're now less than twenty miles from the coast and I have my eye on a naval vessel ahead and slightly to the left. Actually, it's a sloop, HMS *Erne*, and there's another one nearby as well, the *Leith*, but I don't learn this till later. I'm relieved to know that if we have to bale out in a hurry, we'll soon be rescued; it'll have to be soon because our 'mae west' life-jackets won't be much help for a long stay in the water. When we get to about 1,500 feet, the port engine loses power and I have to close the throttle on the starboard one to prevent the Hudson from going into a diving turn to the left—it has no rudder control and very little aileron, let alone elevator. It stays more or less level, but is going down rapidly, so I leave my seat and scramble back through the cabin towards the escape-door.

"Everyone else is already there. I haven't been able to contact the crew to tell them to abandon the aircraft, but seeing me leave my seat is enough and out they go: not without difficulty because our combined weight is now all at the rear of the cabin and the Hudson is very nose-up and banking to the left, making the escape-door face up, towards the sky. I can't recall their order of departure, though I do remember helping Neville out. I have difficulty levering myself over the edge, then fumble for the ripcord and pull it at once. It works, giving me a moment of pure joy, and hanging there I look down in time to see the poor old Hudson in a steep diving turn, just before it plunges into the sea with a mighty splash. In a matter of seconds, I'm in the water myself.

"After what feels like a very deep dive, I undo my harness, float up under the parachute, swim out of that and inflate my mae west. The sea's calm and I seem to be all alone. I think of salvaging the parachute—girls like a supply of free silk, so I've been told. Then I begin to wonder if I really will be rescued—you can't see far when your eyes are only six inches above the surface—and forget about girls for once and parachutes. Although normally a bit of a 'water baby', I quickly begin to feel very chilled and miserable, so I must be shocked. However, the ship I saw—HMS *Erne*—is in fact close by and one of her boats soon picks me up. I try to persuade the captain to look for the U-boat's remains, but of course he has his own job to do and the wreckage is quite a long way off. They fill me up with rum and put me in a cabin to sleep—which I do, to my surprise. The other ship, HMS *Leith*, picks up the rest of my crew, but Neville Atkinson and Cyril Prior are dead. Neville's head struck the fuselage as he baled out and he must already have been unconscious when he hit the water; Cyril's parachute failed to open." Both men were buried at sea after a brief ceremony which Mick was too distressed to attend.

Neither Mick nor Horace Roe ever considered that there was anything but a depth charge explosion under the Hudson. They neither saw nor felt a secondary explosion nor said anything about splitting the conning-tower, as has sometimes been reported. The Hudson was *very* low and 250 pounds of Torpex going off under it was quite sufficient to wreck both the submarine and the aircraft. Mick thought it went off in contact with the pressure hull below the wooden deck and blew the gun into the air. "The wonder is that I ever trusted a hydrostatic fuse again." Looking back on the whole episode, Mick says that it still gives him a sick feeling in the stomach, "and I suppose that I have spent a lot of my life running away from the fact that I was bloody frightened." He seems not to realise, even now, that almost all human beings would have been at least as "bloody frightened" as he was and that many of them would have been quite unable to act rationally—as he did—during such an experience.

However frightened he may have been, it is the considered opinion of one eminent aviation historian, Alfred Price, that in this crisis Mick gave "a display of airmanship and cool-headedness that can have few equals in the entire history of flying". Another historian, H L Thompson, described this incident as "probably the most spectacular attack of the whole war."[7] It was only the second occasion in the Atlantic or Mediterranean campaigns that a depth charge actually struck a U-boat and detonated on impact. No third instance appears to be recorded. About four weeks before Mick's misadventure, on 20 October, a Liberator of 224 Squadron had suffered a similar fate some 600 miles south-west of Ireland. The boat, *U216*, was destroyed and the Liberator severely damaged, but in this case the crew got her home

[7] Alfred Price, *Aircraft versus Submarine*, p. 103; H L Thompson, *New Zealanders with the Royal Air Force* (War History Branch, Department of Internal Affairs, Wellington, 1953) vol. i, p. 311.

after a desperate struggle. They crashlanded at Predannack, near Lizard Point on the south coast of Cornwall. Although the aircraft caught fire immediately, everyone got out safely, one man breaking a leg, the rest no more than scratched, bruised and exhausted. The 1st pilot, Flying Officer D M Sleep, received a most well-deserved DFC. Curiously enough, 224 would be the next squadron in which Mick fought U-boats.[8]

Mick and Horace got back to their squadron at Tafaraoui within a few hours of their rescue. They were told that someone at Coastal Command Headquarters in England wanted to see them urgently, so they were ferried to Gibraltar immediately. No time was allowed for them to celebrate their spectacular success, mourn their dead friends or even make proper farewells to men with whom they had shared danger for many months. It seemed almost as if they had done something disgraceful, rather than amazingly skilful, but higher authority decreed and lower forms of life were required to obey at once. Little consideration was given to their mental or physical condition after their ordeal and not much even to their safety, Mick being required to pilot himself in a battered Hudson (MK-X) that "had been a bit shot up and required repairs" high over Spain from Gibraltar to Gosport. He had Peter Holmes (the New Zealand egg-barterer we met earlier) as his navigator and Horace Roe in the rear turret. Horace, who had left his turret in 'S for Sammy' to throw out all moveable equipment in an attempt to lighten the Hudson and so help Mick keep it aloft, would be awarded the DFM on arrival and sent for officer training. Deep regret was expressed in the squadron's Operational Record Book for the loss of two "very popular and very experienced aircrew" and a warm tribute paid to Mick's "superb display of airmanship". Everyone was sorry to learn of his departure from the squadron.

On the night of 24-25 November, then, just nine days after that bitter victory, Mick was on his way back to England. A flight of nearly seven hours, it was the sixty-seventh and last operational flight of Mick's career with 500 Squadron. It brought his record as a first pilot in that squadron during sixteen months (from July 1941 to November 1942) to just over 500 hours in total. His operational flights amounted to exactly 357 hours at an average of five hours and twenty minutes each. Of these operations, nearly one-quarter (sixteen) were flown wholly or partly at night. On arrival in England, he learned that he

---

[8] *The RAF in Maritime War*, vol. iii, pp. 504 & 511; Franks, *Search Find and Kill*, p. 74.

was to become a Companion of the Distinguished Service Order. At the same time, he was promoted to the acting rank of Squadron Leader. Mick was the third New Zealander to complete the 'hat trick' of DSO, DFC and Bar. The other two, Wing Commanders E P Wells and T O Freeman, were at that time back in New Zealand. Mick was also the youngest, by far the most junior in rank and the first member of Coastal Command to achieve this triple distinction.

At that time, Mick's record against U-boats amounted to one certainly sunk, one certainly suffering serious damage and three certainly shaken up, if not damaged. It is a record of which Mick is justly proud. "There weren't too many crews in Coastal Command who had attacked more than one U-boat; we had five attacks in eight months." Mick had also hit one ship with bombs and another with machine-gun fire as well as bombing targets at St. Nazaire on the south coast of Brittany. In addition, he had damaged an Italian aircraft. Quite apart from these varied achievements, he had carried out many anti-submarine sweeps, escorted convoys (attempting on occasion to round up scattered ships) and looked for lost aircraft and dinghies. In return, two crew members had been killed, one Hudson destroyed and another seriously damaged. Mick himself had been decorated three times and both the original members of his Andover crew had been awarded the Distinguished Flying Medal.

Denis Spotswood, Mick's CO, later recalled that Mick was "a quite outstanding pilot and Captain of Aircraft—as results indicate. I recall that in 500 Squadron we initiated an internal training scheme concentrating on crew co-operation and Mick was assiduous in his attention to this." He would not otherwise have survived the attack on *U259*. Spotswood suspected that "Mick's depth charges were imperfectly fused and that a 'dry hit' caused one to explode on impact. His was a remarkable piece of airmanship thereafter." Personally, concluded Spotswood, "I think he was as great as any of the U-boat killers, and not with the best equipment."[9]

Eastern Air Command repeated to 328 Wing Headquarters on 22 December 1942 a signal received by the AOC (Air Marshal Sir William Welsh) from the Admiralty, requesting him to convey "the congratulations of their Lordships to No. 500 (GR) Squadron on the successful destruction of *three U-boats* on 14, 15 and 17 November." Welsh added: "This is high and well-deserved praise. The work of the squadron, entailing long hours flying over the sea can be, at times, extremely tedious. It is, however, vital and I am glad it has been

[9] Letters, Spotswood to Spooner, 16 January and 2 May 1988.

crowned with success and I know that more will come." The three
boats were *U595* on the 14th (which, in fact, was later to be attributed,
quite correctly, to Flying Officer G. Williams of 608 Squadron, though
several crews from 500 Squadron also attacked it, helping to drive it
ashore); *U259* on the 15th (which Mick Ensor sank, no question); and
U331 on the 17th (immobilised and obliged to surrender by Mick's
fellow-New Zealander, Ian Patterson, it was later sunk by Fleet Air
Arm aircraft). However, 500 Squadron is still to be allowed its three
victories within a week because on 13 November Squadron Leader
John Ensor, Mick's namesake, sank *U411* "west of Gibraltar", a feat
wrongly attributed at the time to a British destroyer.[10]

Neville Atkinson, Mick's navigator and good friend, was married
and Mick had met his wife, their baby and his parents. As soon as he
returned to England, Mick visited Neville's parents, but they were still
so distressed that they refused to let him enter the house, angrily
telling him to clear off and leave them alone. His wife, however,
received Mick calmly, got the baby ready and went for a long walk
with him in a nearby park, chatting easily about old times and future
prospects. Even so, that day was for Mick an experience no less
dreadful in its own way than the plunge into the Mediterranean.
'Another part of war's hardening, I suppose', he reflected sadly.

On 14 December 1942, Margaret Douglas wrote to Mick's mother
from Hindhope, near Jedburgh in Roxburghshire, Scotland. She had
been John MacGillivray's fiancée "and saw quite a lot of Mick in those
days. Then when Johnny was killed, Mick was simply grand to me and
came up to Calrossie. Since then I had not seen him for quite a time,
till last month when he came up to stay with us for a bit of his leave."
Margaret thought Mrs Ensor might welcome news about her son from
another source, Mick being such an infrequent correspondent. He had
been out in North Africa for the past six weeks or so, she wrote,
"which turned out to be rather an unhealthy spot, as he had an
involuntary swim in the Mediterranean and lost either two or three
members of his crew. In spite of this, he is looking terribly well and
full of life and I am glad to say is off operations for a while and has a
job at Coastal Command HQ at Northwood, just outside London. It
will at least be a relief for you to know that he is out of danger for
about six months anyhow and he is fortunate in being so near the
Strangs at Amersham. I went to visit them with Mick not long ago and
Dorothy has asked me to go down this weekend and see them, so I
hope to see something of Mick then too, if he can get any time off."

---

[10] Letters, Coppock to Spooner, 18 March and 29 July 1988.

Margaret was working as a physical education teacher at a girls' high school in Rotherham, Yorkshire, "but we get our Christmas holidays in less than a week now so after I've been to London I'm going home to Scotland for three weeks—my father has sheep farms in the south of Scotland—so it is a grand change after living in an industrial area like South Yorkshire. Mick was just saying the other day how strange it was that the country people always seem to collect together and it is quite true—I suppose it is because we have so much in common."

Mick had gradually become very fond of Margaret after their second meeting at John MacGillivray's funeral in January 1942; too fond, for her peace of mind. "At that stage", she wrote later, "that was the *last* thing I wanted—and I also felt I'd never again get involved with anyone in the RAF and go through all that shattering experience. In fact, I was quite numb." And yet, as Margaret recognises, Mick was "probably a great help to me—on looking back—as he came up to Yorkshire to visit me and drag me out. I asked him home to Hindhope, as he was a farming boy. My parents had quite a few overseas boys to stay and it was what we did, to write to their parents which was always much appreciated. Hence my letter to Mrs Ensor and that was all, as far as I was concerned.... Apart from Mick's visit to my home, it was always parties and beer in London and I met a lot of New Zealanders. I was very grateful to Mick for making me get up and go again, but ... I didn't know or wouldn't let myself know how much he cared.... We didn't ever talk about his experiences except briefly or he'd write a letter, such as 'we ditched in the Mediterranean last week.'"[11]

The account Mick sent his parents in December of his "very interesting trip to North Africa" certainly wasted few words. "It wasn't too hot," he told them, "but the nights were a bit cold as we had no beds or bedding for the first week. I would still be there if the unfortunate thing that happened to me hadn't occurred. It was very bad luck on my navigator and my gunner, both of whom were killed, as we had done a great deal of flying together. However, war is war, I suppose, and one must just learn to accept these things as they come. Sgt. Roe and myself were only in the water for 20 minutes before being picked up, which wasn't bad considering. I must say I don't like jumping out by 'chute, but I really thought the wings were going to fall off at any minute and we had hardly any control over the aeroplane anyhow. When one engine cut it just went down like a rocket, but by that time we were all ready to jump and it took no time at all. I was last out.

---

[11] Letter, Margaret Goss to Spooner, 18 March 1988.

Pete Holmes and I flew back here together some time ago, but he has gone back now, the lucky devil." Aware that his family would be anxious to know more about this tragic triumph than he cared to write, Mick added: "no doubt you will get all the news from Malcolm MacFarlane when he gets home, as I saw quite a bit of him in London while I was on leave this time. Hope you are all well, please give my love to all the rest of the Rakahuri and Double Hill outfit. From your loving son, Maechel Ensor." Years would pass before he felt able to write or speak in any more detail about his last wartime flight over the Mediterranean.

CHAPTER VII

PW'S PLACE
JANUARY TO JULY 1943

BY Christmas 1942, Mick Ensor had already made his mark as a brave, skilful and cool-headed aircraft captain. At the end of that year, only six per cent of attacks upon U-boats were resulting in destruction and there was continual argument between squadron crews blaming poor weapons and Operational Research Section staff at Command HQ blaming poor aiming.[1] Wise men on both sides of this argument agreed, however, that the realistic answer lay in practice and yet more practice, as well as the development of more efficient weapons. "That the solution lay here", recorded Captain D. V. Peyton-Ward, RN (author of the RAF's authoritative history of the maritime war), "was supported by the successes scored by certain squadrons and individuals in those squadrons. During the past year, three squadrons were outstanding in numbers of U-boats killed and damaged—Nos. 120, 202 and 500. All these squadrons had good records in practice bombing and all had been heavily engaged with the enemy, thereby getting still more practice. The outstanding individual pilots at this time were Squadron Leader T M Bulloch of No. 120 Squadron and Flying Officer M A Ensor of No. 500 Squadron. Both had a natural eye for bombing (comparable to that possessed by a good shot-gun performer) and, aided by painstaking practice, this had resulted in a very high standard of attack." Their endeavours, concluded Peyton-Ward, "showed clearly that the existing weapon was perfectly adequate to sink U-boats, provided the pilot put it in the right place."[2] Mick was now to come under the command of Peyton-Ward and to this day finds it

---

[1] *The RAF in Maritime War*, vol. iii, pp. 537-9.
[2] *The RAF in Maritime War*, vol. iii, pp. 528-9. For a biography of Terry Bulloch see Tony Spooner, *Coastal Ace* (Kimber, London, 1986).

difficult to believe that 'PW' (as he was known to humble and great alike) returned his high regard.

Not yet twenty-one years old, there lay ahead of Mick plenty of remarkable adventures and achievements in dangerous operations, but first he must spend six months behind a desk, away from the cockpit. In early January 1943, he went to Coastal Command Headquarters at Northwood (near Watford, about twenty miles north of central London) as a staff officer. There he met a great many men and women whose work with pen, paper and maps admirably complemented the efforts of aircrews in one of the war's most critical campaigns: that against U-boats threatening vital shipping traffic across the Atlantic and through the Mediterranean.[3] It was, of course, office work; too quietly undramatic at first for the taste of so active a young man, but he would learn to respect and admire the achievements of his new colleagues. When Mick returned to operations, he certainly had a far clearer understanding of everyone's contribution, on the ground and in the air, to the command's *constant endeavour*.

Coastal Command Headquarters were housed in a handsome country residence situated on rising ground and surrounded by several acres of woodland, the whole being known as Eastbury Park. Numerous camouflaged huts scattered among trees provided working or living accommodation for the people employed there. The air staff and the C-in-C's personal staff all had offices in the main building. When Mick reported for duty, after some much-needed leave, he found that he had joined a department named Plans Anti-Submarine. He was told that he was now an acting Squadron Leader with the substantive rank of Flight Lieutenant and had been awarded an immediate DSO to go with his two DFCs. Although rightly proud of his array of decorations, they did rather embarrass him at times, as he confessed in a letter to his parents. "I feel now that it is not really me that is walking round in a uniform at all," he wrote, "everyone looks at it as if it were some sort of curiosity or something and I don't really feel that I have earned all this."

Mick had been interviewed by the BBC on 7 January and his mother enjoyed the entirely unexpected thrill, half a world away, of hearing her youngest son's voice as he spoke quietly and modestly about his achievements. She wrote at once to tell her eldest son the good news. Jimmy, then helping to pursue Rommel as he fled westward to Tunisia, was delighted. "He has done wonderfully well, hasn't he?

---

[3] Air Ministry, *The Origins and Development of Operational Research in the Royal Air Force* (HMSO, London, 1963) pp. 76-103.

There can be only a very few who have been decorated three times in twelve months. I hope after all his success he doesn't become rash. His judgement seems to be pretty good, so I think he will be alright."

Group Captain Narbrough Hughes D'Aeth (known to his friends as 'Jimmy') was Mick's new boss. He made him very welcome over a good lunch and even gave him a desk in his own office. Jimmy was a good listener with a prodigious memory and an inexhaustible interest in the problems of finding and destroying U-boats. He told Mick that he had been added to the staff at the particular request of the C-in-C, Air Marshal Sir Philip Joubert de la Ferté, and was retained there by Sir John Slessor, who succeeded Sir Philip on 5 February. Mick came to regard Slessor as "the most approachable very very senior officer I ever knew" and Slessor later wrote: "I have never known a happier headquarters and no Commander-in-Chief can ever have been better served."[4]

Mick was there to contribute his extensive recent experience in actual operations to the planners' deliberations. However, he had no experience whatever of RAF administration. For example, when Jimmy gave him a policy file to look through, he started at the first page, as if he were reading a normal book, until Jimmy kindly advised him to turn to the back, where the earliest document was placed, and work forward to the most recent document, at the front. Jimmy then revealed to him the existence and purpose of minute sheets attached to the inside of the front cover. Thus began Mick's staff training, very much 'on the job.' Being totally ignorant had some advantages because he was able to talk to anyone with complete informality and later write an account of his talk in a free and easy style. "I was thrown into some pretty deep situations", Mick reflected later. "From being an ordinary pilot in 500 Squadron, I suddenly found myself at a huge headquarters dealing with just about the highest in the land on the one hand and a lot of able people on the other. It didn't worry me; I was able to accept life in the more rarified atmosphere quite easily." No doubt this apparently wild colonial boy was helped by the advice and support of his several worldly-wise relatives in that part of England.

Mick soon became familiar with a small, standard hut, perhaps thirty feet by twenty, connected to the main building by a passage-way. This anonymous hut housed Coastal Command's key figure: the indefatigable Captain Peyton-Ward. Officially, PW was the

---

[4] MRAF Sir John Slessor, *The Central Blue: Recollections and Reflections* (Cassell, London, 1956), p. 486.

Admiralty's representative, but in fact his main concern was the efficient use of aircraft in co-operation with surface vessels against U-boats. He had a bunk near the hut and as far as Mick observed (and later learned), PW worked all the hours that God sent throughout the war, despite almost constant pain from an arthritic hip. He was "a very gifted ex-submariner, much loathed by the Admiralty," remarked Sir Edward Chilton, one of Coastal Command's outstanding personalities, "which is why we got him as their liaison officer. He turned out to be first-class for Coastal Command; he understood the German mind, he understood submarines—and we couldn't have got on without him."[5] Slessor agreed. PW, he wrote, had "an insight into the workings of the air/sea war that must have been unparalleled."[6] Although the hut may have had an official name, it was always known as 'PW's Place'. It was equipped with 'scrambler' (secret) telephones to the Admiralty plotting room and all the command's operations rooms. These could be linked to provide conference facilities. The informality of the daily meeting, in Mick's opinion, would provide a salutary lesson for some highly-trained, but stiff-necked, staff officers in post-war days.

By the time of his twenty-first birthday, on 5 January 1943, Mick had achieved his very own office, which he needed to prepare some documents and study others, but he spent a great deal of his time in PW's Place and his mind was always working on unanswered questions. He never wrote "loose minutes" or "papers" on situations, preferring to get about and study them on the spot. In this way, he made some good contacts. The drill was that first thing each morning PW would obtain from the Admiralty what was currently known about the whereabouts of all U-boats, plus suspected movements and any educated guesses about the intentions of their commander, Gross-admiral Doenitz. It is no secret now that much of this information was absolutely accurate, thanks to the work of codebreakers at Bletchley Park in Buckinghamshire who were able to provide the Admiralty with translations of signals passing between Doenitz's headquarters and U-boats at sea. PW had a large softboard map of the Atlantic on which he built a display of the day's situation in a simple but extremely effective way. As Mick put it, "even I could tell what was going on." There was, he recalled, only one WAAF officer on view (PW's assistant, Phil) who guarded everything—including herself—like a delightful but tiresomely efficient mother hen.

---

[5] Contribution to symposium on the Battle of the Atlantic, *Seek and Sink* (RAF Historical Society, 1992) p. 69.
[6] Slessor, *Central Blue*, p. 486.

At about 9 am, the Senior Air Staff Officer (second only to God, in Mick's ranking) would arrive and discuss the situation with PW. A telephone conference followed with all relevant group commanders or their principal advisers, during which the SASO briefed them on areas in which there were probably U-boats in transit or on patrol and gave a general picture of the Atlantic convoy situation and any combined Admiralty-Coastal Command priorities for air cover. Subject to the latter, group commanders planned to use their squadrons as they saw fit, in consultation with local naval commanders. In a matter of thirty minutes or so, the command was given its tasks for the next twenty-four hours. Naturally, the system changed gear during a flap, when matters were handled by operations room staff at the various Group HQs.

PW's consuming interest lay in analysing attacks on U-boats by Coastal Command aircraft and presenting his conclusions at the regular meetings of the Attack Assessment Committee in London. Sometimes he took Mick with him, when he thought Mick might have something useful to say. Detailed reports of all U-boat sightings and attacks, however inconclusive, arrived at PW's Place within a few days of the event and PW, assisted by the capable Phil, would reconstruct the event—with diagrams—in his own standard form. Like most great men, his genius lay in his ability to keep things simple while overlooking nothing important. Such reconstructions could not be complete without a direct input from the crews concerned and it fell to Mick to arrange for them to visit PW's Place as soon as possible after the event. Some would arrive looking as if they were about to visit a dentist, but once inside the hut and served with tea and biscuits they always relaxed.

A most important member of the team was Lieutenant Commander Andrew Brookes, until recently a submarine captain who had been grounded—or is it 'shored'?—for health reasons. Brookie spent a lot of time visiting squadrons. He was immensely popular, said Mick, because he often went on operations with crews and did his best to put them in the big picture. Sadly, he lost his life on 3 June 1943 in a Bristol Beaufighter which was intercepted off the north-west coast of Spain by several Junkers Ju 88 fighters while carrying out an antisubmarine patrol. Mick knew the pilot well and he was terribly cut up about losing Brookie, but Mick told him—blunt as ever—"that he'd done jolly well to save his own life in such a hairy situation and not to fuss about what couldn't be helped." His place was taken by Lieutenant Commander Dickie Raikes, a man of similar background and qualities. Squadron Leader C. W. P. Selby of Intelligence

would usually come into PW's Place at some stage. Another remarkable and charming man, Selby had been an observer during the Great
War and lost an arm when jumping out of a crashing aeroplane
without a parachute. Selby also died off the north-west coast of Spain
while seeking frontline experience. He was a passenger aboard the
sloop *Egret* when she was sunk on 27 August 1943 by a glider-bomb
launched from a Dornier Do 217 bomber.

Mick was already well aware that air crews were rarely forthcoming
even within their own squadrons about any dramatic or alarming
incidents during operations. This was partly because they naturally
feared accusations of line-shooting from other air crews, but it was
also partly because they found it difficult to grasp the overall shape of
events in which their own part was so fleeting and often bewildering.
But PW and Brookie never failed to win their confidence and get
them talking. If they had all been in civilian clothes, said Mick, these
meetings could not have been more 'rankless'. Brookie and he used
to look after the officers at lunch-time in the Mess, which sometimes got rather expensive because no entertainment allowance was
available. Mick always made certain that the NCOs were being
similarly looked after in the Sergeants' Mess. It was often possible to
rope in the SASO and even the C-in-C, Slessor himself, to talk to
these men. Slessor readily followed the custom already established by
his predecessors of chatting informally with crews and staff officers
about problems which were, after all, of absorbing mutual concern.
These visits by crews to HQ provided an invaluable link at the tactical
level and whatever the crews had done—or tried or failed to do—they
at least went back to their squadrons feeling that their endeavours
were appreciated in high places. The same should have been true
for Bomber and Fighter Commands. Being so much larger, it was of
course much more difficult to create a similar 'family atmosphere', but
officers well placed to know assured Mick, then and later, that if he
had to serve at a headquarters in wartime, Coastal Command was
the pick.

A scientific research officer—Mr E C Baugham—was working on
bombing errors that occurred in attacks on U-boats and seeking a
means of increasing the probability of causing fatal damage. He
concluded that the spacing between depth charges should be increased
from fifty to one hundred feet, thus doubling the margin for error in
release distance, but the change did nothing to solve the long-standing
problem of late releases resulting in over-shoots; a problem very
common with Liberators in the Atlantic. The new depth charge
spacing nevertheless went out as a Tactical Instruction that was

mandatory; other matters were written up as Tactical Memoranda and were merely advisory. Mick had quite a lot to do with documents issued in both categories, as well as articles appearing in the 'house journal', *Coastal Command Review*. His main tasks, however, were to ensure that the material made sense to an 'average' aircrew member (by casting himself in that role) and if it puzzled him, finding a literary artist with technical knowledge to "unpuzzle me and, I hoped, all those unlucky airmen who were no brighter than me." Mick's own particular hobby horses were aircraft concealment and the need for accurate bombing. As for Brookie, he was a mine of information on the shortcomings of aircraft look-outs aboard submarines.

"This weekend," Mick told his mother on 27 January 1943, "I am going up north to see my little Margaret as she is now back in Rotherham. You will probably hear more of her later on. We are very much attached to each other at the moment. I have known her for one and a half years now and our friendship seems to grow all the time.... I don't really think that I will be going back to NZ for quite a long time yet. I had the chance, but refused because I am really rather enjoying life over here now. (That is, of course, when I am not working.)" In April, he spent a week's leave with Margaret and her parents at their home near Jedburgh in Scotland. It was, he informed his parents, "about the only place where one can get a real feed of mutton these days, the whisky hasn't run out either!" The Jedburgh district reminded him of Hawarden, in North Canterbury, and he spent much of his time either riding over the hills or walking "and so I feel very much fitter than I have for a long time."

A few days later, on 11 May, Mick paid his second visit to Buckingham Palace, this time to be admitted to the Distinguished Service Order. He again invited Lady Campbell to accompany him and also Margaret, who came down from Rotherham. After the ceremony, he told his parents, they had a splendid lunch at Simpson's in the Strand, joined by Mick's former CO, Denis Spotswood. The rest of the day's celebration, he confessed, did not bear relating. Mick then reverted to a subject that interested him far more than decorations or even wild parties. "Very soon I shall be going to war again," he exulted, "this time with four engines instead of two." Thinking of his brother Jimmy, at that moment enjoying the part he had played in the Allied triumph in Tunisia, set him off again. "My biggest regret", he wrote, "is that I have been stuck here in England most of the time and have hardly seen anything of the real war at all."

Mick believed that his friendship with Margaret Douglas was ripening into love, on both sides. In fact, Mick's chances of persuading her to marry him were nil. His letters home are full of grumbles about being grounded and presumably he also told Margaret how anxious he was to leave the security of Northwood and risk his life yet again. Quite apart from her still-acute memories of John MacGillivray, Margaret was not prepared to be emotionally devasted a second time. As with his frequent and apparently casual references to the deaths of fellow-airmen in accidents or combat, Mick seemed entirely unaware of the effect his words might have on those who read or heard them, a family far away or a girl-friend close at hand.

Early in his time at Northwood, Mick escaped briefly to Aldergrove, near Belfast in Northern Ireland, to have a good look at a huge, four-engined machine with which Coastal Command was being re-equipped—and in which he hoped to fly, after his stint as a staff officer. This was the Consolidated Liberator: "by far the most complicated and expensive combat aircraft the world had seen", in the words of a leading aviation expert, Bill Gunston, "it was built in bigger numbers than any other American aircraft in history, in more versions for more purposes than any other aircraft in history, and served on every front in World War II and with every Allied nation."[7] Mick managed to fly one, unofficially, from the co-pilot's seat and take part in a practice bombing exercise. Thinking about this exercise, he wrote: "I have never had any reason to change my opinion that a pilot who trains himself properly is the best low-level bombsight in daylight", far more accurate than any gadget. "At night, however, particularly if a searchlight was being used," he readily admitted that "disorientation could occur. Having hit the sea myself in such circumstances, I was acutely aware of the problem!"

Mick returned to Northwood, grateful for Aldergrove's hospitality and the opportunity to fly in this immensely impressive aircraft, but disappointed by the appalling lack of forward and downward vision for its pilots. The long flat nose with an astrodome sticking up at the front limited their view of the sea to a sector between the captain's left and the co-pilot's right. Pilot's eye bombing of the style that Mick had found so effective in the Blenheim and the Hudson was simply impossible in the new machine. The answer, he thought, would be a compromise. If the target remained visible to the left because drift was causing the aircraft to crab in that direction, release by the captain was feasible; if to the right, the co-pilot could see what to do and when. But the time had not yet come for Mick to concern himself with

---

[7] Bill Gunston, *The Encyclopedia of the World's Combat Aircraft* (Salamander Books, London, 1976) p. 42.

the Liberator's problems or to appreciate its many advantages as a submarine hunter.

Group Captain D'Aeth chaired a weekly meeting on anti-submarine warfare and Mick was responsible for the minutes. At least thirty people attended, including boffins with whatever specialist knowledge was thought might be helpful. At first, Mick scarcely knew what minutes were, much less how to produce them. Fortunately, D'Aeth had a marvellous secretary—Miss Burrows—who not only had that skill in abundance but also a comprehensive grasp of all the subjects under discussion and could even remember everyone's name. The minutes were always circulated no later than the following morning and although Mick checked and signed them, he felt distinctly uneasy whenever any complimentary remarks about them came his way.

Mick found it instructive to observe the way various factions sought to pull policy one way or another. The Chief Scientific Officer, for example, together with some of the Admiralty people, had a myopic defensive mentality whereas those in favour of such special projects as the Leigh Light often over-sold them without much regard for thorough technical development or crew training in their effective use. Jimmy D'Aeth, however, steered a sound middle course and could often be seen at lunch-time soothing ruffled feathers with a gin and tonic.

The need for a practical low-level bombsight had been evident for some time and numerous scientists were giving it their attention. One of them was a regular train-traveller (so the story went) and one day, while watching a long paling fence passing the carriage window, he noticed that it appeared to stop for an instant at a certain point. He quickly realised that the illusion was a result of a special combination of angles and velocities that might be related to the low-level, high-speed bomb-aiming problem with which no current sight could cope. He was right and eventually a handy sight, no bigger than a small football, was produced. The optics consisted of a glass plate about four inches square, facing forward and slightly down, mounted on a bracket and gyro-stabilised. Onto this, using the same principle as that for reflector gunsights fitted to fighters, a vertical centreline and about twenty horizontal lines were projected. A control box was provided into which the co-pilot fed the length of the stick of bombs or depth charges, height and groundspeed. The latter was always a guess, but a long stick would compensate for inaccuracy. When the sight was switched on, the glass screen would take up the correct angle and the horizontal lines moved down, like a ladder being moved down outside a window. During a bombing run, the target would first appear to move slower than the lines; then for an instant at the same speed; then faster.

The device was produced for inspection at one of Jimmy's meetings and Mick remembered it being welcomed with open arms. Some concern was expressed over a red notice on it reading *handle like eggs*, but in fact it proved very robust. It certainly gave Liberator crews a better chance, once they had mastered it by lots of flying practice. Most of the problems had been solved in a truly ingenious way, but as Mick later learned, 'vigorous fireworks' from a U-boat under attack could persuade any pilot into making rapid changes of altitude, causing his navigator to mis-read the sight and consequently the depth charges would be released either too soon or too late.

Another valuable piece of equipment then coming into general use was an airborne radar that would scan all around the aircraft and 'paint' a picture of any objects 'seen' on a circular screen in front of the operator. He was given a wealth of information simply not available from the earlier, fixed beam, radars. Having read about it, studied reports from air crews using it and observed it in training use, Mick became increasingly eager to see it tried out on operations, with himself in the cockpit.

Until the employment of a handful of Wellingtons equipped with both radar and searchlights in June 1942, there had been no serious aerial threat to U-boats at night.[8] Consequently, they had used the long hours of darkness during previous winters for safe—and speedy— surface travelling; at the same time, of course, they had little need to risk being spotted in daylight. Mick watched the performance of radar/searchlight Wellingtons with somewhat mixed feelings because of the presence of their ardent patron, Wing Commander Humphrey Leigh, who never let one forget them, even at breakfast-time. Humphrey was then working on a light suitable for VLR (Very Long Range) Liberators, which were much more powerful aircraft than the Wellington. As soon as airborne radar indicated the presence of a U-boat, the pilot would switch on the light at a range of about two miles. The hope was that this sudden, alarming light would panic the U-boat's gunners into opening fire too soon, giving away their precise position and expending their loaded ammunition before the aircraft came within dangerous range. The gunners would then be changing clips with dazzled eyes—and ears straining to catch the first note of the dive klaxon.

The Liberators—with or without searchlights—were already

---

[8] *The RAF in Maritime War*, vol. iii, pp. 83-4.

performing admirably in the Atlantic, denying U-boats freedom of movement on the surface in the vicinity of convoys. They sank, damaged or at least gave a bad fright to enough U-boats to make them so cautious that the old, deadly wolf-pack tactics became rare. However, it would be better still if fewer U-boats even *reached* the convoy areas and so the navy formed independent escort groups— more accurately described as 'U-boat attack groups'—to operate in the Bay of Biscay. Under Captain F J ('Johnny') Walker, the group proved successful and woke everyone up, in Mick's opinion, to the fact that offence was the best means of defence, given that U-boats could not operate effectively far from their bases if they were obliged to travel submerged—and therefore very slowly—to the convoy areas.

Another exciting weapon which Mick observed was the HVAR (High Velocity Aircraft Rocket), then being developed for tactical ground attack and anti-shipping strikes. There were two types: one with a 60-lb explosive head that was said to have the power of a six-inch shell, the other with a 25-lb solid head. The latter had a higher velocity with great penetrating power and if the motor was still burning when it entered the water, it would drive on at a lethal pace for about a hundred feet before failing. This was a weapon that greatly appealed to Mick, even though it was no use at night or when there was a heavy cloud cover. Better still, a Liberator could carry a good load of these rockets (in addition to the standard depth charges and homing torpedoes) with very little reduction in its cruising range. The day would come, as we shall see, when Mick used this weapon with tragic consequences.

The squeeze was increasing for the U-boats everywhere and Mick remembered Brookie saying to him that if they wanted to remain effective in the Atlantic, they would have to *fight* their way through the transit areas. How right he was! Later in 1943, this became (for a time) U-boat policy and they were provided with extra guns and sometimes an extra 'bandstand' on which to mount them. "I could go on describing the aircraft versus U-boat tactical see-saw for ever," wrote Mick, "but by August 1943 I had joined 224 Liberator squadron as a flight commander and there I sat on the bumpy end of it." By that time, however, the U-boat was no longer able to strike serious, let alone devastating, blows against Allied shipping. Until the end of 1942, the 'exchange rate' was still in German favour: eight ships and 45,000 tons per U-boat lost. By April 1943, the rate had fallen to 28,000 tons and by the end of May had collapsed to a mere 5,000 tons.[9]

---

[9] Air Ministry, *Operational Research in the RAF*, p. 81.

It did not recover. German captains were becoming more concerned to locate and avoid powerful enemies than to find and destroy the precious freighters, tankers and troop transports that those enemies now guarded so carefully.

Month by month, this situation worsened, from the U-boats' viewpoint, but they remained at sea in a successful attempt to keep very large Allied naval and air forces fully occupied away from Germany. "You have had to combat a strong air menace with, up to date, little chance of success", admitted Doenitz in a signal to all boats in November 1943, "but your fighting has led to a very large deployment of enemy resources in the sea war. Keep fighting so as to continue to tie down these forces and so prevent their use against the Fatherland even though the battle seems fruitless to you." No doubt his captains read this signal with mixed feelings, but the fact remains that they obeyed. Even in the last two months of the war, U-boats actually sank as many as forty-four Allied ships.[10]

Meanwhile, Mick's social life at Command HQ was "civilised and pleasant". During the long summer evenings, staff officers would gather on the terrace outside the ante-room of the Mess to enjoy each other's company, the refreshments and the lovely view over Eastbury Park. "This was my first experience of English society, with men and women mixing easily, and altogether superior to station life," in Mick's opinion, "which had not so far impressed me." In general, he thought navy women (WRN or 'Wren' officers) were more assured than air force women (WAAF officers) who could be overawed by rank unless their upbringing was such that they were able to ignore it on social occasions. "Thanks to good teaching by my parents, I was able to handle most formalities easily. Some of the older ladies mothered me and, I'm glad to say, readily introduced 'young Mick' to new arrivals."

Decorum was not, however, invariably observed. One party given by the WAAF officers in their Mess—another large house in the woods—became memorable for the vigorous, though unsuccessful, efforts of a senior female spoilsport to prevent some of the younger persons from enjoying themselves more than she thought proper. A story got around next day that Mick had climbed the ivy to a certain bedroom. No-one believed his strenuous denials and Mick could hardly tell the truth—which was that he had not needed to climb the

---

[10] Hessler, *The U-Boat War*, vol. iii, pp. 61-3; John W R Taylor, 'The Crow and the Mole', *RAF Quarterly*, vol. xx (January 1949) p. 6; *The RAF in Maritime War*, vol. iv, p. 198.

ivy. The heavy furniture from the Mess had been temporarily moved to the garages and his friend of the moment suggested that one of the sofas there would serve them admirably, and so it did.

There was, of course, the occasional sortie to central London (about forty minutes away by Underground) to meet friends on leave or just to visit the *Wings Club* in Piccadilly. "A revolting dive really, but we always met someone we knew there and had plenty of fun." The *Sherlock Holmes* in Shepherd's Market was more interesting and served a good meal while the *Sussex*, somewhere up from Trafalgar Square, as Mick recalled, attracted a lot of New Zealanders. It was airy and pleasant, not far from New Zealand House and the New Zealand Post Office in the Strand was within easy walking distance. Sometimes he would go 'up market' and dine out properly—or as properly as was possible in those days of strict rationing—and go on afterwards to a show. The Underground line to Northwood terminated at Amersham, about half an hour farther on, and Mick twice slept past Northwood and awoke only at Amersham. On neither occasion did he feel brave enough to impose upon his relations who lived there and made do with a kip in a Home Guard hut.

Then came the shocking news, on 3 June, that Mick's father had died suddenly. Hugh Ensor was only sixty-three and although he had already suffered one major heart attack, Mick took it for granted that he was indestructible—at least for the foreseeable future. Neither Hugh nor any other member of the family was given to revealing, let alone expressing, deep feelings. Nevertheless, Mick was well aware of his father's quiet pride in the exceptional achievements of his youngest son and some part of Mick's enthusiasm for 'front line' duties lay in an equally quiet desire to keep on justifying that pride. Half a world away from Rakahuri, a beloved home, Mick found it difficult to believe that his father was really dead. Not even his mother's departure from Rakahuri some fifteen months later wholly convinced him; only his own return to New Zealand, long after the war was over, did that.

Meanwhile, during June 1943, Mick had high hopes of returning to his old squadron in North Africa as a flight commander. "I don't really want to leave England again for any length of time," he had told his parents in March, "but it would be such a good opportunity to do a bit more towards the 'war effort' that I would go like a shot if sent. It is really rather stupid keeping me in a job like this because I am not much good at it and am really getting a bit fed up." The people in charge of officer-postings were very polite, but did not agree that he had been 'resting' (from operations) long enough. To his unconcealed astonishment, he was solemnly assured "even by people who damn well knew better" that he was in fact a good staff officer and could not be spared for some time to come. Nevertheless, Mick maintained a determined campaign and was at last posted (celebrated by a memorable party) to the Liberator Conversion Unit.

After the night of 24-25 November 1942, when he landed at Portreath, and until 27 July 1943, when he had his first flight in a Liberator III at the Operational Training Unit, Mick did very little flying. In those eight months, he managed only about eighty-four hours in the air: thirty-nine in single-engined aircraft (usually a Miles Whitney Straight) and forty-five in various multi-engined aircraft, among them Liberators: thirty as 1st pilot and fifteen as 2nd. Although Mick missed the friends he had made, male as well as female, by July he knew a great deal about the theoretical aspects of anti-submarine warfare and was anxious to put into practice the ideas he had been playing around with for so long. He now felt he had a bird's eye view of Coastal Command's work to supplement the worm's eye view his service with 500 Squadron had given him. Not least, he wanted to show PW how much he had learned at his feet.

CHAPTER VIII

AN ASTONISHING COMPANY
JULY 1943 TO SEPTEMBER 1944

MICK ENSOR served a full 'sentence' at Coastal Command Head-quarters because, he said, "the 'powers-that-be' reckoned six months' rest from operations was the minimum I needed. But a Liberator squadron was being built up in the command. Things were getting pretty active in our particular job and I was desperately keen to get back into the cockpit—and especially into a Liberator cockpit because it was by far the best aircraft available for sub-hunting. Nothing else was up to the job: the Hudson and Wellington had insufficient range, the Sunderland was too slow and the Catalina lacked fire-power." Mick therefore gladly relinquished his acting rank of Squadron Leader on 19 July 1943 and was posted next day as a Flight Lieutenant to No. 1 Operational Training Unit at Beaulieu, near Lymington in Hampshire. There he would be trained to fly the four-engined Consolidated B-24 Liberator. Some of these American-built, high-level, long-range day bombers had been modified for Coastal Command use into low-level, *very* long-range sub-hunters, able to operate day or night.

That aircraft greatly appealed to Mick and not only because there were ashtrays in the pilots' armrests. "It had a beautiful laminar-flow wing," he wrote, "ideal for easy and graceful flight, with four very powerful Pratt & Whitney engines that were known to be entirely reliable. Up to eight .5-inch machine-guns offered a realistic defence and for offence there was a heavy load of depth charges, homing torpedoes and rockets. Early models had a practical range of no less than sixteen hours, but later marks carried more and more equipment until they became too heavy for safe take-offs when fully loaded. By 1944, therefore, the maximum sortie had been cut to thirteen and a half hours—which was quite long enough, especially when most of that time was spent on exacting, low-level work in darkness."

According to Tony Taylor, an eminent wartime test-pilot, the Liberator was "the progenitor of the 'modern' aeroplane ... and it could not be handled safely without a flight-deck crew of two competent pilots—though an experienced flight-engineer might be adequate as a second pilot in good weather on shortish flights." The Liberator demanded far more expertise from pilots than the relatively simple British aircraft it replaced. The controls were heavy, it was hard to fly accurately in windy conditions such as prevail over water, while lining up for a safe landing took plenty of time and space. Its tricycle undercarriage, very rare in those days, was a distinct asset on take-off or landing, but on the ground the Liberator was sensitive to centre-of-gravity changes and liable to sit suddenly and expensively on its tail. Some crews, Taylor recalled, "rightly refused to budge from the forward area until a tail strut had been put in place by the ground crew." However alarming the Liberator might seem on first acquaint-ance, it proved a reliable friend to those who knew it well. It was the first aircraft operated by Coastal Command able to close the 'Atlantic Gap', that ocean area where U-boats had hitherto sought victims safe from aerial attack.[1]

Mick collected a crew, all of whom came direct to Beaulieu from training in the Bahamas, and most of whom, he believed, were New Zealanders. That crew "never really developed and I did a rather awful thing in transferring them to a new captain (Phil Hill) and in due course they were all lost." As on other occasions in his life, Mick here makes an unnecessary rod for his own back. Hill's crew was not lost until November 1944, long after he transferred them, and his personal responsibility for that loss is nil. Not that it matters, but only three of the ten men who died were in fact New Zealanders. However, Mick later thought he should have farmed all ten out, one by one, into other crews because collectively, in his opinion, they never became "war conscious". By that he meant that they lacked the capacity for prolonged concentration (as opposed to professional skill) and so caused him to lose radar contact with several U-boats. Worse still, from a personal viewpoint, they came perilously close to allowing themselves to be surprised by German fighters.

Although far from uncaring about casualties, Mick had schooled himself to be ruthless. "In fact, each one—starting with John

---

[1] H A Taylor, 'Flying the Consolidated Liberator', *Air Enthusiast* (February 1972) pp. 87-90; James D Oughton, 'Coastal Command Aircraft, 1942-1992', *RAF Coastal Command Yearbook* (IAT Publishing, RAF Fairford, Gloucester, 1992) p. 20.

MacGillivray—just built another block of ice in me and strengthened both my determination to survive and my intolerance of stupidity and incompetence." Mick felt he *had* to be successful in this deadly profession, "and when it became clear to me that I could not nurse my crew any longer and survive in the Ju 88-ridden Bay of Biscay, let alone find U-boats, I had no conscience about gathering the best: Joe Addington, George Carter, Butch Pugh, Bill Andrews, etc., although the selfishness of it came home to roost when the others were lost from Milltown."[2]

Mick flew from Beaulieu under dual instruction with Flying Officer Kimmins in a Liberator III for a couple of hours on 27 July. That model of the B-24D had standard fuel tankage, either American or British armament and no ASV radar.[3] Next day, he flew the same aircraft himself with Kimmins and various crew members on three occasions. Practice in take-offs, landings, low flying, steep turns, bombing and air-to-air firing continued until 23 August in several different Liberators. Apart from that one dual flight, he accumulated over thirty hours as a 1st pilot in daylight, but only a little over three hours in darkness.

From Beaulieu, Mick joined 224 Squadron at St. Eval in Cornwall on 26 August 1943 as a flight commander, flying there with his own crew in a Liberator GR V (letter G). This was the definitive Coastal Command model of the B-24D and had extra outer wing fuel tanks as well as American ASV equipment in either ventral or nose (known as 'Dumbo') positions.[4] The CO was a fellow-New Zealander, Wing Commander Arthur Clouston, a pilot famous for long-distance flights in the thirties. "I don't think Arthur particularly welcomed me," Mick wrote later, "because I had no experience on Liberators," but it did not take long for such a superb pilot as Clouston to recognise in Mick a man who knew what he was about in the air. Clouston was also impressed by Mick's enthusiasm for his duties as a flight commander. Mick did not fuss himself unduly over paper work, except to delegate it to anyone unwise enough to show the slightest interest in administration, but he was never slack when it came to examining any problem, human or mechanical, that affected the Liberator's performance as either a flying or a bombing machine. And Clouston certainly stood by his flight commander, as we shall see, when a tragic accident threatened Mick's career.

---

[2] Letter, Errol W Martyn to Orange, on fate of Hill's crew, 21 December 1993.
[3] J D Oughton, letter, *Air Enthusiast* (October 1972) p. 202.
[4] Oughton, p. 202; Larry Davis, *B-24 Liberator in Action* (Squadron/Signal Publications, Carrollton, Texas, 1987) p. 23.

Group Captain J. M. D. Ker became station commander at St. Eval. Mick had first met John at Coastal Command HQ and a close friendship would grow between them even though their backgrounds were so different: John was more than ten years older, a pre-war regular officer with a BA degree (and would retire in 1960 as an Air Commodore). "John was in Ops. Requirements at HQ and very receptive to technical ideas, even from a juvenile upstart like me. With his support, I was able to carry out some very interesting detection trials under various guises without putting anything on paper except for one navigator who would do private plotting with appropriate *red* dots. Over the years, we developed a bond that was not only technical and professional but also personal." They often served together in future years and gradually became firm friends. In February 1973, John and his wife Anne visited New Zealand and one day Mick was flying them over the Southern Alps in his Cessna 172 when the side door suddenly burst open. Nobody actually fell out, however, and the alarm did not end their friendship.

Meanwhile, on 3 September 1943, in Liberator GR V (H), Mick carried out an anti-submarine patrol in the Bay of Biscay: his sixty-eighth operation in total, but first for more than nine months. It was also by far his longest flight, lasting for eleven hours and fifteen minutes (including two and a half hours in darkness). "The Bay", wrote Sir John Slessor (head of Coastal Command in 1943) "is the trunk of the Atlantic U-boat menace, the roots being in the Biscay ports and the branches spreading far and wide, to the North Atlantic convoys, to the Caribbean, to the eastern seaboard of North America".[5] The German occupation of ports on France's west coast had given them an admirable springboard for ventures into the Atlantic, far more favourable than the long haul round the north of Scotland from German or Norwegian bases. Moreover, there was no need for U-boats to surface in daylight while crossing the Bay of Biscay either outward or homeward bound because they could surface to re-charge their electric batteries by night. It therefore became necessary for Allied aircraft to find and attack them in darkness. This they were able to do on a regular, large-scale basis, from the winter of 1943-4 onwards, with the help of more sensitive, wider-looking radars and very powerful Leigh Lights. Daylight patrols remained necessary to ensure that U-boats remained submerged (and therefore travelling very slowly) for as many hours as possible.

By the end of September, Mick's feat of endurance was already

---

[5] Quoted in Price, *Aircraft versus Submarine*, p. 154.

routine: he had completed five more operations, each lasting on average more than eleven hours (including four hours in darkness). During daylight hours, there was usually something to see on the water: huge patches of oil, numerous pieces of wood, abandoned rafts, dinghies or lifeboats. Occasionally, he came across a wallowing boat that had not been abandoned. Numerous seabirds gathered around these, picking clean the corpses. Mick circled above, he and his crew staring down silently. There was nothing to do, nothing to say, so they flew away. He never had the luck to find a boat from which men looked up and waved. All six September patrols were officially "uneventful". More cheerfully, Mick and his crew practiced bombing, the use of rocket projectiles and their flying skills. He flew in various Liberators, distinguished only by single letters, and usually with the same crew, though leave, illness or special training caused individuals to drop out from time to time.

During October, Mick completed five more operations. On one, an anti-submarine patrol in the Bay of Biscay on 2 October, he "homed on a contact from 19 miles", according to his log book, but "Lost contact at four miles and found nothing", to his unconcealed exasperation. There was rarely any cheerful singing on the way home with this crew. A few days later, on another patrol over the bay, Mick sighted a Junkers Ju 88 and two unidentified aircraft. He promptly turned west, out into the Atlantic, to discourage pursuit. Well armed though the Liberator might be, no prudent captain would willingly mix it with German fighters. Only after fifteen anxious minutes was Mick convinced that he had lost them. He then warily resumed his search for U-boats. Flying Liberators in those waters, Mick remembered, "we knew we'd very likely meet up with Ju 88s, but on the whole we were careful—and we had radar: it was only the unlucky or careless fellows who got caught. Usually we'd spot 88s if they were about and get into a cloud. One chum of mine got caught up with half a dozen of them, but he got into a cloud and said later he was certain that one wing must have been sticking out because every time he put his nose out, the bloody things were still there. He did get burned a bit, but eventually made it home alright."

Unlike his comrades in other commands, Mick was largely spared, from start to finish of his wartime career, the fear—let alone the actuality—of aerial attack. For this wonderful boon, given that he never flew an aircraft capable of seriously defending itself from fighter attack, he had Hermann Goering to thank. As head of the Luftwaffe, Goering provided only the smallest and most grudging support for the U-boat campaign. Wholehearted support in the early war years might have transformed the U-boat from a potential to an actual warwinner; it would certainly have multiplied its already serious impact on Britain's capacity to keep fighting. Goering was also Germany's economic overlord in those years and refused to give high priority to U-boat production, encouraged in this attitude by Grossadmiral Raeder, head of the Kriegsmarine and a devout big ship enthusiast. Hitler, fortunately, chose not to exert his overwhelming personal authority to ensure either effective sea-air co-operation or an adequate supply of U-boats. "It was hard enough to find a U-boat anyway," remarked Mick, "given the limitations of our equipment and flying conditions that were rarely clear. I doubt if we could have done any good at all if German aircraft had been systematically pestering us north of Scotland or out in the Bay."

Spanish trawlers, fishing for tunny, roamed at will in the Bay and Liberator crews learned to hate them. "The Germans realised our radar would lead us to the trawlers just as much as to their submarines", explained Arthur Clouston. "Formations of eight or ten Ju 88s would fly out from their bases in occupied France and wait for us high up in the sun, above the trawlers. It happened so often that we could not help thinking there was a liaison between some of those neutral ships and the enemy aircraft."[6]

Liberator patrols often lasted for up to thirteen hours and pre-flight preparation started a couple of hours before that, followed by at least one and a half hours on return for reporting and feeding. In all, "out of bed for sixteen hours and most of the job was at night, but if you took off at midday in summer, you'd fly through the night and be landing next morning. As flight commander, my routine after such trips was to look in at my office and see if there was anything stirring that really needed attention. If it was near lunchtime, I'd have enough grog to send me to sleep by the time I got down to the Watergate Hotel. There was no possibility of doing anything else on such days." That hotel, about five miles from St. Eval, was where the officers lived. It had its own private beach and plenty of comfortable furniture as well as views of the Atlantic, especially at sunset, that residents other than Coastal Command airmen would have rightly thought magnificent. "But we saw much better ones, stretching half way round the horizon, pretty well every time we flew", said Mick. "You can get sick of sunsets." It was less easy, in wartime, to get sick of fresh fish and an ample supply was a consequence of diligent training. An air-sea rescue launch would lay smoke floats to simulate a U-boat about

---

[6] A E Clouston, *Dangerous Skies* (Cassell, London, 1954) p. 159.

fifteen miles out to sea. The Liberators would then attack these floats with depth charges, observed by the launch which would then sweep up thousands of fish killed or stunned by the explosions and deliver them to the hotel and customers elsewhere.[7]

Mick's seventy-sixth operation on 10 October 1943 lasted for just over fifteen hours, the longest of his career so far, and ended in the tragedy of an attack upon a friendly submarine. He had picked up a convoy north-east of the Azores and escorted it for an hour and a half as it made its way towards Britain. About 300 miles west of Brest, he sighted a submarine on the surface and attacked it, firing eight five-inch rockets carried on small winglets affixed to either side of the fuselage below the cockpit. It turned out to be a French boat, the *Minerve*, which had surfaced where it should not have done. Russell Laughland, a squadron pilot, remembered the incident very clearly. The squadron was then experimenting with rocket projectiles and Laughland flew a training detail with Mick, firing these weapons. Later, while flying over the Bay of Biscay, wrote Laughland, Mick "spotted a submarine on the surface and attacked it with RPs. It turned out to be a Free French Navy sub, off course and not reported as being in the area. Mick visited the sub in harbour [at Falmouth]: very brave, considering there had been casualties including some killed."[8] It had large white letters painted on the conning-tower and Mick thought they read P.35. Actually, *Minerve*'s number was P.26 and no French boat bore the number P.35. In any case, seeing letters at the last moment before going in to depth charge his damaged victim, Mick realised it could not be a U-boat because they were never marked in that style. The recognition flare set off in the conning-tower had been seen by Mick, but taken for a fire: "we did not see the colour", he said, "only the smoke." The *Minerve* was a boat with an honourable record, having served alongside British forces since early in 1941, but now she suffered serious damage in addition to two men killed.[9]

Arthur Clouston described this incident in his memoirs, published in 1954, referring to Mick only as "one of my flight commanders". At that time, Mick was still serving in the RAF and presumably Clouston did not wish to embarrass him, even though Mick's conduct was blameless. According to Clouston's account, Mick hit the submarine

---

[7] Clouston, *Dangerous Skies*, pp. 159-60.
[8] Letter, Laughland to Spooner, 8 January 1988.
[9] Rear Admiral Paul Auphan & Jacques Mordal, *The French Navy in World War II* (Greenwood Press, Westport, Connecticut, 1976) pp. 162-3 & 293; letter, Rodger B Haworth to Orange, 16 November 1993.

with two rockets before it had fully surfaced. Both rockets punctured the hull, but fortunately only one hole was below the waterline. Squadron aircraft spent nearly a week escorting it back to port. A Royal Navy liaison officer was on board and Clouston thought he should have known better than to allow the French captain to surface in daylight to repair a diesel motor. Clouston went with Mick to visit the *Minerve*. "Our Group Commander", he wrote, "made us wear plain clothes as, understandably perhaps, the crew of the French submarine were feeling very hostile towards the RAF. At the time of the attack two French mechanics had been leaning over the diesel motor, and one rocket had cut them clean in half. Their bodies were still down below and the stench was unbelievable." Mick, however, was "completely exonerated", as Clouston emphasised. "The submarine captain admitted to us before we left that he had disobeyed orders by surfacing in daytime, and he fully accepted the blame." Mick apologised personally, but some crew members glared angrily at him and he left the boat hurriedly, more upset than when he arrived. One more gut-wrenching episode that seemed not to trouble him unduly at the time. Only years later would he pay the price of his apparently calm acceptance of yet another tragedy in his young life.[10]

On 12 October, Mick flew with his crew and five passengers from St. Eval to Ballykelly, near Limavady in Northern Ireland, for further practice in the use of rocket projectiles. He then flew from there to Reykjavik in Iceland—a flight lasting over five hours—on the 16th. Everyone had high hopes of a chance to use the rockets in anger, but after freezing for nearly a week and achieving nothing, they returned to St. Eval via Ballykelly. During November, Mick flew only one operation, an anti-submarine patrol lasting fourteen hours (ten in daylight), but he also spent time practicing with the Leigh Light in darkness and handling the Liberator on only three engines. The light, he found, "had the advantages and disadvantages of a precise weapon. There was little margin for error. Your radar indication and flying had both to be spot on because although the light was very powerful it gave only a very narrow beam. Either you saw something beautifully lit up or you saw nothing at all." The fact that the light could be aimed was a great help, but its weight and location (outboard of the engines on the starboard wing) added to handling problems at low levels. Mick flew two more operations in December, one an anti-submarine patrol on 23 December lasting thirteen hours of which eleven were in darkness (by far the most he had yet flown at night) and the other a "search

---

[10] Clouston, *Dangerous Skies*, pp. 167-8.

for a blockade runner". Wing Commander Clouston assessed him as an "exceptional" General Reconnaissance pilot on 11 January 1944, adding that he was "experienced in bad weather flying."

On 5 January 1944, his 22nd birthday, Mick's crew again found a U-boat in darkness in the Bay of Biscay—and again lost it. From then on, Mick began to look out for more alert men. During that same month, Wing Commander Terence McComb succeeded Clouston as CO of 224 Squadron. Terry was "a delightful Irishman," says Mick, "well liked by everyone. Looking back now, I can see how jolly lucky I was to serve under such men as Denis Spotswood and Terry McComb. Both were quite outstanding as airmen and administrators, but what really impressed me, then and now, is how *easy* they made it seem to run a squadron. Never angry, never in a flap, always knowing everything they needed to know and not fussing over details. When my turn for command came, I'm sure I worked twice as hard as they did for half as good a result. Inspiration beats perspiration every time." All of which may well be true, but the fact remains that both Spotswood and McComb formed a high opinion of Mick's capacity to handle a squadron as well as an aeroplane.

Mick flew four more operations in January, almost wholly in darkness: over forty-six hours out of a total flight time of some fifty-two hours. All four operations were uneventful, despite his aggressive hunting "and a few sharp words to the troops before take-off. I said I wanted them to get their fingers out and keep them out." He searched for a blockade runner without success; he obtained a contact that might have been a U-boat but lost it; he sighted the odd "suspicious" aircraft and ducked smartly for cover; and he endured some "very rough" weather. He also spent a little time on bombing practice.

During February, he carried out no operations, but took part in an exercise code-named *Oasthouse* on the 21st. It lasted four hours in darkness and Mick managed to light up the target submarine four times: an excellent performance by an alert, disciplined crew and one not matched by any other crew. "They *could* do it," Mick says, "but they couldn't *keep on* doing it, not hour after hour, which is what Coastal Command work was all about. One or two of them simply couldn't concentrate for long enough, but I still feel uneasy about getting rid of them as a job lot." On the 24th, he spent ninety minutes in darkness on Leigh Light training, making six runs across Barnstable Bay. In March, Mick completed two more operations. One was an anti-submarine patrol, mostly in darkness on 6 March off the Spanish coast, looking for a Japanese submarine making its way to Germany under very strong escort by Ju 88s and torpedo boats. This was the *I-29*, a huge boat (2,584 tons surfaced, 3,654 tons submerged), more than three times as big as a standard Type VIIC U-boat and with twice as many crew members. Only four Japanese boats reached a French port during the war and of these only one got home to Japan: the *I-29* would be sunk in the Philippines by an American submarine on 26 July 1944. Much to his regret, Mick failed to find this exotic intruder, which reached Lorient safely, though some of the escorting aircraft were shot down. "That really would have been something to dine out on," he muses, "sinking a Japanese boat in Biscay—but who'd have believed me?"[11]

The other patrol, mostly in daylight on the 10th, was a convoy escort: "convoy met and R/T communication established without trouble", he recorded in his log book. During that month, he also carried out various tests and exercises, including night photography. Two operations followed in April. A daylight reconnaissance of the French coast from the Brest peninsula south ended early—after only four hours and twenty minutes—owing to a rare absence of cloud cover and the sight of two enemy aircraft. A typical patrol followed: mostly in darkness, several contacts were investigated, but none proved positive; plenty of flotsam observed, some of which didn't bear close examination. Mick flew only one operation in May, but he also did a good deal of test and practice flying. "After seventeen days and nights of intensive radar, bombing, Leigh Light, air firing and fighter affiliation practice," recalled Tom Cockeram, his new wireless/radar mechanic, "we finally did our first op together in the Bay of Biscay on 28 May 1944; twelve hours and forty minutes; uneventful, no enemy sightings."

Edmund Charlton Andrews, known as Bill, had been chosen by Mick as his new 2nd pilot earlier that month. A Christchurch man, some five months older than Mick, he also attended St. Andrew's College in 1937 and could just remember a plump, round-faced schoolboy; a real country boy with no interest whatever in "city delights—such as they were in Christchurch before the war." As 2nd pilot, there was not a great deal for Bill to do (the Liberator having an excellent automatic pilot) apart from keeping a sharp lookout to the right, monitoring instruments, synchronising engines and calling out the speed during take-off and landing while Mick was looking

---

[11] *The RAF in Maritime War*, vol. iv, p. 474; Dorr Carpenter and Norman Polmar, *Submarines of the Imperial Japanese Navy* (Conway Maritime Press, London, 1986) pp. 38-40 & 101.

ahead. Bill thought Mick very mature for his age (all of twenty-two) and an absolute master of flying, calm and precise. He certainly helped Bill through the paralysing fears of his first operation—which happened to be Mick's ninety-first—without for a moment "playing the old soldier or making me feel the absolute passenger I was." According to Bill, Mick was not at all a talkative man, even during the longest flights, but on one occasion he suddenly astounded Bill by confessing "right out of the blue" that since his tragic triumph in the Mediterranean he had become much more careful in the air. If so, Bill thought, he must have been a real tearaway in those days because Bill never noticed any reluctance to stay away either from enemy waters or bad weather.

By this time, May 1944, the Western Allies were ready to attempt decisive action on the Western Front: Operation Overlord, the campaign to liberate Occupied Europe. That great campaign would have been impossible without victory over the U-boats in the Battle of the Atlantic during 1942-3. Having played his part in that victory, Mick now enjoyed the rare satisfaction of helping to exploit it. Overlord began on 6 June 1944 and for weeks before and after that date 224 Squadron flew numerous 'Cork' patrols, so named because they were intended to 'cork the bottle', i.e., prevent U-boat access to the western flank of the sea passage from England to Normandy. This corking was vital: at first to permit the actual landings of men and vehicles and later to safeguard the transport of essential reinforcements. Throughout the critical period it proved entirely successful. One avoidable hazard was 'friendly fire' from Allied ships. The fact that the Liberators were operating in agreed areas and flashing agreed identification lights made little difference: flak came up just the same, though fortunately it was always inaccurate. Nevertheless, it puzzled Mick that an aircraft as distinctive and numerous as the Liberator was evidently not recognised by navy gunners as late as the summer of 1944.[12]

Mick made a copybook attack, as he described it, on a U-boat in the English Channel just after midnight on D-Day plus one—7 June— but his bomb-aimer undershot. Unlike in Hudson days, Mick could no longer release depth charges himself because the Liberator's long nose obstructed his view. He therefore depended, much to his exasperation, on the judgement of someone else at the most critical moment. "Perfect radar approach", lamented Cockeram, "everything spot on to one mile, then unfortunately the bomb-aimer got it wrong (some

---

[12] *The RAF in Maritime War*, vol. iv, p. 581.

damage, no kill)." He may well have been put off, as Mick fairly acknowledged, by a vigorous exchange of gunfire with the boat. It was a Cork patrol, flown five times from the Scilly Isles to Ushant Island, just off the Brest peninsula. Bill Andrews thought the lighthouse on that island had a cannon on the balcony and told Mick. "That was a mistake," he soon realised, "because whenever we went back there after that Mick was keen to get close enough to have a go at it: not a great idea in a place where Jerry was still thick on the ground and we were in a lumbering whale of a Lib."

During June, Mick carried out as many as six operations. On one, his customary rendering of "Onward Christian Soldiers" was rudely interrupted near Ushant by a sudden burst of flak. "Dammit", he complained, "a chap can't even sing without being interrupted these days." Then turning to glare back at the island, he yelled: "Just for that, we'll bloody well have it again" and belted out those stirring words louder than ever. Everyone on board appreciated the senti-ment, if not the sound. Flying another Cork patrol on the night of 11-12 June, he saw a Sunderland flying-boat of 228 Squadron shot down while attacking U333 (commanded by the famous Peter Cremer) some fifty miles west of Brest. Obliged to surface in order to re-charge his batteries, Cremer had been caught by the Sunderland's radar, but he decided to stay up and fight back. "The aircraft did not keep us waiting long", wrote Cremer. "As though drawn by a thread, it came straight towards us out of the darkness", until the U-boat's gunner hit an engine and the Sunderland plunged into the sea. "On impact the bombs exploded in blazing columns. For a while the wreck stayed afloat, the flames lighting up the surrounding sea and U333 as well, while behind in the darkness other planes were already circling, not daring to come closer." Mick *did* approach, as quickly as he could, but the flames were gone by the time he reached the scene. His first thought, however, was to seek survivors of the Sunderland. Unfortun-ately, his searchlight revealed only smoke and what seemed to be wreckage; he saw no sign of either survivors or a U-boat.[13]

A fortnight later, on the 26th, Mick had the satisfaction of watching the crew of U971 (commanded by Walter Zeplien) being picked up by the destroyers *Eskimo* and *Haida*. Fifty-two very lucky men had already survived four separate aerial attacks in nine days before Zeplien took refuge on the seabed. He decided to scuttle his badly damaged boat and was both *able* to surface and *permitted* to by the

---

[13] Peter Cremer, *U333: The Story of a U-Boat Ace* (Triad Grafton Books, London, 1986) p. 247; Franks, *Search Find and Kill*, p. 114.

destroyers, which chose not to destroy him where he lay.[14]

During that month, Mick achieved a long-held ambition. After much pleading, he was permitted to make his first flight in a Supermarine Spitfire—on 18 June, for thirty-five exhilarating minutes. "It was certainly different! Nobody sitting in the back to worry about, tremendous power at the front, both weapons and engine. I would like to have fought the war in fighters. However, if life has taught me anything it is that we have to take whatever God sends us and make the best of it. Who knows, I might have been shot down on my first op." Mick also flew in a Beaufighter as 2nd pilot on the 26th and lst pilot next day. And he had two long flights in his first love, a Tiger Moth, to remind him of what now seemed to have been carefree days so far away in New Zealand.

The New Zealand-born author Hector Bolitho was invited by the Air Ministry to spend a few weeks with 224 Squadron in the summer of 1944 and produce a book about its daily routine. This he did, casting it in the form of a diary, and *Task for Coastal Command* (Hutchinson, London, 1944) is the result. At Mick's suggestion, it was dedicated to Captain D. V. Peyton-Ward, "as a small sign of the devotion and gratitude of Coastal Command." Bolitho considered the aircrew of that squadron "an astonishing company". It was certainly a mixed company: 137 Britons, forty-four Canadians, thirty-three Australians and eight New Zealanders as well as an American, a Swiss, a Chilean, a Brazilian and an Australian-born Chinese.[15]

Bolitho first mentions Mick by name on 4 June, calling him "Mike" throughout the book, even though he was "Mick" to everyone who served with him during the war and after. "Mike Ensor," he wrote, "who comes from a placid farm in the South Island of New Zealand, said that he did not like civilisation as he finds it in the old world. He wishes to return to the innocent hills and the silence of New Zealand. I tried to tantalize him into argument by pointing out that the percentage of lunacy was higher in New Zealand than in any other English-speaking country, and that it did not seem such a swell civilisation to me. But he would not bite. Then he said that all he wished for was a solid, respectable married life. [Hubert] Jessell and I pulled his leg by telling him that marriage was a defunct institution in modern civilisation, as was proved by almost every case we could quote. Mike did not like this so he walked away." What he really disliked was Bolitho's opinion that life on a great High Country sheep station

[14] Franks, *Search Find and Kill*, pp. 115-116.
[15] Bolitho, p. 15. Subsequent quotations are from the same source.

was placid: "it's not the first word I think of to describe a routine of lambing, shearing, mustering, feeding-out and coping with washed out roads and bridges."

Bolitho later wrote (more to Mick's taste) about the bond between the ten members of a Liberator crew which was, he thought, "one of the silent strengths of Coastal Command, easy to comprehend when one realises what the ten men share as they fly: boredom, disappointment and hope, for twelve or more long hours over the sea, with death as their near companion. It is an unspoken bond in which rank has no place or importance. But this is a solemn estimate of something which expresses itself in laughter. We drank too much, laughed and talked too much."

Mick's beloved dog, Liberator (given to him by Margaret Douglas), appealed mightily to Bolitho. Mick had asked her for one of the border terriers her family had at Hindhope, near Jedburgh in Scotland, "so Dad put Lib on the train at Hawick and I collected him at Sheffield and took him to Rotherham. I had to take him to school in my bike basket for two or three days and then took him down to London to Mick, who was on leave."[16] This well-travelled dog, wrote Bolitho, had "the aloofness of a cat and an irritating habit of treating me as if I were an interloper. He catches buses alone and knows what time they leave and where they go, which is more than I do. About once a fortnight he disappears from the mess and joins his friend, Freddy Bell-Scott's cocker spaniel, who lives two miles away. After two days of her refreshment he comes back alone, by bus, like an Edwardian roue coming home from Paris. If he is bored when Mike takes him up to the aerodrome he withdraws, goes to the bus stop alone and comes home." Mick took Lib everywhere, even to London theatres. At the cloakroom counter, Margaret recalls, Mick would simply hand over his coat, gloves and cap with Lib curled up inside. The attendants never objected and seemed indeed to welcome Lib's company; Lib made no objection either, accepting close attention as part of life. He would spend his last years with Pat Green's sister and her husband, departing painlessly in due time.

"The newspapers", thought Bolitho, "give too much space to the glory and heroics of war and not enough to the misery; the days of slow starvation in dinghies, the horrors of mutilation and the cries of men being burned. The mass mind fights shy of these things, naturally preferring the heroism. There is too much limelight on the gallantry, which encourages war, and not enough on the despair and pain, which

---

[16] Letter, Margaret Goss to Spooner, 18 March 1988.

might put a mute on the trumpeters who cry: 'He died a hero.' That he was a hero is merely incidental to the fact that he died in pain, that he was robbed of life and that he is lost to his generation. There is glory in living for an ideal as well as in dying for it. The aircrews themselves are resilient when the bad news comes, but they are also vindictive. Their hatred of the German is not emotional. It is terrible with purpose. They go about their business hoping that next day will give them the chance of revenge but knowing that the crop of deaths among themselves is inevitable. My older heart starts when I see the dismal ritual; the disappearance of faces from the mess table, the packing of the dead man's possessions, the pile of his luggage in the hall; and the new man, fresh from his training, walking up the stairs to occupy the empty room."

Reflecting on these words, Mick recalled that several members of the squadron spoke freely (usually when full of beer) about the likelihood of being killed—in the Pacific, fighting against Japan, if not in the Atlantic—though this, he thought, may have been no more than an ancient human device to dispel a fear by voicing it. Mick was never one of these, drunk or sober. He had learned to bear the deaths of other men calmly and refused to allow himself to believe that he too might be killed. He personally has no memory of occasions when Australians and New Zealanders in particular anxiously discussed their career prospects after the war, as Bolitho alleged. "Didn't happen in my hearing. Ops, leave, wine, women and song, money and promotion were what we *talked* about. Other matters might have been *thought* about, privately. 'Sufficient unto the day is the evil thereof' was, I think, the motto for most of us."

In Mick's opinion, Bolitho's account of his time with the squadron is "rather over-blown; he was more of a novelist than a historian." Mick agreed, however, that there was merit in Bolitho's belief that Australians and New Zealanders, more so than Canadians, seemed "unconscious of their value; of the store of experience and judgement they will take back with them, not only because their courage has been proved but also because of the widening of their mental horizon. Those who have been here three or four years realise that however independent the new countries have become, their roots lie in Britain. Some of them yearn to go home soon because they are poor travellers and unwilling to learn, but most to whom I speak realise that their language, their civic consciousness, their democratic intentions and their integrity owe a debt to the English system."

Mick has always felt equivocal about Bolitho's emphasis upon his own achievements. "Proudly embarrassed" might best sum up his attitude. After describing both the Heligoland Bight raid and the destruction of *U259* at length, Bolitho asked: "What kind of man emerges from this terrific experience? He looks more than twenty-two. If the war had not come he might still be sitting on a five-bar gate on his father's New Zealand sheep farm. Mike is a tiger for work, yet capable of ridiculous boyishness. His pleasures are as fierce as his labour. It has all made him a little intolerant of fools, self-contained and mentally secretive, with a wise sense of cold justice which many a man in his fifties has missed. He still plods along the road, shoulders bent, like a sheep farmer climbing the hills. His decisions now come in instinctive flashes, fortified by experience, so they are usually right. He is stern, ruthless and free of vanity. He has the assurance of leadership and the respect of the squadron, especially of his crew. How good it would be to see such a crew translated, with their experience, their loyalties and their absolute inter-dependence, into industry or some walk of life where the value would not be lost! The man of big business would be wise if he could convey such a crew into his works or his administration and allow their loyalty, mutual respect and loathing of all humbug, to inspire their tasks in peace. But I don't suppose it will happen. They will part at the end, go back into a world which will not comprehend the value of their mutual experience and something of terrific value will perish and thus be lost to the world."

During July 1944, Mick flew two more operations with the crew he had gradually assembled for himself since April. 'Butch' Pugh was a New Zealander and became a particular friend. He was posted to 224 Squadron from 75 Squadron, the New Zealand squadron in Bomber Command. A man never lost for words, he and his wife Mary used to borrow Mick's open Austin Seven (named 'Belinda') as often as they could. Butch was a very good radio man and became the squadron's chief signals officer. "He also helped me a lot with flight and then squadron administration", added Mick, "with particular emphasis on booze-ups." Butch is "round as a tub", observed Bolitho, "and his voice can pierce three floors of solid Victorian brickwork." He had an ancient motorbike which looked like "a very old rusty harp with a pair of Aberdeen Angus horns on top."

Mick added three more operations to his tally in August. On the 3rd, he returned from escort duty over HMS *Ramillies*, last seen in Halifax harbour, when Mick was beginning his first Atlantic crossing. The battleship was sailing westward through the English Channel from Portland Bill (on the Dorset coast) to the Scilly Isles, off Land's End, a total distance of about 175 miles. That evening, Bolitho met a member of his crew, Flight Sergeant Bill Moses, "who said that he had seldom seen anything as magnificent as the battleship steaming over the smooth sea at fourteen knots. 'She gave me a feeling of great power.'" Bolitho then said to Mick: "I would like to see *Ramillies* from the air. She must look grand on a calm sea." Aware of the author's delight in fine sentiments, dramatically expressed, Mick chose to reply bluntly: "When you have been watching the bloody thing for eight hours you get sick of the sight of it." Mick's hundredth operation was a patrol off Bordeaux on 8 August in a Liberator V (letter X) with Bill Andrews as 2nd pilot and his usual crew. It lasted for exactly eleven hours (nearly six and a half in daylight, the rest in darkness). No particular celebration followed his safe return, because Mick was not a statistically-minded man and had no idea how many operations he had completed.

At this time, 53 Squadron (also equipped with Liberators) was based at St. Eval under the command of Squadron Leader Tony Spooner. He and Mick used to meet in the Intelligence Office to study "those excellent 'Red Books', which gave the details of how specific U-boats had met their end" in addition to a wealth of information about tactics, personalities, limitations, armament, performance, construction and morale. Tony learned that the most useful Coastal Command HQ paper on how to deal with U-boats had been written (dictated, actually) by Mick. He was even more impressed to learn, years later, that the author was only twenty-one. "The Mick Ensor I personally remember", wrote Tony, "was *not* a fast and loose party boy. He was a quiet, intelligent, youthful Squadron Leader with an acute tactical brain and a determination to excel at the responsible tasks assigned to him. We tried to know everything about our enemies and to prepare ourselves against as many eventualities as we could think of. I think we both also tried to lead by example and enthusiasm." In Spooner's opinion, Mick was never a "press on regardless" type nor an "eat drink and be merry for tomorrow we may die" fanatic. He seemed "admirably balanced."[17] That opinion was evidently shared by higher authority because 224 Squadron was now to move north, to take part in the final onslaught against the U-boat, and Mick would soon be entrusted with its command.

---

[17] Letter, Spooner to Ensor, 11 May 1987.

CHAPTER IX

FROM THE FAEROES TO THE KATTEGAT
SEPTEMBER 1944 TO MAY 1945

ON 11 September 1944, 224 Squadron was suddenly transferred from the south-west corner of England to the north coast of Scotland: from St. Eval in Cornwall to Milltown in Morayshire, near Lossiemouth, a distance of more than 500 miles. It took Mick three hours to fly there, with his crew and six passengers. Milltown, a former 'Q-site' (that is, an imitation airfield, designed to lure Luftwaffe raiders away from the genuine airfield at Lossiemouth), had gradually been turned into the real thing. Mick's squadron was sent there to counter U-boats then operating from Norwegian bases.[1] Milltown had no WAAF establishment of its own, but Lossiemouth more than made up for this deficiency as far as Mick was concerned, for he would meet—and marry—a WAAF officer based there.

A week after moving to Milltown, on the night of the 18th, Mick found a U-boat off Bergen. It was *U1228* (a Type IXC/40) commanded by Kapitänleutnant Friedrich-Wilhelm Marienfeld, who had been ordered to search for *U867*, a boat in serious trouble: both its diesel engines had broken down. The IXC/40 was much larger (at 1,144 tons surfaced, 1,257 submerged) than the Type VIIC; it had a longer range, superior equipment and this particular example had an experienced, determined and (not least) a lucky crew. "Butch Pugh got a good blip," recalled Bill Andrews. "So Mick put up the speed from cruise of 135 knots to attack speed of 160. I turned on the Leigh Light. Then we hit a patch of fog. Only one we found all night. The U-boat could see our light, but we couldn't see the boat. Not until it started firing, then we saw it alright. We were too close, too low and off to the right.

---

[1] David J Smith, *Action Stations 7: Military Airfields of Scotland, the North-East and Northern Ireland* (Patrick Stephens, Cambridge, 1983) p. 151.

We certainly took some hits; probably more than we gave, I'm afraid."

Mick damaged Marienfeld's *schnorkel* gear (a retractable air pipe, permitting use of the diesels while travelling submerged) and obliged him to abandon the search for *U867*, which eventually scuttled itself, and take refuge in a fiord south of Bergen. There he managed to patch up the gear sufficiently well to enable him to make his way to Bergen for a proper refit. Marienfeld had fought back so skilfully that the Liberator (in Mick's words) was "thoroughly ventilated". He therefore broke off the attack and everyone aboard endured a long and increasingly anxious journey back to Milltown—none more so than Mick, who had already crossed the North Sea once in a damaged aircraft and well knew it to be an unhealthy habit. In Tom Cockeram's memory, although "there were no casualties, one side of the mid-fuselage looked like a colander, the gyro compass was put out of action and one gunner's trousers had been slit by shrapnel. We couldn't assess any other damage in the dark, so returned to base and landed safely." Next morning, it was seen that the Liberator had sustained hits in the fuselage, one tail fin and through an empty fuel tank. By great good fortune, no control cables were hit.[2]

And yet Mick was off again to the same area, between the Shetlands and the Norwegian coast north of Bergen, only two nights later. This operation was carried out in "shocking weather": a phrase nowadays devalued, but used rarely and always with feeling in Mick's log book. "A black night," he recalls, "rain coming down sideways. Big and heavy as the old Lib was, especially with a full war load on, she bobbed about like a Tiger Moth in a nor'wester. Kept her well off the sea that night, I can tell you. Bloody silly to be out there anyway in such conditions. I mean, all the boats would be a mile down and our radar wasn't clever enough to spot any that were stupid enough to be up top, not in all those waves." Nevertheless, Mick and his crew stuck it out grimly, doing their best to find a target, for more than nine hours: a classic example of *constant endeavour*.

During October, Mick carried out three more operations, mostly in darkness. One was flown east of the Faeroes, the other two off Norway. In addition, he managed a couple of brief flights in a Hurricane (on 2 and 3 October). "Another treat. Not as exciting as the Spitfire, of course, but I did enjoy single-seat fighters. Everything happened so much more quickly and easily than in the dear old Lib

---

[2] *The RAF in Maritime War*, vol. v, p. 90; Hessler, *The U-Boat War*, vol. i, pp. 109-110. *U1228* sank a Canadian corvette off Cabot Strait in November 1944 and was still serving on the American coast at the end of the war (Rohwer & Hummelchen, *Chronology*, pp. 297, 316 & 353-4).

and it was nice to have something other than sea underneath. Mind you, I've always enjoyed flying anything with wings, with or without engines." Mick completed three more operations in November. One was over the Skagerrak, mostly in darkness; one was off the Norwegian coast and one north of the Faeroes. He and Bill Andrews agree that among the world's loveliest sights must be the Faeroes in moonlight on a calm, clear night from about 5,000 feet: "what's more, we even got paid for enjoying it." Mick flew no operations in December, only tests and training flights. Shortly before Christmas, copies of the November issue of *Contact*, an RNZAF magazine, reached Milltown and exposed Mick to some good-natured banter (as well as some that was barbed) by describing him as the "air-sea war prodigy of the RNZAF", decorated three times at the age of twenty-one. At the end of 1944, this prodigy had more than 1,600 flying hours to his credit.

Peter Cundy, a squadron pilot, got to know Mick at Milltown in 1944 and recalled one memorable night when Mick tried to tap a barrel of beer. "The Mess was in a castle-type building known rightly or wrongly as McGinty's Towers and what I can only imagine was the ballroom in pre-war days had become the ante-room and decorated as a dungeon with primitive weaponry hanging on the walls. Anyway, Mick's attempt proved quite disastrous—we did our best to stem the flow, taking it in turns to be plumber or consumer, but after umpteen pints in quick succession had to admit defeat. I suppose he could have had a pretty hefty mess bill for that month!" As it happened, the officer members of Mick's crew insisted on helping to pay it while the NCO members kindly expressed their deepest sympathy.

On New Year's Day 1945, Mick was consoled for this disaster by news that he was to succeed Terry McComb as CO of 224 Squadron and be promoted to the acting rank of Wing Commander. "Terry was a lovely bloke," recalled Bill Andrews, "quiet, yet attractive, greatly admired and respected. Mick modelled himself on Terry and couldn't have chosen a better model." A month later, he was decorated yet again. Awards were never made lightly and a single DSO, second only to the Victoria Cross among decorations available to officers, was a mark of very high distinction. To receive that award for a second time admitted Mick, at the age of twenty-three, to a most select inner circle. The citation for the award of a Bar to his DSO states that he "has taken part in many operational sorties during his second tour of duty. During this period, he has attacked enemy U-boats on three occasions. One of the submarines was probably seriously damaged and, from one of these engagements, Squadron Leader Ensor's aircraft was severely damaged by the heavy and accurate anti-aircraft fire encountered. This officer has displayed outstanding enthusiasm, tact and courage as flight commander and officer in charge of squadron training. He has contributed much to the development of new and successful methods of attacking enemy submarines." H L Thompson, author of an official history of New Zealanders in the Royal Air Force, regarded Mick as "the outstanding personality" in 224 Squadron, "where he won commendation for his work as flight commander both in the air and on the ground."[3]

There were two flights in a Liberator squadron, each of twelve crews, ten men to a crew: 240 fliers in total, quite apart from a large force on the ground of experienced technicians in many trades, and Mick had been in charge of half of them. Terry trained Mick in man-management and when he left the squadron at the end of 1944, "I was very surprised, though not completely nonplussed, on being told that I would be promoted to Wing Commander and given command of the whole squadron." In sensitive or complicated situations, Mick simply asked himself: "What would Dad have done?" And the answer came: "Be honest, straightforward and don't change your mind." Mick had almost completed a second tour with Liberators when Terry was posted, "so instead of being taken off operations I started again—though in a new position—and this suited me very well. The upshot was that from the time I went onto Blenheims in the middle of 1941 until the end of the war in Europe, I only had six months away from an operational squadron." And in all that time, he proudly records, "I never had an accident in the air, though I did have a few on the ground."

Mick flew his first operation as CO on 9 January 1945, in Liberator VI (R). Terry McComb had not yet left Milltown and *asked* Mick, much to his delight and embarrassment, if he might fly with him as 2nd pilot. It was an anti-submarine patrol over the Shetlands and Faeroes: by Mick's standards, a relatively short patrol, lasting under eight hours (half the time in daylight). As CO, Mick need never have flown another operation. Such a very large squadron generated more than enough paper work to imprison its commander permanently in the office and in fact Terry had rarely escaped. But Mick made determined efforts to break free as often as possible. Although he did this mostly because he enjoyed flying so much, he also had in mind the poor example set by his first CO in 500 Squadron at Bircham Newton: "We all thought Gilbert should have led from the front much more

---

[3] H L Thompson, *New Zealanders with the Royal Air Force*, vol. ii, p. 269.

than he did and many of the crews told each other loudly. The ground staff and even the admin people knew what was going on and the whole atmosphere there became really poor. I wasn't going to have such things said about me and see this squadron fall apart." On the morning of 18 January, after a night of total abandon, Mick flew Terry south to Northolt, west of London, with Flight Lieutenant Tom Storey as his new 2nd pilot. The flight, recorded by Mick in his log book as "worst trip ever (bad weather and hangover)", lasted four hours that felt like four years and was followed by days of total abstinence. To his lasting regret, Mick never again served with Terry McComb and rarely enjoyed the pleasure of his company.

During February, Mick flew only one operation, an unusually dangerous one. It was a patrol begun on the 12th and intended to cover the Skagerrak, between Denmark and Norway. The weather became so dreadful during the journey home that Mick was obliged to steer south and seek refuge at Middleton St. George, near Darlington in County Durham. He flew back to Milltown next day. Tom Storey, his 2nd pilot, had experience as a Liberator captain and on that patrol, wrote Mick, he "probably saved me from another disaster. At that time, the Germans had trawlers flying balloons in the Skagerrak. Of course, we homed onto and illuminated every contact, but had to be very smart about recognising and avoiding balloon-flying trawlers: hitting a steel cable at 130 knots would solve all one's problems." Mick was fully occupied, "sculling around in bad weather at 400 feet", when Tom realised that the engines were rapidly losing power because of ice forming around the nacelles. He took the appropriate action on his own initiative, there being no time for a discussion, and the Liberator narrowly escaped becoming a statistic: "missing in unexplained circumstances". It was one occasion, Mick reflected afterwards, when his enthusiasm for the hunt almost got the better of him. He flew no operations during March or April, only a few brief air tests and the odd flight in an Oxford which reminded him of ancient days at Wigram.

Mick worked closely with Squadron Leader J C T Downey (who ended a distinguished career as an Air Vice-Marshal) while at Milltown. Downey wrote a little book on the use of the Leigh Light. "It was a very good one", thought Mick, "two years too late. We both worked on it and it contained most of my ideas because we knew we had to get the squadron weaned off Coastal Command procedures and theories—at least the more hopeless ones." In particular, Mick argued that crews were not receiving nearly enough realistic training in the proper use of this light. During operations, therefore, it was often switched on much too soon, when the aircraft was still too high and too far from the target. The light was positively dangerous to use in foggy conditions because it was simply reflected back into the crew's eyes and nicely illuminated the aircraft if the target were a surfaced U-boat preparing to fight back. In all circumstances, Mick emphasised, the closest co-ordination between the radar and light operators was essential.

Then, in the last week of the European war, on 5 May 1945, flying a Liberator VIII (letter T), Mick attacked and sank another U-boat. On 2 May, all boats in German ports that were capable of diving had been ordered to sail to Norway, away from the threat of low-flying aircraft and to a position where, in the words of Fregattenkapitän Gunter Hessler (formerly a U-boat captain, later a staff officer at HQ and, incidentally, Grossadmiral Doenitz's son-in-law) "it was thought that their presence, in large numbers, might strengthen the hand of the German representatives in their negotiations with Field Marshal Montgomery." More than eighty boats departed, including several that could not in fact dive, and they were soon spotted. In the absence of German aircraft or escorting flak ships, Allied aircraft enjoyed "a last bloody massacre". During the five days from 2-6 May, twenty-one U-boats, most of them unable to dive, were sunk.[4]

Mick's victim was *U579* (a fully-functioning Type VIIC, commanded by Oberleutnant Hans-Dietrich Schwarzenberg), sailing from Kiel for Norway and caught in the Kattegat north of Zealand, between Denmark and Sweden. "I felt a bit guilty about the loss of life so close to the end of the war," Mick told the historian Norman Franks in July 1988, "although I did not know how close it was that day." He had only been in the patrol area for fifteen minutes before making contact with *U579* at a distance of eight miles. Until that day, throughout numerous patrols, Mick had never before seen more than a single U-boat and never another aircraft in a position to join the attack. Now he had as many as five boats in view as well as a Liberator of 547 Squadron (flown by Flying Officer Art Bruneau, a Canadian). *U579* was the rearmost of three boats travelling line astern and about six miles off to port Mick could see two more. His first problem was to

---

[4] Hessler, *The U-Boat War*, vol. iii, p. 100. Among the victims of this massacre was *U534* (commanded by Kapitänleutnant Herbert Nollau), sunk off the Danish island of Anholt by a Liberator of 86 Squadron on 5 May, but another Liberator (of 547 Squadron) crashed while attacking. No fewer than fifty-three men aboard the U-boat survived. It was raised in good condition on 23 August 1993 by a group hoping to discover secret documents and Nazi loot. Water and mud were pumped out and rusting shells removed. The raising was watched by eight German survivors and four of the airmen who helped to sink it (*Guardian Weekly*, London, 29 August 1993).

ensure that he and Bruneau did not attack the same boat and risk a collision.

As soon as Mick realised that Bruneau was aiming at the second of the three boats in a line, he set himself for "a standard daylight attack" on the first. It was turning and beginning to dive as he roared over it almost at sea level, dropping six Torpex 250-lb depth charges spaced one hundred feet apart. His rear gunner saw the second and third charges straddle the conning tower as it disappeared from sight. Mick climbed away and turning, he saw both black oil and white air bubbles gushing to the surface, followed by yellow planking and other debris. As for Bruneau, his target was *U1168* which chose to remain surfaced and fire back, but it too was sunk. These boats were among the last of 784 destroyed during the war. Of 40,000 highly-trained men who served in U-boats, nearly 28,000 died and 5,000 were captured. Shore-based aircraft, British and American, sank 41.5 per cent of these boats by their own unaided efforts and assisted surface forces in many other victories. The price for these vital achievements was very high: Coastal Command alone lost 1,777 aircraft and 5,866 men were killed.[5]

U579 went down about 4.30 pm and some crew members survived, though twenty-four did not. Serving as a training boat throughout the war, *U579* consequently had no victories to its credit. Neither did Mick's other certain victim, *U259*, and he now finds it "rather sadly ironic" to reflect that at least two of the boats that got away from him had better records: *U458* (which he did damage) sank two steamers and *U1228* (which nearly shot him down) sank a Canadian frigate. "I suppose they were too good for me," he says with a wry smile, "so I'll have to console myself with the thought that the one we got in the Mediterranean *might* have sunk some shipping if we'd not spotted it." Next day, 9 May, Mick was out again, photographing surrendering U-boats north of the Shetlands in dreadful weather. He encountered one boat on the wrong course and dropped depth charges near it as a warning. "It was interesting to have nothing better to do than observe what a terrific upheaval a stick of these good depth charges caused. I thought we'd dropped them far enough away to do no harm, but the poor old boat rocked about and I suspect everyone aboard really got the wind up. First and only time I frightened a U-boat without meaning to!"

Mick's list of victims destroyed or damaged may seem a short one, but the fact is that most Coastal Command crews went through the

---

[5] Hessler, *The U-Boat War*, vol. iii, p. 101; Franks, *Search Find and Kill*, pp. 61-3; Terraine, *The Right of the Line*, p. 456.

entire war without even sighting a U-boat. On the other hand, the endeavours of Mick Ensor and all other crews must be weighed in the light of this comment in the RAF's official (though unpublished) history of that command: "During the whole war there was never produced a large long-range aircraft specifically designed for action against U-boats."[6] The Blenheims, Hudsons and Liberators flown by Mick were all makeshifts, so too were the Ansons, Sunderlands, Catalinas, Wellingtons and other types flown by his colleagues. Moreover, the same source adds that an efficient low-level bomb sight did not "eventuate" until June 1943. Until that date, release of depth charges depended entirely on the pilot's eye, helped by "practice, experience and any natural aptitude for judging heights and distances." This remained largely the case until the end of the war.

Also the mind-numbing *noise* of operations lasting for many hours in a cold, comfortless, unstable metal tube must not be forgotten by those who write or read about them: and add to these miseries the time spent preparing for take-off and the time spent in de-briefing after landing. Although crews faced far less flak than those of Bomber Command, those forced to abandon their aircraft by enemy action, storm damage or navigational failure were certain to endure extreme hardship even if rescuers came in time; many would die, slowly and painfully. And finally, as Sir John Slessor wrote: "one of the main enemies was boredom, the endless monotony of patrolling apparently empty wastes without ever sighting a U-boat or getting the chance of a kill." But kills, he rightly emphasised, "were not the only yardstick for success in anti-submarine warfare: the object of the exercise was to prevent our own ships from being sunk, to ensure the 'safe and timely arrival' of the convoys. The mere presence of aircraft, circling the convoys and patrolling the U-boat transit routes, saved an uncountable number of Allies ships."[7]

The attack upon *U579* was Mick's 114th and last operational flight of the war: sixty-seven with 500 Squadron, forty-seven with 224 Squadron. His sixty-seven operations with the former amounted to exactly 357 hours (thirty-eight and a half of these hours in darkness), an average of five hours and twenty minutes each. His forty-seven operations with the latter amounted to nearly 522 hours (almost equally split between daylight and darkness), an average of just over eleven hours each. In sum, his 114 operations amounted to 879 hours

---

[6] *The RAF in Maritime War*, vol. iii, p. 2, note 3.
[7] *The RAF in Maritime War*, vol. iii. p. 42 & note 3; contributions to RAF Historical Society seminar, *Seek and Sink*, pp. 78-80; foreword to Price, *Aircraft versus Submarine*, pp. xi-xii.

(585 in daylight, 294 in darkness), an average of seven and three-quarter hours.

By the end of the war, Mick had 108 hours in single-engined aircraft to his credit (eighty-three as pilot, twenty-five under instruction). In multi-engined aircraft, he had 1,195 hours in daylight (1,088 as 1st pilot, fifty-eight as 2nd pilot, forty-nine under instruction). In darkness, he had flown for 382 hours (369 as 1st pilot, six as 2nd pilot, seven under instruction). All told, he had amassed 1,685 hours in the cockpit, plus fifty-five hours as a passenger. He had served for eight months in New Zealand and four years and three months in Britain. Incidentally, two of the three ships on which Mick sailed were later destroyed by enemy action: the *Awatea* and the *California*. Only the ferry, *Royal Ulsterman*, survived. "Never did fancy a life on the ocean wave," he admits, "and now I know why." Mick's decorations appear in the *London Gazette* on the dates stated: DFC, 20 February 1942; Bar to the DFC, 27 October 1942; DSO, 16 February 1943; and Bar to the DSO on 6 February 1945. All four had been earned by the time he was twenty-three, together with promotion from the rank of Pilot Officer to that of Wing Commander. And yet he has said: "I am not proud of my wartime performance. I could have done better, but I feel humble to have been so honoured by the King and later the Queen." Mick's meeting with the Queen came in 1954, when he was awarded a fifth decoration, the Air Force Cross.[8]

For 350 of his flying hours (250 on operations), Tom Cockeram was a member of his crew. "Mick Ensor", in his opinion, "as a captain was second to none. He had an uncanny way of weighing up situations and applying his expert judgement as to the feasibility of an attack or discretionary observation. I well remember the Germans at one stage had a number of small flak ships, sprayed with rubberised paint, which they put out at night just off the French coast. The radar return from these was not much more than a *schnorkel* at over five miles and woe betide any patrol aircraft that made an unsuspecting run on them. Mick always feigned to pass close by to tempt them into exposing their firepower because a U-boat commander would never give his presence away unless he was certain of being attacked."

"Every member of his crew had complete confidence in him at all times", continued Tom. "He maintained a certain discipline which was strict but not oppressive and could let his hair down with the best of them when the occasion called for it. He had no time for incompetents, eccentrics or any kind of inane foolishness, yet would

---

[8] Letter, Ensor to Spooner, July 1987.

join in a game or a bit of fun with crew members or other immediate fellows. But he always seemed to maintain a certain aloofness around other junior ranks, which was the order of the day at that time, and consequently was thought to be rather snooty to other men who didn't know him as well as we did. As a pilot, he had a natural ability and could handle the Liberator with great skill in every situation. I never recall a bad landing, even with one engine out and engine cowlings full of semi-barbecued lapwings. The only incident of any gravity I recall was when the 2nd Navigator, Bob Tate, opened the bomb doors when the Flight Engineer was standing on them, arming practice bombs. We nearly lost him and Mick wasn't best pleased about that."

Like everyone else who knew Mick at St. Eval late in the war, Tom was enchanted by the dog Liberator, whom he described as "a little Norfolk Terrier". Liberator, he recalls, "hated flying and preferred to mooch about the camp, looking for anything interesting like bitches, and when he was fed up would catch the bus all on his own back down to the Officers' Mess at the Watergate Hotel, some miles away. Liberator bit sailors to order, when they shot down our crews (by mistake of course). Mick also had an old Austin Seven Tourer (canvas-topped) which he always seemed to keep maintained and fuelled. I remember his batman (whose name escapes me now) drove it loaded with gear, all the way from Cornwall to Morayshire, when we were posted to Milltown."

On one famous occasion at Milltown, Mick took seven members of his crew in that little Austin, plus some crates of beer, to Urquhart, a nearby village. His navigator (Joe Addington) lodged there with his wife and children in the fine old home of a Presbyterian missionary's widow. Both ladies had gone to shop in Aberdeen, some fifty miles to the south-east, and stay overnight. Unbeknown to them, Joe had hidden a beer barrel in the coal cellar and invited his comrades to help empty it. "I can still see the scene now," wrote Tom, "a roaring log fire, beautiful royal blue carpet and matching velour table cloth. Joe's barrel, on newspaper and two bricks, coal dust and all, on the table. We all lying around in front of the fire, in various stages of inebriation, playing poker dice, when in walked the two ladies, who hadn't got accommodation in Aberdeen and had come home. Well, if the looks from Joe's wife could have killed, the war would have ended for us all, there and then. We all mumbled slurred apologies and prepared to leave. But the old lady would have none of it and immediately got food going. The old dear ended up playing dice with us on the carpet and a very convivial evening was had by all, except for Joe's wife, who kept him in the dog house for sometime after. Mick drove us all back safely to camp along those winding lanes (God knows how) and it was business as usual the next day."

True friendships, Mick found, rarely developed in wartime: one or other partner would be killed, wounded or posted away before a promising closeness could mature and after this happened once or twice, most people became wary of exposing any deep emotion. There was also a barrier between officers and NCOs. Mick's Blenheim and Hudson crews were made up of NCOs who were "extremely loyal and we were friendly, very friendly; we wouldn't have survived otherwise. But deep officer-NCO relationships didn't develop for obvious reasons. Too much mingling off-duty was discouraged and if you started favouring one NCO against another it put the backs up of the others and so one of the first lessons you really had to learn in the service was the subtle line of demarcation." Mick also thought Gilbert and Sullivan were quite right when they said that every time an Englishman opens his mouth he makes some other Englishman despise him. "Scotsmen, Irishmen and Welshmen are not so easily classified by voice, though no doubt their class systems are also strong."

As for relations between air and ground crews, Mick had the greatest respect for ground crews who usually lived and worked in conditions that were appalling: "at least by our standards of living. Aeroplanes were invariably dispersed to all corners of the airfield, as protection against bombing or strafing, and only came into hangars for major servicing, so ground crews had to work on them where they stood in all weathers, day or night; they had it pretty tough." Pilots got to know the NCOs in charge of frontline servicing very well indeed because they had to sign the Form 700, accepting responsibility for an aircraft's condition, and no sensible pilot would do that without making his own personal checks. Such NCOs were often much older than the pilots who were their seniors in rank and this could make for difficulties unless there was mutual tact and respect. A farm up-bringing had taught Mick a natural respect for 'the workers' and he was well liked by the ground crews.

For example, at a re-union of 500 Squadron members after the war, Mick was confronted by one notable expert, Flight Sergeant Wilson, who greeted him as a long-lost brother and said: "You know, you were the only one on the squadron who never turned an aircraft down for some technical fault." In fact, Mick did sometimes change planes and once or twice landed back with a full load to get another, but the compliment remained valid because several Blenheims and Hudsons developed mysterious 'mag drops' if the weather was bad or the job looked a bit tricky. Mick had never wanted either to niggle or find an excuse to miss an operation: "aeroplanes have been very good to me, on the whole, and I rarely had cause to complain. In fact, one of the greater pleasures in my life, having taken off and got everything sorted out, was to look out at those propellers turning and listen to the engines purring away; I just loved it."

Meanwhile, as the war in Europe drew to an end, Mick looked to his future. On 29 March 1945, he wrote that he hoped to remain in the RAF or the RNZAF and attend Staff College, but he would also go into civil aviation "if opportunity offered." Group Captain J A C Stratton, station commander at Milltown, described Mick on 30 April as an "officer with an outstanding operational record who possesses high qualities of leadership both in the air and on the ground. He has tact and a pleasant personality and gets the best out of people. A most efficient Squadron Commander in every way." Air Vice-Marshal Sturley Simpson, head of 18 Group, added on 4 May that Mick was "a most capable and efficient officer with a very fine operational record" and he "strongly" recommended him for retention in the postwar services. Not surprisingly, given the warmth of such testimonials from these and other senior officers, Mick chose to remain in uniform. For at least a decade after the war, he never doubted that he had made the right decision.

CHAPTER X

THE MOST USEFUL JOB I EVER DID
JULY 1945 TO MAY 1949

MICK ENSOR's hopes of marrying Margaret Douglas had gradually died during 1943. "I doubt if she would ever have married me", Mick reflected many years later, "though I asked her often enough. After I went to Milltown with 224 Squadron I took very little leave and also I think I might have been just an extension of John MacGillivray." In late 1944, Mick introduced Margaret to Captain Bill Goss, New Zealand Army, in charge of the New Zealand Post Office in London throughout the war and, strangely enough, also an old boy of St. Andrew's College. "Older than me", said Mick, "but obviously a sound, reliable chap. They got married and I grew a moustache in protest." They eventually settled in Christchurch, New Zealand, where Bill died in August 1990. "Now I can understand, but then I could not.... My view of the world was hardening. But aeroplanes never argued with me or let me down. Not just flying them; *managing* them, the air crews and ground crews directly."

On 6 July 1945, Mick married Patience Wellsted Reith Coote at her home, the Old Rectory in Badingham, Woodbridge, Suffolk. She was the second daughter of Marguerite Wellsted and Colin Reith Coote: "a man greatly esteemed by his peers," according to an obituary, "a most gallant officer in the First World War"; a man whom "shrewd judges forecast that he would surely one day be Liberal Prime Minister."[1] In fact, Coote became editor of the *Daily Telegraph* from 1950 to 1964 and among the most influential men of his generation in British political life. Although his marriage with Marguerite soon ended (both re-married), he remained close to Patience throughout her life. Mick wrote to his mother (now living at Paihia, in the Bay of

---

[1] *Daily Telegraph*, 9 June 1979, pp. 8 & 18.

Islands in the North Island of New Zealand) from the Old Rectory on the day before the wedding. "It would have been much easier for guests and relations if we had been married in London," he said, "but we have decided that London weddings have much too much of a mass-production air about them. Anyway, Patience wants to be married at home and she is quite right.... We had drinks with Sir George Hamilton, MP, and Lady Hamilton on Sunday. Major Borthwick, Conservative candidate for this district, who was born in Christchurch NZ was also there.... The Best Man is to be Flight Lieutenant Carter (George, the perfect Englishman), my old rear-gunner and now one of my staunchest assistants in the squadron."

"On Thursday", Mick continued, "I am going to look at a job with British Overseas Airways which has a good prospect. It will mean leaving the RAF, but I would willingly do that for £1100 per year which is, I think, the initial salary.... I do not want to throw away the chance of a good and interesting job for a holiday just now. In a few years, when I have some money, and after all it will be seven years before I am thirty, I would like to go back to farming in NZ if things have settled down by then. What do you think?" Mick then reverted to a subject currently more interesting than his future. "I am very lucky indeed to have met such a sweet and perfect person. Do you know, we knew each other for three months before either of us summoned up courage to make any more than the politest of conversation, because I thought Patience could never be interested in a rather disreputable little NZ Air Force officer and she thought she could never be good enough for me to take an interest in! Isn't life crazy?" Heather Dalton White was Patience's cousin and a very close friend. She described her as "a placid, stoic, unemotional person and very loyal", a woman who loved the outdoors, hunting or sailing. As for Mick, "he was a quiet, shy, unassuming, very modest man."[2]

Patience and her friend Vivienne (who later married George Carter) had been WAAF officers together at Lossiemouth and only met Mick in late 1944. Patience was an equipment officer and obtained a good supply of salt for Mick's runways at Milltown when Coastal Command supplies failed him. Naturally, he had to go and thank her in person and matters developed from there. "We had the Huntley and Palmer's seaside house as our Mess, housing ten WAAF officers", Vivienne recalled. "Pat was a great character and her amusing sayings became part of our vocabulary." She was, however, short-sighted and reluctant to wear her glasses, so Vivienne had to be on hand to tell her

[2] Letter, Dalton White to Spooner, 28 March 1988.

when Mick arrived at any social gathering. Vivienne thought her "an odd mixture with some highbrow interests including books and music, which at the time was unusual in our Mess life. She was very popular with the girls and thought great fun by the men."

Patience was never very interested in makeup and clothes or even in an expensive engagement ring. After agreeing to marry Mick, she asked Vivienne to go with her to a jeweller in Elgin and help her choose a ring costing much less than Mick wanted to spend. Later that day, she and Mick returned to Elgin and Patience insisted upon that very one and no other. Later, Vivienne went with her to Aberdeen to choose a wedding dress. The wedding itself, Vivienne remembered, was "beautifully done". Patience, added George, "had a mind of her own and wasn't going to put up with too much nonsense. She certainly had a lovely sense of humour and was tremendous fun, but she was not perhaps sophisticated.... She was essentially a very homely sort of girl with no interest whatever in clothes or a great social life." As for Mick, George thought of him "very much as the country boy who had never had any real experience of life until coming to England." By "life" George evidently meant "urban customs", but Mick's achievements on the ground as well as in the air during the past four years were only possible for a man of strong character, able to get along with men of various backgrounds and face exceptional hazards calmly.[3]

Looking back on his application to BOAC, Mick thought he would have been taken on, "but my AOC (18 Group) and others persuaded me to apply for the RAF, which of course I got. Thus to Transport Command. Really, I did not have the maturity to make the best decision for *me* and I did not seek mature advice; furthermore, Patience was all for my staying in. I simply did not try for Empire Test Pilots' School, although I did think about it. The possibility of becoming a very senior officer did not enter my head. As a matter of interest, I was caught—later—in an age versus seniority juggle that put me at a serious disadvantage compared to the postwar Cranwell graduates." As for the RNZAF, Mick correctly saw no future there. Its leadership was Pacific-orientated and had little time for men whose service had been in the European theatre. Ian Patterson advised him to try for TEAL, the New Zealand civil airline, "but by then I seemed to be committed to the RAF." Mick had been given a free hand to pick his own captains for postwar service in 224 Squadron and when he asked Pat Green to join him, "I really didn't hesitate." And so that

---

[3] Letter, Carter to Spooner, January 1988.

"postwar period of euphoria when some dies were cast", in Pat's words, came to an end. The squadron returned from Milltown to its old home at St. Eval and Mick remained in command.

Between June 1945 and January 1947, when he left both St. Eval and the squadron, Mick flew as often as he could, but his hours in the air were few indeed—and distinctly undramatic—compared to wartime: no more than 203 in twenty months and of that meagre total only ninety-five minutes were in darkness (en route from the Azores to Cornwall on 23 July 1946). In October 1945, he had made a week-long tour from St. Eval to Lyneham in Wiltshire and thence to Castel Benito (near Tripoli) with 5,000 lbs of freight; from there he flew to Cairo West with more freight, returning to Castel Benito with eight passengers and bringing ten back to Lyneham; his attempt to fly home to St. Eval that day was foiled by fog. That was his only spell of intensive flying during this whole period.

Once the war was over, Mick had to face the fact that most members of his squadron wanted to get out of it and return to civilian life. They had enlisted for 'the duration' and now received a release number, calculated on age and length of service. When their number came up, out they went. Good for them, but not so good for the maintenance of Mick's aircraft and equipment, to say nothing of morale. As he put it, "People always say you shouldn't command a squadron at the start of a war, when your equipment and state of training will be poor, but it isn't too much fun at the end either—once the thrill of victory wears off." Most of the ground personnel who left were of junior rank, accustomed to helping out wherever needed and doing dirty jobs in cold or wet conditions, whereas many of those who stayed on were of senior NCO rank. Mick understood the reluctance of such skilled, experienced men to take on routine, elementary chores in addition to ever-increasing responsibility for keeping the squadron flying safely, but he never flinched from pressing them. "I was straight with all the technical people, telling them what Group HQ told me about the shortage of tradesmen. I would always put our case (ours, not theirs, I emphasised) to Group, but meanwhile they'd just have to get on with it. I never stood for any bitching." This approach, he remembered, had been his father's when dealing with aggrieved shearers or musterers and Mick made it his own.

A training programme was nevertheless devised and crews went periodically to a school at Ballykelly near Limavady in Northern Ireland where determined efforts were made to keep alive the spirit of co-operation between air and surface forces. A round-the-clock standby for Air-Sea Rescue duty was also maintained. In addition,

224 Squadron carried men and supplies to Lagens in the Azores and Reykjavik in Iceland. Pat Green made three round trips to Lagens in the summer of 1945. Another was cancelled, presumably because "our load appeared to consist of a pot of paint and a copy of the *Daily Mail* for the CO." The RAF had acquired a base there during the war, thanks to an ancient treaty with Portugal, but by 1945 (wrote Pat) "it was virtually an American base; the US Navy aircraft based there had RAF roundels on them, in addition to their own markings, as a sort of sop to the fact that the agreement with Portugal had only been for British aircraft to operate from the airfield. However, there was a small RAF contingent based there and our job was to fly out replacements and bring the old hands home." Being newly married and also responsible for the whole squadron, Mick was unable to make any of these flights himself, but he and Patience shared the benefits from the barely-remembered peacetime shopping available to his crews in Lagens: such exotic fruits as pineapples and bananas as well as such rarities as civilian clothing (under and outer) and, above all, silk stockings were brought home. Less popular flights were also made to Reykjavik for the same reason: to relieve/replace British personnel there and bring home any available American products.

During 1946, Mick did escape twice to Lagens (though somehow he never found time to go to Reykjavik) and went once to Ballykelly. Otherwise, his flying was mainly to keep in practice, to test equipment and crews, to pay visits (official and otherwise) and once or twice to take part in exercises or searches for missing aircraft. Several Lancasters, each equipped with a large lifeboat, were assigned to Mick's squadron for rescue duties and gave everyone some agitation on take-off and landing when they had to remember how to handle a large aircraft with a tailwheel instead of a nosewheel. They also had the rare treat, for Coastal Command airmen, of climbing to high altitute once a day in order to collect weather information. Although he usually flew Liberators, Oxfords and Proctors, Mick did manage several flights in Lancasters and one hour in a Spitfire on 7 November 1945. His last flight in a 224 Squadron Liberator came on 24 October 1946 as part of a formation flypast in honour of the AOC and lasted a mere half hour; his last flight of any kind in that squadron was an air-test in an Oxford on 13 December.

Mick had found time to take up his old hobby of building model aircraft at St. Eval and Pat Green vividly recalled an occasion when the two of them were out in the middle of the airfield preparing the latest model for an air test. "This was before the days of radio-controlled models and was, in fact, one of those days when low cloud drifted over from the coast. Mick rather overdid the fuel with the result that instead of the engine stopping before reaching cloud base, his precious model continued climbing and disappeared into cloud. 'Quickly', cried Mick, 'back to back and look up. When the engine stops watch for it gliding down.' The engine noise ceased and after a pause Mick shouted: 'There she is!' And there she was, in a shallow glide, heading in the general direction of the Fleet Air Arm airfield at St. Merryn. We retrieved her from a field a mile or so to our north." Mick also found time to take up a new hobby, dinghy racing: coached (and goaded) by his friend and Station Commander, Group Captain John Ker.

"I had a totally wrong attitude towards my service career", Mick now believes, "in that when I joined the RAF in 1947 I thought I would be out and returning to New Zealand by the age of forty [in fifteen years' time], having had a full flying career and that was when a middle-ranking officer could expect to get out." He had not allowed for the fact that he would then have four sons to educate and limited prospects of a second career, nor for the fact that an increasing amount of non-flying duty would drive him to drink too much. At the time, however, he was perfectly content. "So, as soon as I got back to England after war-service leave in New Zealand, I went to see Air Marshal Baker (C-in-C Transport Command) who knew me and asked for a job with the York force. He fixed it up, but in order to get flying again I had to go down to Flight Lieutenant. That was an obvious move, but plenty of my contemporaries were hanging on to temporary Squadron Leader rank in non-flying jobs, making a future that had no appeal for me. It was not that I deliberately ignored the career aspects of my decision, I just never thought about them."

"I have never thought of myself as a brilliant pilot", Mick added, "but I have always felt competent and strove, often against considerable odds, to remain so. I became an Instrument Rating Examiner when the scheme was introduced in 1946 and remember fouling up steep turns on limited panel while being tested for the qualification in an Oxford at the Central Flying School. I could do them OK in a Lancaster though! When I joined Transport Command, I had to tidy up my flying considerably, but I seemed to learn fast. I remained an IRE until I finally left Kinloss in 1960 and it became clear that there would be no more active flying for me—the Air Ministry having told me that I had done more than my share. I also did instrument flying training work with the US Navy, although never particularly happy with radio range procedures: I thought it a very inexact science."

Mick was granted war-service leave to return to New Zealand for six months from 6 March 1947. He relinquished his commission in the RNZAF on 10 June on being granted a permanent commission in the RAF next day as a Flight Lieutenant, two ranks below that in which he had served for the past two years. His total service as an RNZAF officer amounted to six years and four months, of which five years and eleven months were spent overseas. Mick enjoyed his return home enormously, after more than six years away. He and Patience now had a son (David, born in 1946) and the prolonged reunion with his large family remains one of the warmest memories of his life. Naturally, he found time to fly: four flights in a Tiger Moth and four in a Whitney Straight (NZ576). All were over the South Island's High Country, often with his beloved Double Hill in view. His brother Peter was his usual passenger, but one fine September afternoon he took his mother up to see her old home. Peter recalled enjoying his first close look at the top of Mount Cook, the highest point in New Zealand. "On the way the airspeed indicator froze up, which would be a bit disconcerting to most pilots in that type of country, but Mick was quite unperturbed and carried on."[4]

Mick was posted to HQ 46 Group on 28 October 1947, to Transport Initial Conversion Unit on 18 November and had his first RAF flight in more than a year on 3l December. It was in an Avro Anson at Bircham Newton, the old home of 500 Squadron and thus a place for him of bitter-sweet memories, where he underwent a week-long course of instruction in the mysteries of the Blind Approach Beam System (BABS). Having been assessed as "proficient", he went to No 241 Heavy Conversion Unit at Dishforth (Yorkshire) in January 1948 and there spent two months learning to fly the Avro York, usually with Flight Lieutenant Hathaway, Signaller Chester and Flying Officer Yates among his crew. The course included a trip to Malta, several exercises in darkness and at its end Mick was once again found to be "proficient". He then joined his third squadron, No. 206, in Transport Command at Lyneham (near Chippenham in Wiltshire) on 10 March.

Squadron Leader J C Blair was the CO and Mick's flight commander was Flight Lieutenant John Taylor. Both were officers who would have been subordinate to Mick in rank and experience when he last served with a squadron. It was an embarrassing situation for all concerned and one in which Mick had to steer a careful course between imposing upon his nominal superiors and permitting them to undervalue his professional expertise. As it happened, both Blair and

---

[4] Peter Ensor, 'Many Good Years, Some Not So Good', p. 63.

Top: Hudsons of 500 Squadron being re-fuelled at Tafaraoui, near Oran in Algeria, on 9 November 1942. Operation Torch, the Anglo-American invasion of North-West Africa, had just begun and the squadron was working hard: Mick flew eight operations in eleven days before his luck ran out on the 15th.

Middle: Neville Atkinson (right) became Mick's navigator and a good friend after Bertie Paige returned to Canada in February 1942. Neville was killed in November, following the attack on *U259*.

Bottom: Wing Commander Denis Spotswood and Squadron Leader John Ensor (third and fourth from the left) outside Buckingham Palace. Mick regarded Spotswood as an ideal squadron commander and when he himself reached that position, deliberately chose Spotswood as a model for his own conduct. As for Ensor (no relation), Mick thought him "a very rare bird indeed, excellent both at operations and instructing. I'd gladly have owned him as a cousin at least!"

Top sequence: On 10 October 1943, Mick found a surfaced submarine about 300 miles west of Brest and attacked it with eight small rockets, hitting it once or twice. Only when closing in for the kill did he realise that it was not a U-boat, but a French submarine, the *Minerve*, which had unwisely surfaced in a forbidden zone. He visited it in harbour: "very brave," thought one pilot, "considering there had been casualties including some killed."

Above: A B-24 Liberator of 224 Squadron with a Leigh Light under the starboard wing seen at St Eval in Cornwall on 28 August 1944. The famous church is clearly visible in the background. Although the B-24 had numerous advantages over the Hudson, Mick hated the immensely long nose that restricted his forward view and the fact that he could no longer be his own bomb-aimer.

Top: Bill Andrews, Mick and 'Butch' Pugh with 'Belinda', Mick's Austin 7, outside the Officers' Mess in the Watergate Hotel, about 5 miles from St Eval. 'Belinda' was as hard-worked as any B-24 and when 224 Squadron was posted from Cornwall to Morayshire, a distance of more than 500 miles, Mick's batman drove her there, heavily loaded.

Above: Mick in the cockpit of a B-24, the place where he was happiest even though patrols often lasted for up to thirteen hours with pre-flight preparation starting a couple of hours earlier. On return, report and feeding took at least an hour and a half.

Left: Mick inspecting the load carried in the B-24's huge bomb bay. These 250-lb depth charges were filled with Torpex (a mixture of TNT and powdered aluminium), much more lethal than the substance used in his Hudson days.

Top: Mick and the crew he personally selected at St Eval just after their return from a 'Cork' patrol in B-24 'S' on the night of 7-8 June 1944. Flt. Lt. Carter and Sgt. Plummer (gunners) in the aircraft; Flt. Lt. Addington (navigator), Mick (captain and 1st pilot), Fg. Offs. Andrews (2nd pilot), Pugh and Muir (radio, radar), stand behind Sgt. Moses (engineer), Fg. Off. Tate (2nd navigator) and Sgt. Cockeram (gunner).

Above: Mick with Arthur Clouston, a fellow-New Zealander, famous for long-distance flights in the thirties. He was CO of 224 Squadron when Mick joined and stood by him firmly over the *Minerve* incident. The dog is a border terrier, given to Mick by Margaret Douglas, and named 'Liberator': much-loved, much-photographed and much-written about by all who knew him.

Right: Wing Commander Terence McComb, who succeeded Clouston as CO of 224 Squadron in January 1944: "a delightful Irishman," says Mick, "well liked by everyone. Looking back now, I can see how jolly lucky I was to serve under such men as Denis Spotswood and Terry McComb." Mick would take over from Terry in January 1945.

Top: On 6 July 1945, Mick married Patience Cooke at her home, the Old Rectory in Badingham, Woodbridge, Suffolk. Patience was a daughter of Colin Cooke, later editor of the *Daily Telegraph* and a man long influential in British public life. George Carter was Best Man: "the perfect Englishman", as Mick described him, and formerly his rear-gunner in 224 Squadron.

Middle: Mick flew exactly 200 missions in Avro Yorks of 206 Squadron between Wunstorf (in the British Zone of Germany) and Gatow (in the British Sector of Berlin) during the Berlin Airlift, 1948-9. "No posh taxi-ways at Wunstorf," he wrote, "this is *mud*."

Above: Gatow, by contrast, had an excellent surface - intensively used. The aim, often achieved, was one aircraft landing in Berlin every three minutes. By the time the Airlift ended, wrote Mick, "we could fly our damned great York to the second and park it to the inch."

Neptune 51-15915 (WX494) – to No 217 Sqn

Top left: Mick at Gatow, waiting for his York to be unloaded. In Mick's opinion, "the assorted smells of previous and present loads wafting through to the cockpit were something no veteran of the Airlift will ever forget."

Top right: Air Marshal Thomas M. Williams (left) visited a York crew which flew into Gatow carrying seven and a half tons of butter and meat. Flt. Sgts. Barnes and Smith flank Mr Arthur Henderson (Secretary of State for Air) with Warrant Officer Fairweather and Mick.

Above: A Lockheed Neptune P2V-5 of 217 Squadron. Of all the aircraft Mick has flown, this is his favourite and the happiest time of his service career was as CO of this "grand little squadron, its crews mostly hand-picked by me" in 1952-3. Led by Mick, it won the prestigious Dunning Cup and Mick was awarded the AFC: his fifth decoration.

Top left: The Ensor family in 1962. From the left: David, Hugh, Patience, Andrew, Anthony and Mick. Patience died in 1975, David lives in England, his brothers live in New Zealand. All four are married and have children.

STUDENTS' SECTION

W/Cdr MIKE ENSOR, FROM COASTAL COMMAND, SAID OF HIS FIRST HUNTER TRIP: "I WAS ABOUT TWO MILES BEHIND MOST OF THE WAY."

BUT TO SEE W/Cdr DENNIS CROWLEY-MILLING, EX-BATTLE-OF-BRITAIN PILOT, STILL IN ACTION, WAS TO PUT THE CLOCK BACK 17 YEARS

Left: The cartoonist Christopher Wren visited Manby in October 1957 while Mick was learning to fly the Hawker Hunter, at that time the RAF's standard single-seat day fighter. Wing Commander Denis Crowley-Milling (later Air Marshal Sir) still remembered Mick's quip more than thirty years later.

Middle: After more than three years as a desk-bound staff officer, Mick was delighted to escape in 1957 to Manby, near Louth in Lincolnshire, where he learned to fly jet aircraft with these gentlemen. George Westlake (third from right, front row) became a particular friend and greatly admired Mick's ability as a pilot.

Bottom: "To many aircrew" wrote Roger Read, an experienced Avro Shackleton pilot, "the old grey lady.... was a dirty, noisy, smelly and supremely uncomfortable home for up to 15 hours at a time". By 1958, when Mick was sent to the Maritime Operational Training Unit at Kinloss as Chief Instructor, he had had more than enough of such machines, especially after a taste of flying modern jets.

Top: The deerhunter, June 1965. Mick out shooting at Double Hill, during a visit to New Zealand not long before he was invalided out of the RAF. "I could still see them well enough, but my trigger-finger wasn't as steady as it used to be."

Middle: The glider pilot, 1970. "Thermal soaring in a sailplane is great fun and tremendously satisfying, probably because it is so difficult compared with the more pedestrian types of flying."

Right: The model builder, 1986. "I have 'modernised' *Phoenix* from my original 1984 design, now six-foot wingspan and tailplane to match. An experiment in low-speed aerodynamics and my building skills - and designing". Learning to fly his models was, he claims, "much more difficult and nerve-wracking than a real one - even a Hunter!"

Taylor were flying men, rather than 'office wallahs', and Mick found plenty in common with them. During the rest of March, Mick made seven more training flights in the York (three in darkness) then, on 1 April 1948 Mick flew York MW248 with a crew of five from Lyneham to Castel Benito, near Tripoli. From there, he flew on to Fayid next day; back to Castel Benito on the 3rd and home to Lyneham on the 4th. During those four days, Mick had spent nearly twenty-eight hours in the air, including more than eight in darkness. Only once in the last three years had he flown so much—in October 1945, when he flew a Liberator to Castel Benito, Cairo West and back to Lyneham.

Mick wrote to his mother at Paihia from RAF Lyneham on 6 April 1948. "I did a trip out to the Suez Canal Zone last week," he said, "getting back here on Sunday. I am not qualified to carry passengers in these aeroplanes yet and have to do one more trip to the Canal and one to Singapore carrying freight, then one to Singapore as 2nd Pilot on a passenger trip. I go to the Canal again on Tuesday, but the other two trips will take two months or so to complete I expect, as we have to wait our turn for the trips." As for their private lives, the Ensors' son David was "starting to wake up at nights" and they had acquired a home at Great Bandfield in Essex, where Patience and David lived while Mick did his flying from Lyneham. Called Orger's Farm, it stood in some fifteen acres of rough pasture and woodland and they already loved it dearly. These early postwar days in Britain were days of strict austerity and, as Mick told his mother, "people who have to live on the rations over here really have a pretty thin time. The food on this station is absolutely grim, the worst I have ever known, and the accommodation is pretty poor also. The only good thing is that we are not actually on the camp very much! Also there is a little cafe just down the road where one can get an egg on toast, fresh bread and butter and good tea for one shilling and threepence. It does a good trade."

On 13 April, Mick made another four-day trip in York MW231 to Fayid via Castel Benito with Flight Lieutenant Mather as 2nd pilot and a crew of five. Having returned to Lyneham on the 16th, he left next day as 2nd pilot to John Taylor in MW303 with a crew of four on an even longer tour that took him to Luqa (Malta), Fayid, Khartoum and back to Lyneham in nine days. Mick's next journey was longer still and took him farther. As 2nd pilot to Flight Lieutenant Roberts in MW262 with a crew of four, he flew to Tengah on 4 May via Luqa, Habbaniya, Mauripur and Negombo. Arriving on the 9th, the return journey began on the 12th and the York called at Fayid en route to Luqa from Habbaniya, where it was grounded for nearly five days. Overall, the journey took eighteen days and Mick spent eighty-three hours in the air, loving every moment: even the noise, smells, draughts and rattles. The ever-changing skies and the self-imposed challenge to fly as *exactly* as the machinery would permit gave him intense satisfaction.

Mick wrote to his mother during his stay at RAF Habbaniya on 16 May. "I have got this far", he said, "on my return journey from Singapore and as all the staging posts are having three days off over Whitsun weekend, we are unable to move on until tomorrow." Habbaniya was "a most remarkable place", he told her, built in "the great wilderness" of Iraq to help the RAF control the Arabs. "This camp now has 8,000 people on it and is situated some fifty miles south of Baghdad. All around is desert, but the camp is more like a huge botanical garden than a military establishment, having been most carefully planned, irrigated and planted with trees, lawns and gardens laid out around all the buildings. There are about eight separate officers' messes, a most luxurious club with swimming pool, large outdoor cinema, outdoor dance floor and lots of soft lights and sweet music. I am glad we are stuck here and not in that smelly hell-hole Karachi."

"We certainly see the world in this job", Mick continued happily. "The Singapore run involves going to the following places: Malta, Habbaniya, Karachi, Negombo (Ceylon) and Singapore with an additional stop at Fayid on the Suez Canal on return. The Nairobi run has stops at Malta, Fayid and Khartoum while we also go to Castel Benito near Tripoli. We are soon to start going right down to Salisbury in southern Africa which should be interesting. I have managed to spend a few days at each of these places in the last five weeks.... After a great struggle, I managed to buy a very large and beauti-ful bath towel in India this time, also shoes for Pat and David in Singapore, tea in Ceylon and a beautiful leather-bound photograph album."

During June, Mick made several more training flights before carry-ing his first passengers—twenty-nine of them initially—in MW234 from Lyneham to Tengah via Luqa, Fayid, Habbaniya, Mauripur (where he brought off a safe landing on three engines) and Negombo. He left Lyneham on the 22nd, reached Tengah on the 26th, had the next day off and was back at Lyneham on 2 July: a round trip of twelve days with nearly seventy-seven hours spent in the air. In just sixteen weeks, he had spent nearly 301 contented hours in the air: 168 (including twenty-five in darkness) as a 1st pilot and 133 (including six in darkness) as a 2nd pilot. These figures well illustrate the truth of Air Commodore Freddie Rainsford's claim that "Transport Command training really was superb. It was due to two remarkable C-in-Cs, I think. The first was Sir Ralph Cochrane, who had the phrase, 'An aeroplane is no use on earth', and he really did push training very hard indeed—I know this because I was on the staff. Brian Baker was the other. The training was absolutely first class and I'm sure that was the main reason there were so few accidents" either on normal operations or during the unique challenge about to face Transport Command.[5]

That challenge brought Mick's career as a long-distance passenger-carrier to an abrupt halt when 206 Squadron was required to take part in the Berlin Airlift. A major battle of the Cold War, the Airlift proved to be a decisive triumph for the Allies. At the end of the European War in May 1945, the Allies had divided Germany into four Zones of Occupation, but Berlin—though within the Russian Zone—was divided into four Sectors. Geography alone made it difficult for this arrangement to work, quite apart from Russian insistence that American, British or French access was a privilege, not a right; that supplies of food, fuel, etc., for the Western Sectors must come from the Western Zones; and that the free movement of people or goods between the western and eastern divisions of Germany or Berlin could not be permitted.

In June 1948, when the Russians forbade western access to Berlin by road, rail or waterway, no-one imagined that a city of more than two million people could be supplied indefinitely by air via three narrow corridors. No stockpiles of food or fuel existed and some public services, notably electric power, depended upon the eastern Sector. The West was short of everything needed to mount an unprecedented exercise on the scale required. It lacked aircraft, crews, airfields, navigational aids, traffic controllers in the air and on the ground, equipment for rapid loading and unloading and much else besides. But the Anglo-Americans had the essential will to try to help the Berliners, so recently bitter enemies, and the Berliners, trusting them, found the essential resolution to hang on. Three years is a long time in politics.

The Airlift required the most precise flying by thousands of American and British aircraft, day and night, for nearly a year before the Russians gave in. As each aircraft landed, it was met by teams of German civilians who unloaded the precious cargo in minutes.

---

[5] Contribution to seminar on 'The Berlin Airlift, 1948-9', *RAF Historical Society Proceedings*, no. 6 (1989) p. 88.

Although a triumph, the Airlift imposed a fearful strain on everyone involved. On the other hand, as Sir Kenneth Cross (responsible for the RAF side of it) has observed, "Compared with war, it was simple: nice flat German plain, one target only, exact weather reporting... and of course the sorties were very short—200 miles out, 200 miles back. So for an operation, it was simple. What had never happened before was the sort of intensity we had on this business. The aim—and it was achieved on a number of occasions for shortish periods—was one aircraft landing in Berlin every three minutes." Three minutes, as a York pilot explained, was the shortest time in which three aircraft could be fitted onto the runway: one approaching, one turning off and one departing. It was a modified version of 'Musical Chairs'.[6]

Simple operation or not, Mick regarded it as "the most useful job I ever did. We knew what was at stake and I believe we were right to help the Germans. That war was over and I wanted it to stay over. It seemed to me that if we gave way over Berlin, the Russians would press on till they reached the English Channel and I didn't think that was a great idea. Anyway, the Airlift was the best flying practice I ever had. By the time it ended, we could fly our damned great York to the second and park it to the inch." Perhaps because he had never served in Bomber Command, Mick had no personal ghosts to lay about carrying food rather than bombs in an air space where friends had been killed. His engineer, Alan Fairweather, *did* have problems—at first. He had served in Bomber Command, been shot down and narrowly escaped lynching by enraged civilians. And yet Alan later married a German woman.

Nevertheless, for all the bravery, skill, determination and ingenuity with which the West developed and maintained the Airlift, it would have failed if the Russians had chosen to find an 'incident' justifying its closure and leaving the West no option to abandoning Berlin other than a declaration of war. The Airlift would also have failed if the winter of 1948-9 had not been exceptionally mild and clear, permitting aircraft to operate on many more days than would usually have been possible. Even so, the amount of food, fuel and other cargo flown in was only just enough to keep the city going. What really mattered, however, was the fact that the West was prepared to send *any* and that the East was prepared to let it happen. The Russians gave up the blockade in May 1949, but by then Berlin had been finally divided in two, the British government had agreed to make bases available

---

[6] Seminar, *RAF Historical Society Proceedings*, no. 6 (1989), pp. 54 & 64-5.

in Britain for American bombers carrying nuclear weapons and the decision to create NATO had been taken.[7]

On 7 July 1948, now CO of A Flight, Mick flew a York (MW232) with a crew of three from Lyneham to Wunstorf (north-west of Hannover in the British Zone of Germany). Next day, he flew MW285 from Wunstorf to Gatow (in the British Sector of Berlin) and back, a round trip lasting nearly two hours, including fifteen minutes for coffee and a cigarette at Gatow while the cargo was being unloaded from his aircraft. A Red Army barracks lay near Gatow and it became customary, especially when taking off early in the morning, to stay low and make as much noise as possible. It was a rare cheering indulgence in an exhausting routine. During the next nine months, even Mick would have his fill of flying. "In the beginning," he said later, when asked to speak about his memories of that dramatic event, "God created Heaven and Earth. Then he created the Berlin Airlift to cure keen pilots of their sinful desire to fly aeroplanes."

Mick's contribution consisted of ten 'bursts of activity' in Germany separated by intervals in England. His ten 'bursts' amounted to 149 days in total and during that time he flew exactly 200 missions (eighty-six of them wholly or partly in darkness) from Wunstorf to Gatow and back. On each mission, he carried about eight tons of cargo: mostly food (flour, dried potato, meat, fish, etc.) but also coal. There were never enough sacks, bags or other containers and those available did not last long. In Mick's opinion, "the assorted smells of previous and present loads wafting through to the cockpit were something no veteran of the Airlift will ever forget." He never had an opportunity to visit the city of Berlin and only once enjoyed a really good meal: on an evening when bad weather caused him to divert to an American base at Celle. As a passionate lover of aeroplanes, it grieved him to see the Yorks worked so hard, although he was delighted to notice how well they stood up to constantly taking off under full power, landing with heavy loads and taxying endlessly through thick mud.

The first 'burst', lasting twenty-two days (8-29 July), saw Mick complete no fewer than thirty-eight missions and the second (after an interval of six days) proved even more intense: twenty-three days (5-27 August) and a further forty-two missions. He often saw Russian jet fighters on their airfields around Berlin and from time to time they would take off and fly "fairly close" to his York, but only when visibility was excellent. "They never *did* anything threatening," he says, "but at the back of my mind was always the thought that they

---

[7] Ann & John Tusa, *The Berlin Blockade* (Hodder & Stoughton, London, 1988).

could knock us off in two ticks if they wanted to. It added an edge to the day." The pace after August was never so hectic, and the system became splendidly well organised, but an increasing number of missions were flown in darkness as winter came on.

On 11 November 1948, Mick was obliged to divert to Lübeck, because of thick fog, on returning from Gatow in MW263 and on 2 December he flew from Wunstorf to Tegel and back, instead of Gatow. On Christmas Day he carried out his 138th mission (two hours and ten minutes in daylight) in MW324 and then, for good measure, tested MW209 in the air for twenty minutes. Next day, Boxing Day, was also just another flying day and so too was New Year's Day when Mick flew the first aircraft of the year (MW331) out of Wunstorf before dawn. On 4 March 1949, he diverted from Gatow to Celle in MW249, returned to Wunstorf and flew from there to Lyneham via Abingdon next day in MW142. In total, these 200 missions amounted to nearly 391 hours in the air (235 in daylight, 156 hours in darkness) and each round trip averaged just under two hours. Mick also spent a further fifty-one hours in the air during this prolonged crisis while flying between Wunstorf and Lyneham, Abingdon or Honington or on air tests. In addition, he spent nine hours as a passenger.

Mick flew MW333 from Wunstorf to Abingdon on 5 April 1949, thus completing—though he did not suspect it at the time—his happy flying days in Transport Command. In later years, he would look back upon this moment as a decisive and unfortunate turning point, both in his career and in his personal life: "All the same, I must confess that that is not how it seemed to me then. I was a very happy man and wished for nothing better than to carry on tomorrow as I had today." Mick had spent sixty-six weeks as a transporter and during that time he had flown thirty-seven hours dual in multi-engined aircraft, 419 as a 1st pilot and 130 as a 2nd pilot in daylight, a total of 586 hours. In darkness, he had flown nine hours dual, 194 hours as a 1st pilot and six as a 2nd pilot in darkness, a total of 209 hours. All told, then, he had exactly 795 hours to his credit while with Transport Command (just over twelve hours per week, on average) plus another eighteen hours as a passenger.

Mick's most frightening experience during that period came one day early in the crisis when he nearly flew his York into the hills near Wunstorf. "I well remember that for the first week or so, very low cloud prevailed and I hardly ever saw the ground and was consequently somewhat unaware of the terrain, as was my navigator, David Barnes. I think that an old Coastal Command habit saved us. This was that even in Yorks I kept the radio altimeter switched on and the bright red warning light selected to 400 feet. Well, we took off in daylight, turned left and into cloud at 1,500 feet for the first short leg to the beacon from where we set course to Berlin. Barnes, of course, would tell me when to alter course. I was not doing any timing, but I thought we were going far too long on that heading when the radio altimeter light came on and the needle was unwinding very fast. I can assure you that no York has ever done such a steep climbing turn to the left (or in any other direction)—and we had a seven-ton load on board. Engineer Fairweather gave me full power. I glanced to the left and saw trees far too close to the wingtip through a bit of a break in the cloud. I returned to my instruments and flew out of a desperate situation. Although very shaken, I never let on—and this is a fault." This incident, together with those in the North Sea and the Mediterranean during the war, have been for Mick recurring nightmares ever since. "Of course, I've faced many tricky moments in the air—and, for the most part, enjoyed them—but these three will not go away."

Mick's next surviving letter to his mother was written from Orger's Farm on 11 May 1949. "You will be glad to hear that I have at last finished with the Airlift", he said. "I came home early last month on normal leave to be greeted with the news that I would probably be required to go and work with the Americans in the Pacific for two years. It has since transpired that I am to go to an American Naval Air Force Wing at Honolulu, of all delightful places." Mick was to leave on the 20th in the liner *Queen Elizabeth* and Patience would follow him in September, with David and their second child, Anthony.

Life as a Flight Lieutenant had been good—Mick never held that rank during the war—"and Pat and I had settled into Orger's Farm in Essex. Based at Lyneham, I got home for decent periods between trips and felt that I was doing what pilots were supposed to do. The Airlift was much harder work, but in May 1949 I went off to the US Navy at Whidbey Island and Pat followed when Anthony was born. She was a wonderful wife and, like me, an outdoors person. An ex-WAAF officer, she understood the Service but shared my dislike of bullshit. A few years later, when the boys went to boarding school—fortunately, my mother-in-law helped with the fees—I began to feel a conflict between Service and family life and this, coupled with feelings of uncertainty and insecurity regarding the Service, did indeed give me a problem which I never solved."

When Mick joined Transport Command, he felt that he was becoming involved in the most useful form of aircraft employment for peacetime and wished that he had been left there. Sadly, he seems to have been *branded* Coastal Command and unable to escape its embrace. He did try, but not as hard as he might have done. And he readily admits that he did not kick against going to the US Pacific Fleet. Although he had a wonderful time with the Americans, that experience undoubtedly confirmed higher authority in its opinion that Mick was to be considered, for the rest of his career, as a Coastal Command man.

CHAPTER XI

A CONSIDERATE GUEST
MAY 1949 TO NOVEMBER 1951

MICK ENSOR left Transport Command in April 1949 and during the last week of May sailed westward across the Atlantic in the *Queen Elizabeth*. He was travelling alone and spent some hours, especially early in the voyage, picking clouds suitable to hide a Liberator in, staring down at the sea's restless surface ("Nothing like so smooth as it looks even from a hundred feet up in good weather") and realising anew how difficult it had been for a U-boat to see *anything* in the sky. "If we had had long-range aircraft to escort convoys all the way across the Atlantic right from the start of the war, even without radar, there'd have been no 'happy time' for U-boats. Forcing them to spend all day submerged would have prevented them from getting into position for night attacks. Easy to see that now, isn't it? Of course, if we'd been properly prepared to defend ourselves in 1939 there'd have been no war anyway, so the question becomes rather academic."

However, Mick was then sailing westward in order to join Fleet Air Wing 4 of the US Navy as part of an Anglo-American attempt to ensure that the free world *was* prepared to defend itself against new aggressors: regimes in the Soviet Union and China that seemed as menacing in 1949 as Germany, Italy and Japan had been a decade earlier. The British and American governments had agreed to exchange a few officers and Mick was among that fortunate handful. The wing he joined comprised several squadrons, all equipped with twin-engined Lockheed P2V-2 Neptune maritime patrol aircraft and based at Whidbey Island, a few miles north of Seattle in Washington State. Far as he was from home, Mick's new base had a New Zealand connection because the island was named after Captain Cook's first mate, Joseph Whidbey.

Few aircraft, in the opinion of professionals, have been better loved by their crews than the Neptune and few have lasted longer in front-line service. It saw little combat, though flying many patrol missions from Japan during the Korean War and it never engaged an enemy submarine: a fact which much amused Mick, who regarded the Neptune as not merely his favourite aeroplane to fly, but far and away the most likely of those he flew in which to find and sink submarines. It was a direct descendent of the Hudson, the first effective warplane Mick ever flew and the type in which he first made his name. "Breeding from good stock", Mick reckoned, works as well with aircraft as with sheep. In September 1946, a Neptune flew non-stop from Perth in Western Australia to Columbus, Ohio, setting a world distance record for piston-engined aircraft of 11,235 miles that lasted for fifteen years. More than a thousand of these superb machines would be built by Lockheed between 1946 and 1962, with a further eighty-two built by Kawasaki Industries for the Japanese Maritime Self Defense Force between 1966 and 1979. Some were employed on intelligence-gathering missions around the periphery of the Soviet Union; some flew patrols over the South China Sea during the Vietnam War; and some were used as late as 1982 by the Argentine Navy to stalk the British fleet during the Falklands War. Of more immediate concern to us is the fact that by the time Mick was entrusted with command of a Neptune, it was capable of taking off from an aircraft carrier loaded with an atomic bomb.[1]

Mick wrote to his mother from the USS *Pine Island* (a Navy Seaplane Tender of 15,000 tons) on 18 August 1949, while en route from Honolulu to San Diego after an exercise. Patience and the children were due to leave England to join him at Whidbey Island early in August and his next best news was that he had been promoted to Squadron Leader with effect from 1 January 1949, just before his twenty-seventh birthday "*without* taking the exam", he told her, "which I would never have passed anyway! I think I have a bit of hard work on the Airlift to thank for that. Anyway, they can't reduce me in rank again without throwing me out of the Air Force, and it is also a substantial increase in pay. I think I must be one of the youngest substantive Squadron Leaders in the Air Force now, which makes me feel that it has been worthwhile staying in, a thing I was beginning to doubt." In addition to his "bit of hard work" in Germany, Mick's exceptional war record (which he has never regarded highly) helped

---

[1] W R Matthews, *Air International* (December 1984) p. 311; Jim Sullivan, *P2V Neptune in Action* (Squadron/Signal Publications, Carrollton, Texas, 1985); Richard P Hallion, *The Naval Air War in Korea* (Nautical & Aviation, Baltimore, 1986) pp. 14-15.

him to a promotion that still left him below the rank he had enjoyed four years earlier. He wanted his mother to visit them. The sea passage from Auckland to Vancouver was easy and the base was only eighty miles from there, but she never did, despite repeated urgings.

"We left Pat Green at Honolulu", Mick went on. "He is attached to Fleet Air Wing 2 there. It is funny how we follow each other about. We first met in training in England in 1941 and have since been in two squadrons together and he was one of my squadron commanders when I was CO of the St. Eval wing, and now this job. He is one of the nicest people and a great favourite with everybody, so I feel a little lost now he has gone." Pat had been Mick's predecessor at Fleet Air Wing 4 and was familiar with the flying and non-flying opportunities both there and in Honolulu. He realised that his friend would get more challenging duties at Whidbey Island. He also realised that Mick and Patience, both great lovers of the outdoors, would find the society and scenery of Washington State far more to their taste than those of the Hawaian Islands. On both counts he was entirely right and is glad that he was able to persuade the naval authorities to send Mick north. In later years, the Ensors looked back on these years as the most contented, at work or play, of their lives together.

Mick told his mother that he thought the US Navy men "among the finest I have ever worked with, but some take themselves rather seriously on board ship, particularly when the Admiral is around (I don't blame them!). However, this cruise has been a great education from all points of view and I am looking forward to doing a similar one next year. I only had one day and two nights ashore at Pearl and in spite of the fact that Pat and his friends made every effort to show me everything, I did not have nearly enough time to take it all in. From the point of view of living conditions (there are some nice houses available), I am rather sorry I was not sent there, but I think that all things considered I will be much better off at Whidbey."

"It is a great eye-opener to come to America", Mick concluded, "where everyone has so much more confidence and faith in the future and, what is more, the will to work hard because they know they can keep what they earn and not have it frittered away in taxation.... Also, the British services can learn a lot from the Americans: that is one of the reasons why I like this job, one gets a different angle on things and although I probably won't be able to do much constructive work while I am here, I personally will pick up a lot that will be of use to me when I have to run an outfit of my own in the future."

Mick was greatly impressed by the high morale of Navy aviators, at a time when rivalry with the Army and the Air Force was extremely bitter and most of the aircraft available to the Navy were believed to be inferior to the latest Russian types. As an old hand in Coastal Command, disparaged throughout the war by 'Bomber Barons' who did their successful best to prevent Coastal from receiving—or retaining—sufficient modern aircraft for its needs, he appreciated the Navy's point of view. And no-one was better able to grasp the argument that long patrols in search of small, alert targets over featureless water in uncertain weather required specialist training that neither an Army nor an Air Force could provide. Mick's expertise, in fact, precisely matched that required in Fleet Air Wing 4. More useful still was his modest, unassuming nature. Naval aviators, already under pressure from their own Army and Air Force rivals, were sensitive to any suggestion that they needed teaching by a 'Britisher', even one from New Zealand. Mick realised all this perfectly clearly and set himself to be a considerate guest. "It wasn't difficult at all. I simply behaved as my parents taught me to when in someone else's home." Before long, even the brashest of his new colleagues observed that Mick could do anything with an aeroplane that they could do and often better.

Mick made his first flight in a Neptune as 2nd pilot to Lieutenant Commander Daily on 30 June 1949. They carried out a rocket firing exercise. The P2V-2 model had a crew of seven, compared with the ten of his old friend the Liberator, and its two engines were more powerful than the Liberator's four. This model was able to carry the same weight of weapons as the Liberator for much further at a much higher speed; in addition, its defensive armament was far superior. The equipment (especially for locating submarines) and overall performance of later models were improved still further. "The Neptune was a new type then," says Mick, "incorporating numerous improvements over all the wartime types I flew, as well as far more sensitive radar equipment. I loved it at first sight and enjoyed every hour in the cockpit, both with the US Navy and later with the RAF. We'd have knocked the U-boats on the head long before the end of the war if we'd had even half a dozen squadrons of Neptunes."

On 2 July, Mick received dual instruction from Lieutenant Hollingsworth in a single-engined SNJ (a Navy version of the North American Harvard trainer), flying from Whidbey to McCourt Field and back. On the 6th, he was 2nd pilot to Lieutenant Cavanagh in a Consolidated Privateer, a four-engined bomber derived from the Liberator. "I didn't care for it", he recalls. "A big heavy thing with a huge single tail fin like a Flying Fortress that was supposed to make it more stable at low levels. It did everything the old Lib could do, only worse and slower, but I didn't like to say so. Throughout my time in the US, I was always conscious that I was the Navy's *guest* and nobody welcomes criticism from guests." Next day, he flew with Hollingsworth in the Harvard to Seattle and back. Mick paid another visit to Seattle on the 8th when Lieutenant Knapton flew him there in a Beechcraft 18, a twin-engined transport aircraft, not unlike a small light Hudson. On the 18th, he had a five-hour flight with Lieutenant Jefferies in a Martin Mariner to Yakutat, Alaska. The Mariner was a twin-engined anti-submarine flying-boat and appealed very strongly to Mick. "I'd seen a few during the war and liked the look of them then. They didn't have the speed, range or weapon load of the Lib, but they were a whole lot nicer to fly. Much less work and the pilot could actually see what was going on! Also, I greatly appreciated the fact that in a flying-boat one could land safely on the water in an emergency. This was an aspect of long patrol flying in land planes that it didn't pay to think about too much."

Six weeks later, on 29 August, Mick enjoyed his second Neptune flight when Daily took him "local flying" for three hours. During September and October, he made nine more flights (with eight different lst pilots) in Neptunes and Privateers to carry out exercises lasting six hours or more in navigation, bombing and co-operation with submarines. In addition, he flew with Ensign Good in a Beechcraft to Quillyute and back on 22 October. "Like all the American machines I flew," recalled Mick, "it was so carefully put together and so well finished off. Comfortable, responsive to the lightest touch and remark-ably quick. Great fun to fly." During November, he took part in three more exercises, each lasting three hours, and managed one more flight in a Beechcraft. He had one brief flight in a Neptune in December and another in January 1950.

On 2 February, Mick took part in a rockets and bombs exercise and then in another bombing exercise on the 8th in the Navy's version of the Douglas DC-3 Dakota, known as the R4D: "it was my first flight in a Dakota, which is strange, because I was always ready to fly anything and there were plenty around in England. Amazingly advanced for its day and so comfortably fitted out, as were all US Navy planes. The British had nothing to beat it in the fifties, let alone match it in the forties." On the 10th, he flew in a Beechcraft and then, on 22 February 1950—after eight months with the US Navy—he was allowed to take command for the first time. He flew another Beechcraft with Lieutenant Commander Langham as 2nd pilot and three passengers from Whidbey to Sandpoint via McChord and back. The journey lasted nearly three hours. On the 24th, he flew with

Lieutenant Gallup and nine pupils in an R4D to practice radar approaches to Ault Field.

During March, Mick had four local flights in a Beechcraft, three of them in command, and on the 22nd flew as 2nd pilot to Lieutenant Williams in a Martin Mariner on an anti-submarine exercise that lasted twelve hours (four in darkness). This experience confirmed his liking for that agile, if rather slow, flying-boat because they found and kept track of the target boat easily. As usual, Mick was quicker to attribute success to the aeroplane than to the crew handling it. He had only three flights in April: two in a Beechcraft (one in command on a flight to Kitsap and back), the other as 2nd pilot to Lieutenant Pressler in a Neptune on an absorbing navigation exercise lasting nearly nine hours. In May, he had five flights: three in a Beechcraft (two in command, all local) and two as 2nd pilot in a Neptune on anti-submarine exercises lasting three hours each.

Then, on 25 June 1950, the Korean War began. Throughout the rest of his service with the US Navy both training and operations took on an urgent edge. Rumours abounded about the prospect of transfer across the Pacific to become directly involved and Mick found the atmosphere at Whidbey on the ground and in the air exhilarating, similar to that at St. Eval in wartime. His own secret ambition, never fulfilled, was to operate a Neptune from an aircraft carrier: "Now that *would* have tested my flying ability. Carrier ops in relatively light fighters were difficult enough, so I believed, but in a heavy bomber! Well, I'd have enjoyed learning how to do it." Mick had no reservations whatever about taking part in this war. He had gone to the United States straight from the Berlin Airlift and regarded events in Korea as part of the same pattern of worldwide Communist aggression. Firm, prompt resistance offered the best chance, he thought, of preventing fighting (as it did in Berlin) or at least limiting it (as happened in Korea). Having worked alongside Americans in Berlin and admired their methods, he was the more willing to work *with* them in this new crisis.

During June and July, however, Mick actually did little flying because he was on leave. Patience and he spent several delightful weeks far from anywhere, introducing their four-year-old son David to the pleasures of camping, hiking, sailing and fishing; Anthony celebrated his first birthday and a third child was expected in October. Mick returned to duty in August, making nine local flights: seven in Neptunes, two in Beechcrafts. On 18 August 1950, he took command of a Neptune (No. 931) for the first time with Lieutenant Koening as 2nd pilot and a crew. The flight lasted six hours because he was running in an engine. From then until November, he had fewer opportunities than he wanted to command this excellent machine. After two local flights in a Neptune on the 13th, he had six flights lasting a total of fifteen hours in seven days (22-28 November) to receive dual instruction aboard a more powerful version, the P2V-3W: an early warning aircraft with the latest radar equipment.

By December 1950, Mick had been with the wing for seventeen months. His masters, both British and American, had originally envisaged for him a purely staff appointment, with little flying. While Mick entirely accepted that he must make himself thoroughly familiar with the organisation of the US Navy's air component, he had for months been quietly agitating to get out of headquarters and into a squadron. At last, with the sympathetic support of a flying admiral, he was assigned to one of the wing's squadrons, Patrol Squadron 2, and made an aircraft captain (Patrol Plane Commander) by the CO, Commander Renfro Turner, Jr., in December 1950. This honour, for so Mick regarded it, was wholly personal. It formed no part of the agreed 'job description' when Mick arrived at Whidbey. It was a tribute to his conduct as a considerate guest and still more to his professional ability. Naturally enough, the US Navy was most reluctant to entrust American lives or its precious front line aircraft to the care of foreign commanders unless and until their skill had been amply demonstrated.

Patrol Squadron 2, equipped with eight Neptunes, was a specialised anti-submarine warfare unit, having taken part in many hunter/killer exercises organised by the Pacific Fleet. It now focused on intensive instrument flight and cold weather operations, including radar exercises with ships. At times, it moved between Whidbey Island and Kodiak Island, Alaska (nearly 1,400 miles farther north), to practice its mobility and self-sufficiency because, as Commander Turner observed, in wartime it may often be necessary "to operate with inadequate facilities." Extreme conditions, with very low temperatures, plenty of wind, snow and sleet, meant frequent engine changes. Hangar space was inadequate and the turnover rate for both air and ground crews was high, partly for medical reasons. Long experience in the North Atlantic prepared Mick well for even harsher weather conditions in the North Pacific and he was never particularly troubled or alarmed while on duty. Off duty in Alaska, however, he was surprised to find that some Navy officers seemed positively to welcome Spartan living. "The Royal Navy was just the same", he thought. "They obviously share a common tradition about making a virtue out of discomfort. Didn't have it in the RAF, I'm glad to say."[2]

During December 1950, Mick made twelve flights in Neptunes (eleven of them in P2V-3s and one in an even more powerful version, the P2V-4) and on seven occasions he was 1st pilot. All were testing, training or patrol flights. Direct Chinese intervention in the Korean War had begun in November and it then seemed alarmingly likely that that conflict would escalate into a worldwide war. In January 1951, Mick made eight flights (in P2V-3 or -4s) with Scheer or Cockerell as his 2nd pilot to practice gunnery, rocket firing, bomb dropping and searchlight training or to gather weather information. On the 23rd, he flew as 2nd pilot to observe crew performance. In February, he made eight more flights in P2V-4s with Cockerell as 2nd pilot on seven occasions and Valencia once to practice gunnery, bombing, anti-submarine and navigation procedures. He also made four night flights from San Diego as Valencia's 2nd pilot in Privateers to carry out searchlight training. In March, he made ten flights in P2V-4s (nine as 1st pilot with eight different 2nd pilots). The last of these was mining training in daylight; the rest were all searchlight training in darkness. By March, he was a qualified searchlight instructor.

For three days early in April (3-5), the Commander of the Fleet Air Wing carried out his annual "Operational Readiness Inspection" and Mick was left exhausted by its thoroughness. It comprised an operation lasting for fifty-six hours under full combat conditions to test the squadron's ability "to search for, detect, identify and develop contacts on submarine targets. The overall performance was officially assessed as "good". Mick at first thought this meant "pretty ordinary", as it would in RAF usage, until he realised that his colleagues were well pleased. "Good", in US Navy usage, meant precisely that. Renfro Turner told him that the Commander's report spoke of "excellent performances verging on the outstanding" by the air crews and congratulated Mick. "In my opinion," he said, "you are up there with the best of them, no question."

During the rest of April, Mick made eleven flights in P2V-4s (eight as 1st pilot with Cockerell as 2nd pilot on eight occasions). These were anti-submarine training or patrols, navigation, instrument or "special weapons drops": dummy bombs that might in a major war be changed for atomic bombs. In May, he made ten flights (all as 1st pilot with Kenney as 2nd pilot on nine occasions). These were devoted to bombing, rockets, instruments or general tests. In June 1951, Mick made thirteen flights, all as 1st pilot; Kenney was his 2nd pilot on

[2] US Pacific Fleet Records: VP-2 Records (Washington Navy Yard, Washington DC).

six occasions, Ginn four times and Jenkins three. These were all operational patrols in daylight, paying particular attention to Russian activity in the north-west corner of the Pacific. They monitored radar activity, identifying airfields, naval bases, surface vessels and submarines at sea and noted communication and operating procedures. They also noted supply routes from the Russian port of Petropavlosk (on the south-east coast of the Kamchatka Peninsula) southward through the Kurile Islands towards Japan.

On 1 June, Mick flew from Whidbey to Kodiak in just over seven hours and from there patrolled westward over the long chain of Aleutian Islands to the extreme limit of American territory, some 250 miles from Kamchatka. He made a "Radio-Counter-Measures patrol to north of Arctic Circle" from Kodiak on the 12th that lasted twelve hours and took him, unofficially, into Russian territory. "That didn't worry us too much, though perhaps it should have done. We were quite sure that we'd pick up a Russian plane on our radar long before they picked us up. Although the weather was mostly clear and sometimes perfect, it changes in minutes up there and I'd already been alarmed by what are now called 'white out' conditions. We used to speak of 'stuffed clouds' and I knew how easy it would be to find one." His route lay north-westward, round the Alaskan coastline and through the Bering Strait as far as Point Hope. It was the most spectacular and exhilarating flight of his life, over snow-covered mountains and a brilliant blue sea, dotted with icebergs looking like vast yachts. In July, Mick made four more long patrols, another across the Arctic Circle and three more along the Aleutians. On the 12th, he had his last P2V-4 flight (a short air test) and on the 24th flew what would become the definitive version of the Neptune, the P2V-5, in which power, range, warload and electronic gadgets were maximised.

During twenty-five months with the US Navy (seventeen with Fleet Air Wing 4, eight with Patrol Squadron 2), Mick enjoyed almost 647 hours in the air, an overall average of six hours per week. Actually, he managed fewer than three hours per week with the wing, whereas in squadron service he raised that to rather more than twelve hours per week. As a Neptune 1st pilot, he was allowed only five local flights with the wing, but no fewer than seventy-five with the squadron and most of these were long-distance patrols lasting five hours or more; thirteen were flown entirely in darkness. In total, Mick flew some 210 hours in his seventeen months with the wing, of which only forty-one (all in daylight) were as a 1st pilot. With the squadron, however, he flew more than twice as many hours in less than half the time: 437

hours of which most (393 hours, including eighty-seven in darkness) were as a 1st pilot.

Mick's tour of duty ended in August and he then began two months' leave. Patience no doubt appreciated having him at home more regularly than usual because their third son, Hugh, was born at Whidbey Island on 21 October 1950. At that time, David was four and Anthony only fifteen months old. Within a few days of Hugh's arrival, the family climbed aboard 'Henry', a large Ford, and set off across the United States to New York. From there, they travelled by sea to England, taking Henry with them. Patience and he had enjoyed camping, sailing and fishing in a very beautiful part of North America, not unlike New Zealand, and were delighted to have in Hugh a permanent memento of many contented days among a friendly, generous people.

CHAPTER XII

HIS NATURAL HOME
NOVEMBER 1951 TO APRIL 1957

WHILE flying American Neptunes around the north Pacific, Mick
Ensor managed to persuade his masters at Coastal Command HQ that
he was "just the chap" to introduce those aircraft to RAF service when
he returned to England. He was therefore attached to 210 Squadron
at St. Eval in November 1951 and allowed to select his aircrew from
existing Coastal Command Lancaster squadrons while awaiting the
arrival of the Neptunes. Meanwhile, after two and a half years as
a US Navy airman, living in comfortable quarters in a wealthy and
beautiful part of the world, Mick and Patience had to remind themselves what it was like to live on the wrong side of the Atlantic. "It
was very difficult for us to re-adjust to life in Austerity Britain after
Whidbey, especially with three young children. David was also old
enough to notice, but fortunately the others weren't. Strict rationing
of food and clothing, no central heating and the winter as bleak as
ever: it made the general drabness and lack of spirit everywhere
hard to bear." Mick also had to re-adjust to service in the RAF and
separation from his family: St. Eval was about 250 miles from his home
at Orger's Farm in Essex.

And not least he had to come to terms with flying a wartime left-
over. Mick had his first flight with 210 Squadron on 12 November
1951, receiving dual instruction in a Lancaster. "It was certainly a
comedown to crawl into an ancient, battered Lanc after flying the
latest Neptune, but I knew it wouldn't be for long and tried to make
the best of it. Apart from the noise, rattles, drafts and total lack of
comfort, the equipment was primitive to say the least. However, I
believed then (and still do now) that *every* flight is a valuable learning
experience. One *never* becomes a master in this business." He
managed nine Lancaster flights (only one as a 1st pilot and one in

darkness, all instrument practice or test flights) amounting to twenty-one hours, plus one flight as 2nd pilot in an Oxford, flying from St. Eval to Debden in Essex, the nearest airfield to his home. At the end of that year, according to an entry in his log book, Mick's flying times were checked "and found suitable for issue of Master Green Instrument Rating".

In January 1952, Mick turned thirty and was appointed Commanding Officer of 217 Squadron at St. Eval, the RAF's first Lockheed Neptune squadron. That squadron, which fashioned a proud record for itself during the war, had been disbanded when the war ended and was now reformed for this purpose. After an interval of five months, Mick once again climbed aboard his favourite aircraft on the 21st to make a local flight of half an hour in a P2V-5 model. These machines were supplied to the RAF by the US Navy under the Mutual Defence Aid Pact in order to help Coastal Command fulfill the reconnaissance responsibilities required of it by NATO directives. The first of fifty-two P2V-5s arrived in England during January 1952 and ultimately equipped three squadrons for the next five years. Problems with obtaining (or affording) adequate spares then ended that fine aircraft's RAF service and Mick's squadron was disbanded again.[1]

He enjoyed his time with 217 Squadron, "a grand little squadron, its crews mostly hand-picked by me. Good enough to win the Dunning Memorial Cup anyway." That cup had been presented to the Air Council in 1922 in memory of a great naval airman, Edward Dunning, who became in August 1917 the first British pilot to land on the deck of a ship under way, but lost his life a few days later while making another landing. It was awarded to the squadron achieving the highest standard during the year on the course at the Joint Anti-Submarine School in Londonderry, Northern Ireland. Points were awarded for performance in tactics, signals procedure and especially in air-sea exercises to find and (notionally) destroy submarines. These exercises lasted for up to twelve hours and a strong emphasis was placed on the quality of co-operation with naval units. "It was at that time a highly regarded trophy", Mick recalled, "and competition was very keen. During and after the Korean War, fears of Russian aggression in the North Atlantic seemed realistic and senior officers in the Air Ministry, the Admiralty and of course NATO were anxious to develop and improve air-sea co-operation. We certainly worked hard to win the cup and got a lot of praise from the top brass for doing so. I'm

---

[1] It came briefly to life again for nine months in 1959 as a search and rescue unit.

sure it earned me the Air Force Cross—that and my time with the US Navy."

After the war, Mick gradually became conscious of "squadron commanders who ran things from the office, mostly by means of local orders incorporated in 'order books' that reached truly stupid proportions. I always deplored this and relied on personal contact with my crews to make my ideas known and respected. When I started 217 Squadron, I made it clear that we had to be accident free, but operate in *all* weathers. I said at the time: 'accident free for at least a year.' In fact, there were no accidents while I was CO."[2]

By the end of January 1952, Mick had completed seven flights in Neptunes, amounting to thirteen hours, all familiarisation exercises in daylight. During February, the squadron transferred to Kinloss in Morayshire, Scotland: a district once very familiar to Mick and one destined to remain so, with diminishing appeal, for the rest of his career. He carried out eight training flights (including one in darkness), one air test, one local flight and one exercise with a near-new battleship, HMS *Vanguard*, amounting to nearly twenty-three hours. "My main memory of Mick at that time", wrote Pat Green, "is that there was really only one topic of conversation—his Neptunes! Dare I say that it became a bit of a bore?"

On the other hand, Mick's crews were all younger men, in love with flying, but accustomed to trundling about in obsolete machines. They shared his enthusiasm for the only aircraft they knew that had a realistic chance of taking on Russian submarines if the war in Korea should spread to Europe and the Atlantic. They also sympathised with his vain efforts to persuade senior officers, Navy as well as Air Force, to consider the Neptune as a carrier-aircraft. "Adequately escorted by relays of fighters, it could have kept every submarine in the world under *permanent* surveillance at sea or in harbour. A valuable deterrent, I thought, considering how much we suffered even from primitive U-boats in two world wars. People listened, said nothing and did nothing. My idea might have been hopeless, but I don't recall being told where or why. It had been different in the US Navy. I found American officers much more ready to argue about professional matters than we were in the RAF."

Mick flew whenever he could during the spring and summer of 1952, often vacating the captain's seat in order to give his pilots as much command experience as possible. He firmly believed that after a certain point in basic instruction had been reached, a pilot learned

[2] Letter, Ensor to Spooner, 29 April 1988.

only by doing. Sitting in the right-hand seat and watching, however carefully, was not enough. Indeed, it could be positively harmful because a young pilot might come to rely on someone else solving a problem. While in the air, Mick said as little as possible, even when a pilot made a mistake (unless it was likely to prove fatal quickly). He wanted to note when the pilot realised his mistake and what he did about it. If he reacted swiftly and accurately, he would lose no credit in Mick's book: "to err is human," he would say, "but to put it right before anyone notices is near enough to divine." As a rule, he made his comments while on the ground: in the office or the hangar, out on the runway perhaps, but preferably in the bar. A squadron commander, he believed, was like a rugby coach: the time for talking was before or after a match or flight, not during it. Amid a great deal of Neptune flying, Mick had his first flight as 2nd pilot in an Avro Shackleton on 22 April, travelling from Kinloss to St. Eval in three and a quarter hours. He would have been astounded, as well as dismayed, if he had known that the Shackleton, a somewhat modernised Lancaster, would long outlive the much superior Neptune in RAF service and that he would spend many hours in that machine.

August was a quiet month, except for a navigation exercise on the 21st that took Mick from Kinloss to Admiralty Lake in Greenland (at 77o 04' W) and back, a round trip of 3,000 miles lasting almost fourteen hours of which six were in darkness. This was the kind of flying that Mick then loved most of all: thundering along in what he called "a precision instrument", responsive to the slightest touch and with an expert crew behind, none of them needing instruction. The possibility of perfect harmony between man and machine appealed to him, so he aimed at *exactly right* engine power, speed, altitude and line of flight, whatever the weather conditions. Nothing on earth, literally, compared with the constant challenge of such flying. In addition, there was the bonus of breathtaking sights in every direction that changed by the minute: sea, clouds and snow-covered lands, all immense and empty. Apart from that exhilarating venture, Mick made one air test and flew as 2nd pilot on an exercise, testing tactics and navigation, that lasted for nine hours. He made seven flights in September (six as 1st pilot) including a naval exercise on the 21st lasting ten hours and two searchlight exercises in darkness. Seven more flights followed in October of which the highlight was a long submarine exercise in darkness. At that time, Mick was relieved to learn, the aircraft was still master of the submarine because he found his assigned target quickly and it could do nothing to shake him off.

Mick's life followed a similar pattern until June 1953. Regular flights, in daylight and darkness, usually solo but sometimes in formation, were made in good weather and bad to practice skills which he hoped never to use seriously. He and his crews learned to find and (in theory) sink submarines and surface vessels and successfully evaded attack (also in theory) by enemy fighters. They mastered numerous weapons of all sorts: radar, radio, searchlights, depth charges, rockets, machine guns and cannons. But in June Mick temporarily abandoned the killing arts in order to help celebrate the Queen's coronation. Many hours were spent rehearsing and then executing a flypast over Glasgow on the 29th as part of the celebrations.

The Glasgow flypast was followed by intensive preparation for the Queen's Review of the Royal Air Force at Odiham, near Basingstoke in Hampshire on 15 July 1953. That preparation included a formation flight from Kinloss to St. Mawgan (near St. Eval) and back, a round trip of over a thousand miles. Several more rehearsals followed and then (as Mick succinctly put it in his log book) came "RAF Review, The Thing": a flight lasting six and a half hours with Flying Officer Kirkup as his 2nd pilot and a crew, leading four other Neptunes in a neat vee-formation. A huge "tented town" had been erected on the south side of the airfield to house some 3,000 officers and men brought into Odiham to prepare for a most spectacular occasion. Forty-nine separate formations flew overhead at thirty-second intervals, starting with a single Sycamore helicopter buzzing along at 86 mph and ending with a Supermarine Swift jet fighter thundering by at 667 mph: no fewer than 631 aircraft in twenty-seven minutes and thirty seconds of unparalleled aerial organisation.

Leading his Neptunes, Mick had been assigned twenty-first place in the queue. He arrived and departed punctually, crossing the airfield at exactly 195 mph and exactly 700 feet. His selection as a formation leader on such a unique occasion, when the Royal Air Force was at the centre of public attention, meant as much to Mick as any of his wartime decorations. They represented, he has often said, luck as well as skill, whereas this distinction indicated his standing as one of the finest pilots in the service. All the Coastal Command aircraft taking part (eighteen Shackletons and three Sunderlands as well as the Neptunes in the air, plus others displayed on the ground) were much praised for their performance and smartness. It was indeed, as Chris Ashworth has written, "a spectacle which will assuredly not be repeated in Britain."[3]

[3] Chris Ashworth, *Action Stations 9: Military Airfields of the Central South and South-East* (Patrick Stephens, Wellingborough, 1985), p. 234; Chris Ashworth, *RAF Coastal Command, 1936-1969* (Patrick Stephens, Yeovil, 1992); *Flight*, 24 July 1953, p. 119.

"Summer War Exercises" followed and on 25 July Mick flew to Luqa in Malta, a journey lasting ten hours. During the next few days, he carried out various air-sea gunnery and submarine detection exercises and returned to Kinloss on 7 August. On 14 September, he wrote to his mother from there, urging her (not for the first time, but as always in vain) to visit them. He then went on to tell her about his recent trip to America, ferrying a Neptune for modification by the manufacturer. It was, in fact, the first time Mick had flown across the Atlantic, as opposed to round and round its northern waters, "and it made a welcome change from routine." They reached Argentia Bay in Newfoundland at five in the afternoon after an uneventful eleven hours, stayed the night and went on to Rhode Island next day. Having fixed some mechanical trouble, they arrived at St. Louis, Missouri, in the middle of a heatwave and returned to Britain a few days later in a BOAC airliner. Mick realised that his time as a squadron commander was coming to an end and wondered what his next job would be. "This one has turned out pretty well," he confided to his mother, "and I am satisfied that it has been done about as well as possible." Mick managed two more flights in September (one to take part in a Battle of Britain Display) and continued to fly regularly until December when he was obliged to leave 217 Squadron. During two deeply satisfying years, he had amassed just over 614 hours in Neptunes, an average of six per week, mostly in daylight.

Mick was busy and fulfilled while with that squadron, but could well have done with being told sometimes that he still had a promising future in the service. "The Army", he wrote, "had a system for annual reports that required COs to show the contents to the officer concerned and, if necessary, discuss them. I don't know why the RAF only required that adverse reports be shown. Maybe there is a good reason, but it is a *negative* approach—and a reporting officer can do a lot of damage without making any strictly adverse comment." Mick felt it was no way to treat a good officer who might need encouragement. He never had an adverse report, but suspected that he was regarded as a bit of an upstart, perhaps because he never tried to curry favour or do the right thing if it ran counter to his beliefs. Moreover, he was in an age group that was being overtaken by post-war Cranwell chaps. "Cranwell", in Mick's opinion, "tended to believe that wartime officers were not really of the quality needed in the peacetime service and I was well aware of that from early on. At the same time, I recognised that we had a duty to teach those who came our way all that we could. Although there was no great age difference between me and some of the

Cranwellians, we certainly came from different worlds!"

Mick formed "a very clear idea" in the fifties "of the sort of flying ability we should be looking for in 1st pilots, but the powers-that-be, while paying lip-service to high standards, had for several years been withdrawing facilities for staff officers to keep in some sort of flying practice. Refresher courses also petered out. A new form of 'limited career' was introduced whereby pilots could keep on, but not rise above Flight Lieutenant or perhaps Squadron Leader. To me, this was just a pansied-up revival of the old system of having Sergeant Pilots available to do the flying. Career officers who were disinclined to fly now had absolutely no incentive to keep up-to-date."

During the past thirteen years, 1941 to 1953, Mick had served in five squadrons (four British, one American) and commanded two of them. All five have distinguished records to which Mick made a memorable contribution, earning five decorations. The squadron was his natural home. It was the only military organisation in which his particular gifts, as pilot and leader, could be fully realised. Another dozen years of service lay ahead of Mick, but he would never again serve in a squadron. Given the structure of the RAF, this was inevitable. Men of Mick's age and experience were needed elsewhere, in administrative and training posts. Ahead of him, in January 1954, lay many good days of valuable and enjoyable service. But the best days lay behind.

In that month, Mick was posted to Coastal Command Headquarters at Northwood, Middlesex. He had not relished his first staff appointment, exactly eleven years earlier, but in 1943 he quickly realised how important the work was and how useful his own contribution was—at least for a few months. It was different now, even though he was able to get home each weekend to his family at Orger's Farm. Mick had no interest in paper work and did not care who knew it. That attitude caused him no harm in wartime and little harm as a squadron commander in peacetime. But Mick was now thirty-two, with a wife and three young sons (a fourth still to come) and quite failed to realise that three options lay ahead: onward and upward, perhaps to Air Marshal rank, a position reached by the pick of his contemporaries; out, into civilian life while still young enough to make another career; or to stick and lose ground. However, Mick had not yet lost forward momentum. In the light of his hitherto admirable record, he would be given every opportunity over the next few years to make the difficult transition from air commander to ground manager.

Whenever possible, Mick escaped from his Northwood office into the cockpit, though finding it much harder to get away than it used to be. He managed only a handful of Neptune flights and during May 1954 even accepted dual instruction in an Anson, but these were mere punctuations in a routine of administration and meetings. In August, however, he spent a few days in New Zealand for the first time in seven years. He was a passenger aboard a large four-engined transport aircraft, the Handley Page Hastings, travelling from St. Eval to Darwin in northern Australia. He flew on next day (as 2nd pilot for some of the time) in another Hastings to the RNZAF base at Whenuapai (Auckland) via Richmond (Sydney), arriving on 4 September. The total journey took nearly sixty-one hours, spread over ten days. Next day, he was flown in a Harvard to Wigram (Christchurch). He flew back to Whenuapai in the Harvard on the 24th.

While he was in Christchurch, Mick arranged to visit his brother Peter's home at Double Hill, taking members of his crew, who were much impressed by the magnificent Alpine setting of that great station. So too was Mick, who had quite forgotten how much he loved the plains and mountains of Canterbury. He now began to wonder seriously when, if at all, he might return permanently. "About this time," wrote Peter, "Mick described the Hastings as the finest three-engined aircraft in the RAF, since one of the four engines was prone to mechanical problems."[4] He left New Zealand in the Hastings on the 27th, arriving at St. Eval on 7 October. This journey, including a return to Darwin with engine failure, lasted exactly sixty-six hours and also took ten days. The *Otago Daily Times* of 7 September 1954 (and other New Zealand newspapers of about that date) reported the arrival of "One of New Zealand's most notable wartime pilots" at Whenuapai. But wartime memories were fading fast and this is the last time that Mick's arrival in New Zealand was noticed by the press.

Mick's total flying hours while with Coastal Command Head-quarters amounted to just under a hundred in thirteen months—only a little over ninety-six minutes a week on average and far below what Mick wanted and perhaps even needed. In addition, he spent 109 hours as a passenger (102 in Hastings, the rest in Shackletons) during these thirteen months: in rather more than thirteen *years* preceeding this appointment, he had spent only eighty hours as a passenger in service aircraft. From Northwood, Mick was posted in May 1955 straight to another staff appointment at the Headquarters of No. 18 Group in Pitreavie Castle, near Dunfermline on the north bank of the Firth of Forth, opposite Edinburgh. "I was practically speechless with

---

[4] Peter Ensor, 'Many Good Years, Some Not So Good', pp. 89-90.

disappointment for days and gave everyone around me a hard time, I'm afraid. As ever, Patience bore with me better than I deserved and got me through."

The long drive north, he told Peter, proved not to his liking and persuaded him to sell his Standard 10, a conventional family motor car. He treated himself instead to "a very good 1950 Sunbeam Talbot convertible (folding hood) ... very nice on the winding roads and quite fast." Patience and the children would soon join him in Scotland and he had rented "a rather awful house", until his turn for married quarters came round. Mick was consoled meanwhile by working under Group Captain John Ker, a good friend from wartime days at St. Eval. The Ensors' fourth son, Andrew, was born at Pitreavie and Mick recalled it as "a *very* happy time. Work was minimal, but fishing and all outdoor sports great." It may be that not all his colleagues and seniors agreed with his assessment of the work load. As for the family's permanent home at Orger's Farm, Mick had seen little of it for months, though he had heard that "the barley is as good as any in Essex at the moment." He certainly hoped that it would earn its keep because he had put "what is to me a lot of cash" into it during the last year or two.

On 25 July 1955, Mick was overwhelmed by his first flight in a jet aircraft: the De Havilland Vampire T11, a two-seat training model. "One of the most exhilarating experiences of my flying life," he recalls, "it ruined me for any other kind of aircraft, except gliders: completely different, but just as exciting." Mick received dual instruction at Leconfield, near Beverley in east Yorkshire. Next day, after two flights devoted to "familiarisation, high-level mach running and general handling" and circuits, Mick carried out a successful solo lasting twenty minutes in this very fast, highly manoeuvrable fighter-type. He told Peter about it in a letter written from Pitreavie on 1 August. "I have just had a few days getting checked out in jet aero-planes and got on very well", he wrote. "Apparently the old hand is as good as the bright young lad any day! However, I am still very much the frustrated staff officer that has to scrounge flying, but that can't be helped I suppose." He had visited Orger's Farm recently and although he was most impressed with the work his partner was doing there, the "simple fact is that we can't send the kids to school without using Double Hill income, so for God's sake keep up the good work! If you want another hand on the place, you really wouldn't have much difficulty persuading me to come back to New Zealand permanently."

Mick flew an Anson from Donibristle (in Fife on the east coast of Scotland) to St. Eval and back on 25 August. During the rest of the year, he flew regularly in Ansons, sometimes in Neptunes to drop practice bombs on a sea target or to take part in a searchlight training exercise, and once more in a Vampire jet. At what then seemed a low ebb in his career, the new year brought him promotion to the rank of Wing Commander: excellent news, which he conveyed at once to Peter. Because he was "on the very young side of the age bracket" for that rank (he was just about to turn thirty-four) "there appears to be some hope for the future." This hope soon strengthened, as Mick told Peter on 5 March 1956, when "new large pay increases, coupled with improved gratuities and pensions" considerably improved his outlook on service life. "The recent services pay rise has helped us a lot," he told his mother in April, "and is sufficient to make staying on over here really worthwhile. However, I still hope to be out in about ten years." Mick would get his wish, though by then his health and circumstances were much poorer.

He soldiered on at Group Headquarters for another year, becoming steadily more frustrated by long hours in the office and short hours in the cockpit. By April 1957, when he left Pitreavie Castle, more than three years had passed since Mick left his beloved 217 Squadron and during all that time he had managed only 247 hours in the air (setting aside his passenger hours) and nearly three-quarters of that time had been spent 'tootling around' in Ansons, en route to or from meetings. His flying hours in darkness were negligible. Mick's restlessness was exacerbated by his knowledge that Coastal Command was very poorly equipped for realistic operations in the absence of American aircraft (with the single exception of the Neptune) or modern British designs. Lancaster bombers and Sunderland flying-boats, obsolete in 1945, still provided the command's main "strength" into the fifties. As far as weapons were concerned, the withdrawal of American equipment meant that the situation was actually *worse* than it had been in 1945.[5] But at last his long ordeal was over. At the relatively advanced age of thirty-five, when tactful friends were already urging him to accept that his days of serious flying were over, Mick was selected, to his delighted surprise, for the most demanding of all flying jobs: in jet aircraft.

---

[5] John D R Rawlings (ed.) *The History of the Royal Air Force* (Temple Press/ Aerospace, London, 1984) pp. 218-9.

CHAPTER XIII

THE WORST THING THAT EVER HAPPENED
JUNE 1955 TO FEBRUARY 1968

MICK ENSOR corresponded regularly with his brother Peter in the
fifties, partly because they shared an enthusiasm for aeroplanes and
partly because their father had left Mick a financial interest in Double
Hill. As Mick became more and more unhappy with his RAF career,
so he became more and more interested in the affairs of that great
sheep station. The brothers became a great help to each other, one
letting off steam or using the other as a sounding board for their
respective family and professional worries. In June 1955, for example,
Mick and Peter discussed two matters of permanent concern at Double
Hill: will the treacherous Rakaia river change its main course again
and how do we maintain all-weather road access in such difficult
country? As for using an aeroplane "as a farming tool", Mick thought
there were "many headaches" with owning, as opposed to hiring, one.
"When I get my place on the plains, I will run an aeroplane for you
all—it is the height of my ambition!"

Mick and Patience were keen to have Peter and his wife Lou visit
them in 1956, "even for a month or so. You could have my car and
caravan if you wanted either or both of them. It would be fun, I would
like you to see our setup and there is a lot we could talk about." In
May of that year, however, Mick learned of serious road trouble at
Double Hill. "Once again I sit here wishing I could be of practical
help," he wrote to Peter. "Double Hill and the others are terribly
important to all of us and I would be delighted to give up the RAF,
out of which I have really had the best." At that time, Mick's "firm
intention" was to return to New Zealand "and put my back into the
transport side. It would be nice for me to get a place in a strategic
position between Double Hill and Christchurch for holding and/or
fattening sheep and maintain a suitable medium-weight general

purpose aeroplane and probably a contract lorry or two. The advantage would be that my pension will be ample to live on and I should be able to operate to the great advantage of us all, possibly assisted in due course by my four sons!"

Meanwhile, Mick warmed to a desire close to Peter's heart. "Your aeroplane idea", he wrote in August 1956, "sounds good to me. After all, half the farmers in the USA have their own aeroplanes, so why shouldn't we? I seem to remember reading some articles on the Piper you mention and there is no doubt that it is a good little plane. Personally, I would go for the tricycle undercarriage every time because for use from normal field surfaces they are easier and safer in every way and there is none of that nasty 'out of control' feeling you get with ordinary planes when the tail comes down just after touchdown. Also crosswinds are much easier to cope with and provided the front undercarriage leg is very robust, you have first-class protection for propeller and engine."

Mick had recently been flying the Dakota and the Shackleton "and I must say that as I normally fly three-wheeled aeroplanes I get more and more fed up with the old layout where you never quite know whether to use brakes, rudder or engines to keep straight and tend to drift all over the runway while things sort themselves out. While the Canterbury Aero Club must inevitably be better informed than I am and you should take their advice in preference to mine, I would think that a second-hand aeroplane would almost certainly be the best bet from any point of view, provided the engine has plenty of life left. I would insist on some sort of guarantee that the aircraft had never crashed, as a re-build is seldom if ever satisfactory, in my experience at least. Also, in choosing an aircraft, you should make certain that it has no unnecessary extras as every little bit of luxury equipment adds weight and the lighter you can keep your basic aeroplane the better. There is a tendency to overdo interior fittings these days, both for noise reduction and looks, to help sales and to suit some people, but it is very costly. Would you keep it at Double Hill? If so, you must have adequate shelter for it, but there again with some attention to the road surface and gales it might be possible to taxi it from the strip to the home area. Don't park near trees: branches blown down can do a lot of damage in a short time!"

On 30 November 1956, Mick told Peter how glad he was to hear that Double Hill had enjoyed another good financial year and thought Peter quite right in suggesting that the aeroplane be bought "as a piece of farm equipment, thus fairly sharing the capital cost and depreciation between us in the right proportion." Mick urged Peter to get on with it: "please don't turn down any chance to get the plane while waiting for confirmation of terms from me." He was currently suffering his "usual British winter depression" and greatly desired to return permanently to New Zealand. But if he did resign, he would remain liable to recall: a distinct possibility at that time, with an Anglo-French invasion of Egypt and a Russian invasion of Hungary both in progress. Peter bought a second-hand Auster V a year later, in November 1957. He had actually learned to fly as long ago as 1932, but since then had rarely managed an average of better than five flying hours a year. During the next decade, however, he put the Auster to good use, not only for his own interests, but also to assist in search and rescue ventures in the dangerous high country around Double Hill.[1]

Mick was sent on an "All-Weather Jet Conversion Course" at RAF Strubby (a satellite of Manby, near Louth in Lincolnshire) which lasted for eight weeks, from 9 May to 4 July 1957, and introduced him to twin-engined Gloster Meteor jet fighters. It also prepared him for a more advanced course at Manby where he would fly even faster jets. "The instruction in Meteors was excellent", he thought, but a considerable "culture shock", even though he had kept his air sense alive while entombed at Northwood and Pitreavie Castle by flying whenever he could and taking instrument rating examinations. He noted, with pardonable self-satisfaction, that he did not have nearly as many problems as some of his brother officers. It was not primarily a flying course, "rather a study course of the practical aspects of air power and the students did exercises in Hunters and Canberras. There were no dual Hunters then and I found the step from Meteors to Hunters about the same as that from Ansons to Meteors."

On 25 October 1957, the *Aeroplane* magazine printed a page of cartoons by Christopher Wren about Manby: that "Valhalla", he wrote, where "lucky and deserving" officers who have completed a staff appointment go to "exchange their seat marks for assorted marks of Canberras and Hunters." Among the cartoons is one showing a Hawker Hunter disappearing into the distance, leaving a beautifully-drawn Mick without any visible means of support and saying ruefully of his first Hunter trip: "I was about two miles behind most of the way." Mick's quip was long remembered, not least by a fellow course-member, Wing Commander Denis Crowley-Milling (later Air Marshal Sir), for he quoted it with great delight and dramatic gestures to the present author thirty-three years later, in June 1990. Though naturally pleased by the reception of his remark, Mick added that once he got

---

[1] Peter Ensor, 'Many Good Years, Some Not So Good', p. 107.

the hang of it he loved the Hunter, which was at that time the RAF's standard single-seat day fighter.

"The Canberra", wrote Mick, looking back on his happy time at Manby, "gave me no trouble and I was privileged to fly Aries IV a few times." That was a famous machine specially modified for long-range work which held the Tokyo to London non-stop record, among others. "One evening flight from Malta to Manby—it was the day of the first Sputnik—I cruise-climbed Aries IV to somewhere near Paris where, from 50,000 feet with the sun going down in the west, the curve of the earth was clearly visible to my right." Sadly, Mick's joy in what was at that time a very rare sight was no longer matched by enthusiasm for specifically military duties and on reflection he thought his inner self was in conflict with what would be required of him to complete a full service career. There was no tradition of military or public service on either side of his land-owning family and somewhere along the line he felt he was losing his sense of direction. "Since school days, I had had something of an inferiority complex where other people were concerned and standing in front of a parade giving orders was always painful to me. Although I could do staff work, I spent many office hours badly irked by the need to stick to set times and often toed the line simply because it was the done thing."

George Westlake, a fighter pilot who earned a distinguished record during the Second World War, met Mick at Manby. "Mick was probably one of the finest pilots I ever flew with", he recalls. "Although his background was heavy four-engines or even heavy two-engines, he took to the Hunter and the Canberra as though he had spent his life in jets! I have never flown with anybody who was so steady and accurate. The needles on his instruments looked as though they had been glued in position. It was uncanny: they didn't waver at all." George was so fascinated by Mick's rock steadiness that he would sometimes lean forward and tap the instruments, to see if they were in fact functioning. At first, this annoyed Mick intensely, but later he accepted George's tapping as a fine tribute to his airmanship, for George was himself an excellent pilot. Mick was no fool either, continued George, "in spite of his slightly deprecating manner."

In George's opinion, "the Air Ministry postings people made a sorry mistake by not putting him in charge of the Comet Squadron or even sending him to be a fighter pilot, especially to a night-fighter squadron—it would have opened up new doors for him and given him new aims. He already was the best and most experienced captain of any of the aircraft flown by Coastal Command, so sending him back there must have been a sad disappointment.... I feel sure that had he been given a fresh interest, he would have gone higher. Sending him back to fly the ponderous old aircraft in Coastal Command after giving him a taste of jets was a ghastly mistake. Mind you, nobody could fly the Shackleton better!" However, it may be that Mick, like the rest of us, was at least partly responsible for his misfortune: he was already drinking too much and, as George admits, "never minced his words when talking to people with whom he did not see eye to eye. Unfortunately, these were usually senior to Mick and his particular bête-noir was a fellow Kiwi, John Morton, the Group Captain in charge of our course."

Mick wrote to Peter Ensor from Manby in October 1957. His course was due to finish in mid-December and he had just learned that he was to return in January 1958 to Kinloss yet again, this time as Chief Instructor at the Maritime Operational Training Unit. Mick tried bravely to conceal his disappointment. Although it was a "good job" and one for which he was specially selected because of his particular knowledge of that work, he did confess to Peter that he had been "hoping for a change, i.e., to an all-jet job, but that is not to be, yet anyway! However, my time here studying and flying modern stuff has given me a valuable background that will help in the future. At least there is one supersonic member of the Ensor family!" He had had no break since 1 May and was therefore looking forward to Christmas, "when I shall have a month without a job—except, that is, to move the family to Morayshire. The trip would be a pleasure in the summer, but we may have difficulty with the caravan in winter weather." Mick had heard that a good many officers were applying for early retirement. He was not eligible, but thought "the more that go out in the medium and higher ranks the better, as far as those of us that are still young are concerned. I am not really worrying about what to do when I retire. Thanks largely to you, I will not be poor and RAF gratuities and pensions are improving all the time. However, I must find a job, otherwise I will rot in five minutes."

Though putting on a confident front in correspondence with Peter, Mick gradually ran into serious trouble with his career from this time on and alcohol began to dominate him. Being posted from Flying College to Kinloss in January 1958 was, he said, "the worst thing that ever happened." He told Pat Green this several times and Pat's main memory of him at Kinloss "is the fact that he was obviously drinking a great deal and didn't seem to be very happy." Mick had been so looking forward to different kinds of challenge, having had enough of cruising around a few feet above the sea, especially after six exhilarating months of hurtling about in modern jet fighters and bombers.

Once in the chair at Kinloss, he immediately ran into problems with regard to students who did not measure up, in his judgement. Some of these were older, more senior men, but Mick was an absolute perfectionist in flying matters and would not tolerate any lowering of standards. He simply refused to allow students whom he considered "inadequate" to graduate. "Flying is no joke," he declared, "it is a deadly serious business" and instructors must decide whether they wanted to be "soft and useless or hard and effective."

The Maritime Operational Training Unit had been formed at Kinloss in October 1956 to centralise all Coastal Command's advanced training and was equipped with twelve Avro Shackletons. This aircraft, a direct descendent of the excellent Lancaster bomber with some features borrowed from the equally excellent Liberator, had entered RAF service in March 1951 and was assigned the maritime reconnaissance role in Coastal Command. It incorporated all the lessons learned in wartime about U-boat hunting and would be progressively improved in engines, airframe, electronic equipment and weapons during the next forty years: an amazingly long lifespan for any aircraft. Too long, Mick thought. The RAF did its ingenious best to disguise the fact that the Shackleton was obsolete when it came into service and had nothing like the Neptune's capacity for effective improvement. In any major conflict with the Soviet Union, Shackleton squadrons would have suffered terrible losses.

Genuine submarines (as opposed to submersible torpedo-boats) were developed postwar by the Soviet and other navies and Shackletons were given the difficult task of locating them: difficult because they rarely surfaced and travelled swiftly at depths undreamed of by Doenitz's crews. Shackletons were also given the no less difficult task of providing early warning should aircraft or missiles threaten NATO countries. Mick's task, then, and that of the crews whose instruction he supervised, was a most important one. Although Mick knew this perfectly well, it was no longer a task he wished to undertake in an inadequate aircraft himself. It also made him increasingly unhappy to help prepare younger men to take his place. "To many aircrew", wrote Roger Read, an experienced Shackleton pilot, "the old grey lady ... was a dirty, noisy, smelly and supremely uncomfortable home for up to 15 hours at a time" and by 1958 Mick had had enough of such machines.[2]

Nevertheless, in April of that year he told Peter that he liked his

---

[2] Flt. Lt. Roger Read, 'Displaying the Shackleton', *RAF Year Book, 1990* (RAF Benevolent Fund, RAF Fairford, Gloucester, 1990) p. 21.

job as a Chief Instructor, "but I got a bit of a bug about jet flying and will try and get into it after this before I become officially too old! I gather that I got quite good results at Flying College, but a nine months' intensive course that combines a lot of expensive social activity is a bit hard on the system. I was rather run down and put on too much weight, but intensive though rather fruitless (so far) salmon fishing has got me pretty fit again and I will return to work tomorrow feeling much better." By 1958, however, Coastal Command was dwindling rapidly. The ancient Sunderland flying-boats and the modern Neptunes both disappeared, leaving only six squadrons equipped with six Shackletons each. By March 1959, the front line strength had apparently stabilised at a grand total of no more than twenty-four aircraft and St. Eval, the command's most famous base, was closed. Many older Shackletons were grounded for modifications intended to extend their lives a little longer and when Mick finally departed, at the end of that year, the command still existed. As the number of squadrons dwindled, a rather pathetic attempt was made to keep the most widely celebrated numbers alive for as long as possible. Of those squadrons in which Mick served, his first (500 Squadron) died first, in 1957; 217 died two years later; 224 lingered on until October 1966 and 206 Squadron, in which, ironically, he served only while it was in Transport Command, later returned to its old allegiance and still flies from Kinloss in 1993. But Coastal Command itself expired in November 1969 and Northwood is now the Headquarters of 18 (Maritime) Group.[3]

More cheerfully, Mick was able to tell Peter in November 1958 that he had just sent him five crooks, as used by genuine Scottish shepherds, to distribute around the family. There was one each for Jimmy, Duncan, Rod and Peter himself as well as a small one for their mother. They were made, he said, "in the old style by a retired Highland shepherd who now lives near Inverness. The hazelwood is hard to get and will last for ever and the crook is carved from ramshorn to a clan pattern. You may think they are too flexible, but I don't think they will break. Anyway, they should be good for a bit of swank at a sheep sale or show!" He went on to say that he was trying to get admitted to the Joint Services Staff College in 1960. "If I succeed, I shall really be quite a well qualified officer. However, decent flying jobs are becoming very hard to get, especially for wing commanders, and unless I am very lucky I shall probably be faced with a tour at Air Ministry."

---

[3] Chris Ashworth, *RAF Coastal Command, 1936-1969*, pp. 212-22.

Almost a year later, in September 1959, Mick admitted to Peter that it had been "a rather difficult year" at Kinloss and they would soon be faced with another major move. He gathered that he had been nominated for the Armed Forces Staff College in Norfolk, Virginia, starting in February. While naturally delighted by this mark of esteem, Mick understood that the course was normally followed by two years in the United States and did not want that. For some reason, he believed it would mean "a serious breakdown in the kids' education" when in fact it offered them an exciting opportunity to experience a different system in a vibrant society. He was concerned that by turning down or at least protesting about the two-year tour, he might have prejudiced his prospects of selection for the staff course. "However, I am due for overseas, but I would like to go somewhere where the kids can come for their holidays. This sort of problem is the main snag with this job when the family starts growing up." He expected to move south to Orger's Farm, "which badly needs attention, for Christmas and with plenty of leave to come I will stay there for six weeks or so and then go to the course by myself. In six months, the next move should be decided." Away from duty, he had enjoyed an excellent summer: "I really do like fishing the fly on a good loch, but I am afraid the season is now at an end." Patience and he had used their caravan regularly, whenever weather permitted—and sometimes when it didn't.

By the end of 1959, Mick told Peter, he was unhappy with his training job because he did mostly check flights plus "a lot of office work and general management which all in all is a lot of worry and very little fun! Particularly as the manpower problem gets more and more acute and no matter how efficient one is it is a battle to keep ahead of circumstances. You are really all very lucky to be where you are." Mick paused here, got a grip of himself and concluded brightly: "In fact, I am lucky too: the rat race of city business life is certainly not for me!" During his two years with the Maritime Operational Training Unit, Mick flew no more than eighty-three times, spending a total of 290 hours in the air (265 in daylight, twenty-five in darkness; 227 as a 1st pilot, sixty-three as a 2nd). Three or four flights a month, each lasting on average about three and a half hours, amounted to far less time in the air than he wanted.

Between 8 February and 1 July 1960, Mick attended the 27th Class of the Armed Forces Staff College at Norfolk, Virginia. "Not really my cup of tea", he reflected later, "and far too much cheap drink, but I got through OK. The course qualified as passing RAF Staff College, Andover (I fixed that when I got to Air Ministry; previously it did not)." Thinking about classroom work or the theoretical aspects of his profession usually depressed Mick. His struggles at Norfolk reminded him that he had "dodged" (his word) the examination for promotion to Squadron Leader "by being on the Air Lift" when in fact his service in Berlin might fairly be considered an extended practical examination in airmanship. His masters apparently had no doubt that he merited an honourable pass and presumably expected him to remedy any theoretical or administrative weaknesses while employed as a staff officer. Mick's conclusion that "I am a bloody old fake, really" is only too typical of the harshness with which, in a low mood, he sometimes dismisses his career.

Patience took the children to Ireland for a holiday in the summer of 1960 and Mick learned that his next job would be in the Air Ministry, as he feared—and as he *deserved*, having asked not to be posted on exchange to the United States. From August, he would be in the Directorate of Flying Training, with responsibility for preparing and amending pilots' notes on the proper handling of all types of aircraft. "I think I will like it," he told Peter. "We will be able to live at Orger's. I was a bit afraid of being put on some dull NATO staff on plans, etc., which would have been awful. However, this job keeps me in the strictly flying world."

The Air Ministry is a fate very few career officers have avoided and one that many have privately welcomed, however volubly they may have complained to their friends about the woes of 'flying a mahogony bomber.' London has its appeal and for an ambitious man service at head office, in the military as well as the civilian world, offers opportunities to be favourably noticed. Mick had reached the rank of Wing Commander at an age young enough to give him a realistic prospect of promotion to the senior rank of Group Captain, if not more, given his superb war record: a record that undoubtedly weighed with 'the powers that be' when considering an officer's personal file. One might suppose that a man nearing forty, with four young children to educate, would need no urging to perform as well on the ground as he always did in the air.

In May 1962, Mick wrote to Peter from the home of Patience's mother, near Bantry in County Cork, Eire. Patience and he were just coming to the end of a ten-day holiday *without* children, the first in at least twelve years, and during a few rain-free intervals, Mick had enjoyed "two or three quite good days on the local lakes with a fly, a sport that I am now very fond of." The cost of educating his children was "hurting a lot" and he depended heavily on the dividend from Double Hill to help him through this difficult period, "but thanks to you I think we will manage in the long run." If the children were not still at school, Mick said he would be "clamouring" for an overseas posting: "living costs are lower and allowances are better in general, but there is not really anybody in England to look after the brats on our behalf. Promotion prospects are grim and if I don't get promoted by 1968 I shall be out on my ear and looking for another job—any prospects in New Zealand?"

Patience's mother died suddenly in June 1963 and Mick had much to do as an executor and trustee. "However, this Air Ministry tour of duty is now finished", he told Peter, "and I am going to the Air Headquarters in Malta in July to quite a decent operations post. It will be a welcome change and I think Pat will enjoy it if the housing and domestic help situation is as good as I am led to believe it is. There are some useful financial advantages and of course in comparison with this nonsense of travelling 55 miles each way each day by car, train and underground that I have been doing for three years, we should be a lot better off. Unless I am promoted, which is unlikely in this contracting air force, I shall retire in five years' time and apply for a job on the New Zealand dole!"

Mick's main task at that time was to get fit for Malta. The doctors had been giving him trouble because he suffered from "the prevalent Air Ministry disease—overweight and blood pressure." Fortunately, six weeks on a strict diet lost him fourteen pounds and he hoped all would be well. He was a little reluctant to leave Orger's Farm, having got it into good order, but Patience's sister was likely to occupy it while the Ensors were in Malta. Mick hoped she would because it was usually "a shambles" when the Ensors returned after a tour of duty in Scotland or wherever. Neither tenants nor partners, no matter how carefully vetted beforehand, cared for it properly.

In 1963, Mick had taken up gliding quite seriously with his son David, who was seventeen that year. Mick had obtained a gliding licence as long ago as 1946, but rarely used it for many years. Now, he found, gliding gave him the "utmost pleasure", in spite of the hard preparatory work required on the ground. "Thermal soaring in a sailplane is great fun and tremendously satisfying, probably because it is so difficult compared with the more pedestrian types of flying." During the sixties, Mick became a gliding enthusiast and later a qualified instructor for the British Gliding Association. His favourite glider was a Skylark IIIF, one of the first generation of high-performance sailplanes. Mick's was a particularly good example, with the most modern inertia-compensated instruments and a fully aerobatic electric artificial horizon (PZL), all of which enabled him to do "lovely high climbs in the rising core of big cumulus, sometimes going up 10,000 feet or more in a few minutes. That would be violent turbulence to you, but I had become a very good instrument pilot able to hold a 45 degree banked turn, keeping in the smooth rising core, and actually enjoying the hail and wondering how much more ice the long slender 60-foot wings could carry. Popping, or being thrown out the top at 15,000 feet, was a fine experience." The highest climb Mick ever achieved came after his return home to New Zealand, when he reached 31,000 feet, on a lee-wave from the Alps. From 12,000 feet (where he was cruising around, smoking cigarettes for one and a half hours before deciding to push forward to look for the main wave) he soared to 31,000 feet in just fifteen minutes.

Two things happened just as Mick was leaving the Air Ministry in July 1963. "Firstly, my Director, while saying goodbye, added very sincerely: 'I hope you get command of a station very soon'; secondly, I got the standard letter informing me that further promotion was improbable, but that I could stay on, if I wished, in my present rank until the age of 55." An important truth had hitherto escaped Mick, as expressed by the First Lord of the Admiralty in *HMS Pinafore*: "Stick close to your desk and never go to sea, and you may all be rulers of the Queen's Navee!" 'Desk Power' was something that this 'simple soul' (Mick's description of himself) never understood; 'Air Power' was a different matter. Nevertheless, his loyalty to the RAF remains "complete and uncompromising. I am just very sorry that I failed to complete my job. Although I have criticised some aspects, better men than me made the policies and many that I did not like were not the fault of the Service; rather, they were forced on it by political or treasury decisions." In early 1963, Mick had called on an Air Vice-Marshal "whom I greatly respected whose job it was to advise on career matters. We had a pleasant chat, but all that he could—or would—tell me was that I drank a lot, though it had not affected my performance. I was well aware that I drank plenty; I did it in company and often unwillingly, as a tool of hospitality if you like, and had no idea of the sickness that was developing in me. There were many times when I wished I was teetotal—and, in fact, I abstained for long periods."

And so Mick went to Malta in July 1963, for what proved to be his last appointment, knowing that he would not be promoted further and, more important, knowing that he would never again fly service aircraft regularly. It is perhaps just as well that Mick did not realise that his RAF flying career had already ended: on 3 October 1962, when he flew a Canberra T. Mk 4 (876) twice for a total of three hours "local, single-engine flying etc." with a two-man crew, as at Andover in 1941, where that career began. The Malta job was "air staff", he wrote later, "involving numerous plans of a somewhat hypothetical nature—or so it seemed to me ... I was totally unsuited to it. So remote from the 1943 HQ Coastal Command. I am just no good as a cog in the wheel, particularly when it is all exacting paper work. The demanding social life and a lot of other things just buried me. Sorry. The kindness of the AOC—Air Vice-Marshal D. C. McKinley—and many others was touching, but by then I was no good to them. They came to see me off on my final trip to England and a hospital. Certainly the AOC had no need to."

Mick wrote to Peter from Air Headquarters, RAF Malta, on 11 June 1964. 'Thank you for your letter of 1 May. I am afraid that my letter writing has slipped rather a lot. Time seems to pass quickly here and I am generally so tired by the evening with the heat and noise etc., that nothing seems to get done.... On the face of it, we have a good time in Malta and should enjoy it, but there are a lot of snags, particularly with three kids at school in England. Travelling to and fro is not too bad and the kids get two holiday trips a year free, but there is a lot of incidental extra expense. In general, the usual perks that go with an overseas tour do not exist here, most prices being higher than in England. My office is more or less in Valetta and I envy all my contemporaries up at Luqa with the aeroplanes, while I sit and do tedious plans about things that will probably never happen!" He and Patience had taken up dinghy sailing, in the absence of gliding. She also played a lot of tennis and was as brown as a berry. David had been living with his parents since Christmas and was expecting to go to Durham University in October. Mick expected to remain in Malta for another two years and would then have only two more before he retired in 1968 at the age of forty-six. "What happens then is a bit of a problem, but most of the education will be out of the way and we should be pretty free agents. I must find something to do, preferably in New Zealand, or I shall go even more to seed!"

Mick gradually collapsed, "from booze and boredom", and in December 1964 he was taken from Malta to an RAF hospital at Wroughton, near Swindon in Wiltshire. He wrote to Peter from there in January to say he was "enjoying a first-class rest with no direct responsibilities, in hospital for my sins. Once in the hands of the specialists it may take some time to get clear of them, but mine is a complaint common to executives and senior staff officers, particularly in the RAF, aged between 40 and 45. Although it is not a nervous breakdown in the crude sense, it is pretty close to it, but I have been caught in time and will be as fit as a fiddle in due course. However, I have had and am still having a long series of tests. So far there is no indication of any serious malfunction, but I am overweight, have excessive but not really serious blood pressure, mental stress, nerves and too much alcohol. So, strict diet, regular meals, mental rest and 'on the dry' are the orders of the day. Actually, I am feeling very well and am of course free to go out or away for weekends, but the doctors in this outfit are specialists and perfectionists and obviously will not let me take up another appointment until I am perfectly fit, so I can look forward to a few months of comparative peace—will probably get bored stiff." He expected to retire in January 1968 and neither Patience nor he wished to stay in England, if they could get a good price for Orger's Farm. David should have his degree in engineering by then and Mick was keen for him to get a start in that field in New Zealand, for he thought he would fit into life there very well.

By March 1965, Mick was staying in the Officers' Mess at RAF Headley Court in Epsom, Surrey, when he next wrote to Peter. He was then planning a brief visit to New Zealand (which took place in May and June), partly to "review the Double Hill situation". He was losing weight and feeling much better. "It is a good thing that I had to give up Malta when I did because now I can do a bit of looking after No. 1 for a change and the general setup there did not suit me in spite of the sailing, etc., being very good.... Of course my gliding lapsed while I was away, but I must get back with the club as soon as possible. It is really my favourite sport in spite of the fact that sailing has a lot in its favour and Pat is keen, so I suppose I will have to do a bit of both if time permits!" He wrote again to Peter from Orger's Farm in November. By then he was engaged in a holding operation there, "which may become very irksome and expensive, but I think it can be managed and should be done in the interest of the kids' education." He had obtained a Skylark IIIF much like the Canterbury Gliding Club one, but with a superb finish and very good instruments. So far, he had done little with it "except get frozen almost to death on a two and a half hour flight in Scotland."

In January 1966, Mick told Peter that the RAF had agreed to give him and his family a free air trip to New Zealand in that year, but Patience was set on a boating holiday instead. Mick agreed with her and was therefore making plans to travel out by sea at the end of 1967. He had begun the new year with a five-hour flight in his Skylark from Dunstable. "Quite a gale and some very heavy rain that had me down to 500 feet over the Chilterns—and nobody else stayed up all day so I felt quite pleased." More than a year later, in February 1967, Mick informed Peter that he planned to return permanently with his family to New Zealand later that year and Orger's Farm was already on the market. "I know that there are difficulties in New Zealand, but believe me there are more here. I am glad to say that I am now extremely fit and want to get on with some constructive job." He was not too worried about his own prospects, but his wife was and this did unsettle him. "All I can say is that as far as I am concerned at the moment, you can have an active partner instead of an inactive one if you want things that way. I am bringing the big diesel Land Rover out and *I know that I can help*, but just how, and where we would live, I don't know."

In March, he wrote again to ask Peter to help in finding a house in Christchurch to rent for about two months from 1 December 1967. David was to stay in England, Anthony was to attend Canterbury University, Hugh *could* leave school and Andrew was down for St. Andrew's College. "I think the boys really dictate that we must live very near Christchurch for the next few years." As for employment, Mick had no doubt that his real interest and aptitude lay in aeroplanes and this was the main reason why he had been learning as much as possible about gliders. He hoped to have the full BGA instructor's certificate before leaving England and if by any chance the Canterbury Club were to offer him a permanent job as resident instructor, he would be delighted. He had already written to friends, asking if there were any possible openings in any capacity in the flying business in Canterbury, but expected a "negative reply."

Mick had taken up oil painting both as a hobby and as a means of financing his gliding. Around Christmas 1966 he had sold as many as five and hoped to have another small stock ready for the coming Christmas. But agitation over the sale of Orger's Farm continued. Patience was booked (and re-booked) to sail to New Zealand on various dates with some of her sons and Mick was to fly before or after her departure with the rest, depending on when the RAF could fly them. David, who graduated from Durham University and married in 1967, would not be accompanying them. "This move of ours to New Zealand", he told Peter, "is a bit like setting off on a cross country. Perhaps I will need a little luck to avoid a field landing! A while ago, I got stuck near the M1 motorway at 800 feet, but had the inspiration to look for a thermal over a big carpark and found one, but it took one and a half hours to get enough height to proceed to Banbury, due to high land blotting out the sun. Perhaps the next year or two will be a bit like that, but I would sooner be in New Zealand even if the lift is poor!" As it happened, Mick arrived with Hugh and Anthony in November 1967 and Patience arrived with Andrew in the following February. "I had been away for nearly twenty-seven years, apart from three brief visits, and oh boy was I glad to put my feet on my own ground!"

EPILOGUE

A STORY THAT MIGHT HELP

"I now know", wrote Mick Ensor, "that I drank because I am an alcoholic." He has no wish to hide this fact and does not flinch from that harsh (but accurate) word. Indeed, he much prefers it to some bland phrase used instead. Neither discreet words nor silence will eliminate the fact that Mick did suffer from this disease. It is a part of his life. One officer with whom Mick served in Malta has written: "I think it would be quite wrong to air the events of that time—they contribute some black humour, as the activities of alcoholics often do—but they serve only to reduce a reputation and blur a proud image.... From the Kinloss to Malta days, I think you will find nothing but fearsome tippling tales and, as I have said, this sad period were best forgotten." No useful purpose would be served by recording those events, but Mick hopes that an account of his eventual recovery from them may be valuable. "If my story could help just one other person, God would want it published and who am I to object?"

The experience of dredging up details about his past has helped him, he says, to realise "that I was a pig-headed and selfish individual who could not accept not getting his own way, nor could I accept that a service career called for much more than a love affair with aeroplanes and the people who understand them." There is, of course, much truth in this typically blunt self-assessment. However, it is also true that Mick's record consistently shows him anxiously concerned about his children's education and about how he might one day employ his hard-earned aviation experience to help his brothers in New Zealand.

Mick is convinced that an alcoholic makes a fatal mistake if he (or she) "starts making excuses about his frustrations, circumstances or associations because if he does he is liable to think he will be able to drink normally if these change. He can't, any more than a diabetic can talk himself out of being a diabetic. I will admit that sometimes circumstances can accelerate these diseases, but once established, there is no way of changing the victim's physical make-up." In Mick's opinion, "a spiritual revival is essential. Anything else—or less—fails in the long run and 'continuation training', particularly with Alcoholics Anonymous, is essential for a happy life. Any damned fool can stop drinking for a while, but the disease is progressive and each return bout of drinking will be worse than the last."

A perceptive article on alcoholism appeared in *Time* magazine on 30 November 1987. "There is only one thing wrong with it," Mick thought, and that was "the search for a miracle cure." Drugs mentioned in the article have been tried and some are still being used. "All that happens is that the victim very soon becomes addicted to them because they are essentially a *substitute* for alcohol and their long-term side effects are very bad. The RAF put me on them and it was fifteen years before I had another drink. At the time, it was believed there were no side effects to Librium or Valium. They also told me that I was not an alcoholic; I just drank too much and might eventually be able to drink normally."

Many alcoholics have fallen into what Mick calls "this trap", kidding themselves that one day they might be able to enjoy a few drinks without causing harm either to themselves or those close to them. Mick had been one of those fools and was still associated with some. "There we were, with a *double* addiction: and a pill plus a drink does not equal two, it is more like five. I nearly died, but I guess I have a strong survival instinct and when I at last found out what I was really fighting, I got to work with the unstinting help of AA friends to beat and re-start my life on a totally new basis. It is a mistake to look for a soft answer where, as any really recovered alcoholic will testify, there is none. Suffering is an essential element of recovery and to cushion it with drugs is to invite a relapse that will be far worse than the original state. AA is successful, but it is tough. People who keep with it seldom fail—and now we also try to absorb drug addicts who really want to change their ways because alcohol is just another drug."

Mick was only too well aware that someone with "a drinking problem" is the last to admit it. He himself denied it or explained it away or became angry at such an unkind aspersion upon his legitimate relaxation, his private affairs "or whatever other justification for getting tight that I could think of." Eventually, he saw himself as his family and friends had seen him for years. "Usually, the only people an alcoholic will listen to are other alcoholics. Even then, alcoholics have to come to terms with God, as they understand Him, and carry on with the AA programme for living with His help. In this way, not only can a much better life be found, but a whole new one. Alcoholism is now recognised as a disease and, like diabetes, cannot ever be cured. But it can be lived with, happily. I had an unhappy time for years— not drinking, even—largely because the RAF medics told me I was not an alcoholic." They may well have done that, he now realises, out of kindness or to protect his pension. In 1982, Mick's resolve never to drink again cracked. He persuaded himself that he could handle a few social rounds and soon learned that he could not. "That was when I really found out that I had a disease. Once I knew that, I was able to recover and experience a whole new world."

In late 1982, Mick recalled, he asked his doctor whether he might safely resume drinking. He was prescribing Valium for Mick at that time and merely said that alcohol could damage his liver. "He should have read the riot act, but had he done so I would still have been living a half life on Valium." Instead, about a year later, Mick had to be admitted to a Christchurch clinic, dangerously ill. "It was only then, after all those years, that I discovered what was wrong with me. Ill as I was, the lectures and discussions triggered some response in my wretched mechanical brain and aroused my natural curiosity. There was no 'soft sell' drug treatment there; most of the senior staff were recovered alcoholics and they knew the score. After three months in the clinic, I had become indoctrinated with AA: 'if you don't get AA, AA will get you.' I would add: 'if you have any sense.'"

Heather Dalton White (Patience's cousin and godmother to David, the Ensor's eldest son) had been in regular contact with the family "in the good times", when they lived at Orger's Farm in Essex, and stayed with them in Malta, "when poor Mick's drinking was at its height; of course it affected all the family, as alcoholism is bound to do." It was, she said, "desperately sad to see such a hero, who had done so much for his country, being rather ignored, though Patience stayed stoic and calm throughout." Heather was sure that Mick only took to drink long after the war, when he was unable to fly regularly and became "an also man", seeing so many contemporaries easily managing the transition from cockpit to desk that was so difficult for him. Who can say what part, if any, his wartime experiences played in all this? Others coped, he didn't. "All very sad," she concluded, "for one who had been so appreciated when guts and courage were required, but to his lasting credit he tackled and beat the disease."[1]

In Mick's opinion, his "great victory over addiction" is worth all the

---

[1] Letter, Dalton White to Spooner, 28 March 1988.

rest of his career put together. In black moods, he finds it difficult to rid himself of the feeling that he has been a failure, personally and professionally, but in better moods he knows that not all his landings were bad ones. He has an equally strong feeling that "if I really want to do something I can do it. I usually win if I know what I am fighting. With RAF career matters, I did not really know. I seem to have a strange streak that drives me in certain directions with intense energy. When I was an aircraft captain with the US Navy, I was once called an 'eager beaver'. Perhaps I just have to see results from my efforts; the demands of the peacetime service were beyond my grasp—or patience."

"Deep down", he wrote, "I did not feel capable of being a good station commander; I am simply not the type. Of course, it would have meant promotion, but subconsciously at least my great desire was to do constructive aviation and this was not compatible with 'career prospects' and a lot of other things." Eventually, the psychiatrists at Wroughton—"my final resting place"—suggested that he simply did not like what he was doing, staff work, and labelled him temperamentally unstable. "They were right in that I *hated* the type of work that I was trying to do in Malta—and I did try to do it. While at Wroughton, I wrote a long report to the Senior Air Staff Officer in Malta about a number of aspects of staff work there and I heard later that some of my recommendations had been acted on." From Wroughton, Mick went on "a splendid physical rehabilitation course at Maddingley Hall where I met some old chums and got quite fit."

Pat Green confessed that he "was not really surprised" when Mick told him that he would not be promoted beyond the rank of Wing Commander. "Something he said to me earlier rather sums it up: 'I never wanted to be a station commander, having to deal with all that sort of stuff.' If he had become a station commander, I am sure he would have done his very best, but his heart would not have been in it. His world was aeroplanes, their weapons systems and the job to be done and he would put every ounce of energy, all his skill and knowledge, his experience and dedication into that job—and sometimes become a bit of a bore in the process!" A good station commander certainly cares about aeroplanes, "but it was all the other requirements of the job that Mick disliked." In retrospect, Pat thought it a great pity that Mick accepted a permanent commission in the RAF instead of joining BOAC after the war. On the other hand, Mick excelled in the appointments he was given for *eight years* after the war: in Transport Command, in the Berlin Airlift, in the US Navy and in command of a Neptune squadron. And for six years thereafter, the

RAF offered him every opportunity to discover whether or not he had it in him to excel in other capacities. Finally, when he collapsed, the RAF did its best to cure him and then eased him back into the civilian world with his public reputation undamaged.

During 1968, after his return to New Zealand, the Ensor family re-organised its financial relations. Mick ceased to have other than an emotional bond to Double Hill, one that will last his lifetime. He was not a farmer, never had been and forty-six was no age to begin. But he loved the outdoors. One day, while he was visiting Double Hill, Lou Ensor (Peter's wife) suggested that he use his big diesel Land Rover to take tourists or hunting parties into the Canterbury high country. Such was the beginning of *Erewhon Courier Services, Ltd.*, "which was", says Mick, "fun and unrewarding (financially) until 1974, when we showed a profit." He established good contacts with others in the transport and tourist industries and particularly enjoyed taking parties of school children far from the beaten track, into country that he had himself loved deeply when he was a boy.

As for Patience, she had lived in numerous homes during almost a quarter of a century and had been required at regular intervals to hand over her 'permanent' home at Orger's Farm to a succession of more or less unsatisfactory tenants. The pressure of Mick's alcoholism, his discontent with his career from 1958 onwards and the various agitations provided by four sons tested her resilience to the utmost. She actually returned once to England. Fortunately, her enjoyment of the active life—playing tennis, riding horses and above all sailing her own boat—enabled her to settle contentedly at Diamond Harbour, opposite the port of Lyttelton, where all those pleasures were available in abundance. She made a home that was, at long last, genuinely permanent. She had plenty of agreeable company; sons who were thriving; and a husband happily occupied. Tragically, she fell ill with cancer in early 1975 and died in October, aged fifty-four. Heather Dalton White wrote that Patience was at first "rather tentative about New Zealand, but felt it offered a future for the three younger boys and went prepared to see how things turned out. I know they were very happy and until Pat's tragic illness and death, were thoroughly enjoying life."

"When Patience became ill," wrote Mick, "I remained at home to look after her and, believe it or not, the chap who was the only regular number two in my little business cut his hand badly in a chainsaw and could not keep it going on my behalf. After Patience died, I tried to recover things, but it did not seem worthwhile and I sold the working part of the company, retaining the investment part. Having more or less enough to live on, I decided to live that way. Patience and I had a nice yacht, a twenty-five-foot keeler (she was really the keen 'yachtie', but I enjoyed it). I did quite a lot of sailing, but maintaining the yacht was a tie and interfered with my trout fishing, so after two or three years I sold it too. After giving up the tour business, I gave up private flying. Really, I did not have a great deal of zest for life during those years." He recovered some of his zest in the eighties, after his last brush with alcohol and as his sons married and began to have families of their own. He took up again a boyhood hobby, one that he had occasionally indulged during the years since: making and flying model aircraft. "Learning to fly these," he claims, "has been much more difficult and nerve-wracking than a real one—even a Hunter!"

Countless books have been published about the stirring deeds of men in wartime, especially since 1918. Few have much to say about the after-life, in peacetime, of those men. No doubt most resumed their old occupations or followed up new prospects, untroubled by any ghosts in their private closets, for *homo sapiens* is an infinitely resilient creature. However, Mick is not unique in suffering delayed damage as a result of exceptional strain. In particular, he was deeply affected (more deeply than he would for many years admit even to himself) by the sudden and cruelly painful death of so many contemporaries, all young men with much to live for; laughing together one day, gone for ever the next. Also, in Mick's case, he endured the prolonged anxieties of operations against a clever and ruthless opponent. He was often flying far out to sea and therefore at the mercy of powerful, unpredictable natural forces that kill men as readily as any human enemy. And Mick had the constant knowledge that other men's lives depended upon his actions.

Mick's frankness about his alcoholism drew these comments from his friend, Archdeacon Alan McKenzie, Assistant to the Anglican Bishop of Christchurch. "No-one who knows Maechel personally could take any exception to what is written, whereas those who may have similar difficulties could find it very helpful and wise. It reflects the honesty of someone who has had to face excessive stress and danger and uses this particular prop to help him overcome." McKenzie concluded, in words with which the present author would also like to conclude, that we see in Mick's constant endeavour "an account of personal courage in the face of physical and spiritual danger, expressed with restraint and humility."

APPENDIX

Mick Ensor's Wartime Operational Record

In 500 Squadron

	Date	Aircraft	Crew	Duration
1.	15 Aug 41	Blenheim IV MK-D	Sgts. Paige, Roe	4h 30m day

Search. Located dinghy three times. Failed to locate motor boat.

	Date	Aircraft	Crew	Duration
2.	11 Sep 41	Blenheim IV MK-V	Same	2h 40m day

Anti-shipping patrol.

| 3. | 17 Sep 41 | Blenheim IV MK-T | Same | 1h 30m day; 4h night |

Night strike St. Nazaire. Four 250-lb bombs dropped on target area.

| 4. | 14 Oct 41 | Blenheim IV MK-W | Sgts. Paige, Prior | 2h 50m day |

Search. Landed Manston.

| 5. | 21 Oct 41 | Blenheim IV MK-X | Same | 4h 30m day |

Search.

| 6. | 26 Oct 41 | Blenheim IV MK-W | Sgts. Paige, Roe | 2h 30m day |

Strike. Nothing sighted.

| 7. | 27 Oct 41 | Blenheim IV MK-Z | Sgts. Paige, Prior | 2h 30m day |

Search.

| 8. | 30 Oct 41 | Blenheim IV MK-S | Sgts. Paige, Roe | 1h day; 3h 10m night |

Dawn Nomad. Bombed small ship & machine-gunned it. Bombs missed. Sighted fighters.

| 9. | 2 Nov 41 | Blenheim IV MK-S | Same | 3h 10m day; 50m night |

Dawn strike to Langeoog Island. No convoy sighted. Flew down coast to Texel under cloud.

| 10. | 15 Jan 42 | Hudson III MK-P | Sgts. Paige, Emberson, Wandon | 3h 35m day |

Search for dinghy.

| 11. | 29 Jan 42 | Hudson III MK-W | Sgts. Paige, Roe, Prior | 5h 5m night |

Nomad to Sylt. Bombed & hit 900 ton ship. Struck rock and wrecked right engine. Gyro direction indicator u/s. ASI u/s. All electrical gear u/s on 24v circuit. Got lost over Holland for half hour. Much AA fire. Struck violent snow storm on way home. Forced-landed in field near Winterton by the light of Very lights fired off by observer.

| 12. | 13 Feb 42 | Hudson MK-M | Sgts. Roe, Prior
[plus one] | 3h 50m day |

Search. Nothing sighted. [The Hudson mark is not indicated here or below.]

| 13. | 16 Feb 42 | Hudson MK-M | F/Sgt. Paige,
Sgts. Roe, Prior | 3h 30m day; 1h 30m night |

Reconnaissance. North Danish coast. Thick fog in patrol area.

| 14. | 19 Feb 42 | Hudson MK-A | P/O Atkinson,
Sgts. Roe, Prior | 1h 20m day |

Reconnaissance. Returned owing to insufficient cloud cover.

| 15. | 24 Feb 42 | Hudson MK-Q | P/O Atkinson,
Sgts. White, Prior | 4h 20m day |

Recco. Heligoland, North Denmark.

| 16. | 26 Feb 42 | Hudson III MK-T | P/O Atkinson,
Sgts. Wood, Prior | 3h night |

Nomad. Returned owing to very low clouds & snow & engine trouble.

| 17. | 28 Feb 42 | Hudson III MK-Q | P/O Atkinson,
Sgts. Roe, Prior | 4h 20m day |

Search for 221 Squadron Wellington.

| 18. | 13 Mar 42 | Hudson MK-M | Same | 2h day; 1h night |

Nomad. Ijselmuiden, Terschelling.

| 19. | 15 Mar 42 | Hudson MK-Q | Same | 4h 40m night |

X-patrol, North Sea.

| 20. | 26 Mar 42 | Hudson MK-V | Same | 6h 10m day |

Atlantic anti-sub sweep.

| 21. | 31 Mar 42 | Hudson MK-Q | Same plus P/O
Barrell | 5h 30m day |

Atlantic anti-sub sweep. Convoy met. Twenty-four merchant vessels with escort.

| 22. | 9 Apr 42 | Hudson MK-Q | Same less P/O
Barrell | 5h 10m day |

Anti-sub sweep (Atlantic) to 16 degrees west.

| 23. | 10 Apr 42 | Hudson MK-N | Same | 5h day; 1h night |

Anti-sub sweep.

| 24. | 25 Apr 42 | Hudson MK-Q | Same | 4h 35m day |

Anti-sub sweep.

| 25. | 27 Apr 42 | Hudson MK-Q | Same | 7h 35m day |

Anti-sub sweep. Large ocean-going sub sighted & attacked with machine-gun & four x 250-lb depth charges. Claim damage.

| 26. | 18 May 42 | Hudson MK-M | Same | 3h 45m day; 1h night |

Anti-sub sweep.

| 27. | 20 May 42 | Hudson MK-M | Same | 3h 35m day; 2h night |

Anti-sub sweep.

| 28. | 22 May 42 | Hudson MK-M | Same plus Wg.Cdr.
Spotswood | 5h day |

Anti-sub sweep.

| 29. | 24 May 42 | Hudson MK-M | Same less Wg.Cdr.
Spotswood | 6h day |

Anti-sub sweep.

| 30. | 29 May 42 | Hudson MK-S | Same | 5h 30m day |

Anti-sub sweep.

31.	5 Jun 42	Hudson MK-S	Same	4h 30m day; 1h night
	Anti-sub sweep.			
32.	7 Jun 42	Hudson MK-S	P/O Atkinson,	5h 45m day
			Sgts. Fugel, Prior	
	Anti-sub sweep.			
33.	10 Jun 42	Hudson MK-S	Same	4h 55m day
	Anti-sub sweep.			
34.	14 Jun 42	Hudson MK-H	Same	5h 30m day
	Anti-sub sweep.			
35.	18 Jun 42	Hudson MK-S	P/O Atkinson,	5h 30m day
			Sgts. Roe, Prior	
	Anti-sub sweep.			
36.	1 Jul 42	Hudson MK-V	Same	6h day
	Anti-aircraft escort to HMS *Renown* and 3 destroyers.			
37.	4 Jul 42	Hudson MK-T	P/O Atkinson,	7h 10m day
			Sgts. Roe, Pearce	
	Convoy escort.			
38.	6 Jul 42	Hudson MK-S	P/O Atkinson,	7h day
			Sgts. Roe, Prior	
	Anti-sub sweep. Sighted & attacked U-boat with four depth charges.			
	Attack good & 300 rounds of machine-gun fired at conning tower.			
39.	10 Jul 42	Hudson MK-S	Same plus P/O	5h 20m day
			Morley	
	Sweep.			
40.	11 Jul 42	Hudson MK-S	Same less P/O	5h 50m day
			Morley	
	Sweep.			
41.	3 Aug 42	Hudson MK-S	Sgts. Robinson,	5h 50m day
			Roe, Prior	
	Anti-sub sweep.			
42.	5 Aug 42	Hudson MK-R	Same plus P/O	5h day; 55m night
			Barrell	
	Anti-sub sweep.			
43.	9 Aug 42	Hudson MK-U	P/O Evans, Sgts.	6h 40m day
			Entwhistle, Roe, Prior	
	Anti-sub sweep. Flora.			
44.	11 Aug 42	Hudson MK-Y	Sgts. Entwhistle,	5h 30m day
			Roe, Prior, Blankley	
	Anti-sub sweep. Rain & low cloud all the way.			
45.	13 Aug 42	Hudson MK-S	P/O Short, Sgts.	6h 40m day
			Roe, Prior	
	Convoy escort.			
46.	18 Aug 42	Hudson MK-U	P/Os Lomas, Dyke,	6h 30m day
			Sgts. Roe, Prior	
	Escort to US forces.			
47.	19 Aug 42	Hudson MK-U	P/O Dyke, Sgts.	6h 5m day
			Roe, Prior,	
			F/Sgt. Greenock	
	Anti-sub sweep.			

| 48. | 20 Aug 42 | Hudson MK-N | Same less F/Sgt. Greenock | 6h 20m day; 1h night |

Anti-sub sweep. Tried to round up dispersed convoy.

| 49. | 23 Aug 42 | Hudson MK-V | Same | 5h 40m day |

Anti-sub sweep.

| 50. | 24 Aug 42 | Hudson MK-A | Same | 5h 40m day |

Anti-sub sweep. Sighted 500 ton U-boat from 5,000 feet. Made low level attack with four depth charges while U-boat was submerging. Direct hit with No. 2 twenty feet ahead of conning tower. Ninety feet of stern rose to an angle of 50 degrees & then sank. Very large oil patch seen five minutes later.

| 51. | 27 Aug 42 | Hudson MK-S | P/O Atkinson, Sgts. Roe, Prior | 6h 40m day |

Anti-sub sweep. Very bad conditions.

| 52. | 1 Sep 42 | Hudson MK-W | Same | 6h 30m day |

Search for damaged U-boat off Spanish coast. Saw one Ju 88.

| 53. | 4 Sep 42 | Hudson MK-W | Same plus Sgt. Butler | 6h 20m day |

Anti-sub sweep in Bay.

| 54. | 5 Sep 42 | Hudson MK-W | Same | 7h day |

Search for U-boat near French coast.

| 55. | 7 Sep 42 | Hudson MK-W | Same less Sgt. Butler | 6h 30m day |

Anti-sub sweep.

| 56. | 9 Sep 42 | Hudson MK-J | Same | 4h 30m day; 1h 30m night |

Anti-sub sweep.

| 57. | 10 Sep 42 | Hudson MK-R | Same | 5h day |

Fishery patrol.

| 58. | 18 Sep 42 | Hudson MK-V | Same plus Flt.Sgt. Merry | 6h 30m day |

Search for Flt.Sgt. Smith & crew.

| 59. | 5 Nov 42 | Hudson MK-S | Same less Flt.Sgt. Merry | 7h 20m day |

Portreath to Gibraltar.

| 60. | 7 Nov 42 | Hudson MK-S | Same | 6h 40m day |

Anti-sub sweep from Gibraltar. U-boat sighted.

| 61. | 8 Nov 42 | Hudson MK-S | Same | 6h 30m day |

Base to Oran. Patrol covering landing of troops.

| 62. | 9 Nov 42 | Hudson MK-S | Same | 6h 30m day |

Oran patrol.

| 63. | 11 Nov 42 | Hudson MK-S | Same | 6h 30m day |

Gibraltar to Tafaraoui aerodrome, near Oran. Convoy escort.

| 64. | 12 Nov 42 | Hudson MK-S | Same | 6h day |

Anti-sub sweep. Attacked [Fiat B.R.20 Cicogna] Iti bomber. Hits seen on starboard engine and fuselage. Smoke seen from starboard engine.

| 65. | 13 Nov 42 | Hudson MK-S | Same | 6h day |

Anti-sub sweep. Attacked U-boat with four depth charges just after it submerged. Damaged U-boat surfaced and manned machine-gun on conning tower. We shot them up with our guns until out of ammunition, leaving several of gun crew dead and wounded. U-boat last seen down at the bows and making little headway (this may be the one that beached on 14 Nov). [It was not. That one was *U595*; Mick's victim was *U458*.]

66. 15 Nov 42   Hudson MK-S   Same   2h day

Attack on U-boat. No. 2 depth charge direct hit, causing U-boat to explode. Own aircraft suffered following damage: elevators blown off, rudders blown off, six feet of each wing bent up, all windows blown in. Flew to Algiers, but port engine cut over harbour and we jumped from 1,500 feet. P/O Atkinson and Sgt. Prior killed. Sgt. Roe and self picked up by destroyer.

67. 24 Nov 42   Hudson MK-X   F/L Holmes,   6h 50m night
                                    Sgt. Roe

Gibraltar to Portreath.

In 224 Squadron

68. 3 Sep 43   Liberator VH   F/O Thorpe,   8h 45m day; 2h 30m night
                                    F/L Morley,
                                    Sgts. Saywell,
                                    Ibbotson, Frayne,
                                    Smolenski, Beck,
                                    Phillips

Anti-sub patrol, Bay of Biscay.

69. 7 Sep 43   Liberator VD   As above, except 8h 10m day; 3h night
                                    F/O Caldwell for
                                    F/L Morley

Anti-sub patrol, Bay of Biscay. Diverted to hunt for U-boat. No luck.

70. 11 Sep 43   Liberator VIII T   Same   8h 5m day; 3h 30m night

Anti-sub sweep & reconnaissance of Ferrol harbour. Nothing peculiar seen. Two depth charges dropped on sea marker for practice.

71. 17 Sep 43   Liberator D   Crew & Sgt. Dawson   4h day; 8h night

Anti-sub patrol, Bay of Biscay. [The Liberator mark is not indicated here or below.]

72. 21 Sep 43   Liberator U   Same   4h day; 7h 30m night

Anti-sub patrol.

73. 25 Sep 43   Liberator M   Same   11h 30m day

Anti-sub patrol.

74. 2 Oct 43   Liberator M   P/O Denny & crew 11h 10m day

Anti-sub patrol in Bay. Homed on a contact from nineteen miles. Lost contact at four miles and found nothing.

75. 7 Oct 43   Liberator H   Sgt. Ashworth &   7h 10m day; 4h night
                                    crew

Anti-sub patrol. Sighted one Ju 88 and two unidentified aircraft. Turned west for fifteen minutes and lost contact with enemy aircraft.

76. 10 Oct 43   Liberator M   Same   12h day; 3h 10m night

Convoy: 42 degrees North, 20 West. One and a half hours with convoy. Sighted and attacked with eight rocket projectiles a submarine, 48 and a half degrees North, 11 West. Turned out to be French ["one hit" added later, with note at foot of page: "alteration certified correct, M. A. Ensor, S/L"]. Bomb bay transfer u/s, so landed with ninety gallons available.

77. 16 Oct 43   Liberator G   Same   5h 20m day

Ballykelly to Reykjavik after instruction in rocket projectile dives.

78. 22 Oct 43   Liberator G   Same plus three   6h day
     Meek's Field (Iceland) to Ballykelly.

79. 23 Nov 43   Liberator P   P/O Dawson & crew   10h day; 4h night
     Anti-sub patrol.

80. 23 Dec 43   Liberator A   Same   2h 10m day;
                                                                 11h night

     Anti-sub patrol.

81. 27 Dec 43   Liberator A   Same   8h day;
                                                                 4h 30m night

     Search for blockade runner.

82. 1 Jan 44   Liberator X   Same   12h 45m night
     Search for blockade runner.

83. 5 Jan 44   Liberator A   Same   1h day; 12h
                                                                 35m night
     Take-off for ops, but No. 4 petrol cap loose, so landed immediately with full load.
     Off again. Night anti-sub patrol to Spanish coast and in Bay. Obtained one contact,
     but found nothing.

84. 13 Jan 44   Liberator P   Same   2h day; 11h
                                                                 20m night
     Anti-sub patrol. Obtained one contact thirty miles north of Spanish coast. Homed to
     four miles, but lost contact. Lit up estimated position, but found nothing. Sighted a
     suspicious twin-engined aircraft near La Coruna.

85. 20 Jan 44   Liberator D   Same   3h day; 10h
                                                                 5m night
     Anti-sub search west of Ireland. Very rough.

86. 6 Mar 44   Liberator A   F/O Liddle, F/Sgts.   3h day; 10h
                                        Saywell, Mount & crew   30m night
     Anti-sub patrol off Spain. Looking for Japanese submarine.

87. 10 Mar 44   VLR Liberator E   Same plus   11h 30m day;
                                        P/O Greenfield   4h night
     Convoy escort. Convoy met and R/T communication established without trouble.

88. 2 Apr 44   Liberator C   F/Os Liddle,   4h 20m day
                                        Tye, Pugh
                                        F/Sgts. Saywell,
                                        Frayne, Smolenski,
                                        Beck, Phillips &
                                        Ashworth
     Daylight reconnaissance of French coast from Brest Peninsula south. Two enemy
     aircraft contacted. Returned early owing to lack of cloud cover.

89. 12 Apr 44   Liberator S   Wg.Cdr. McComb   4h 30m day;
                                        & crew   9h night
     Anti-sub patrol. Several contacts investigated. All fishing boats.

90. 28 May 44   Liberator C   F/Os Andrews, Tate,   6h 40m day;
                                        Pugh, F/Ls Addington,   6h night
                                        Carter, P/O Muir,
                                        F/Sgts. Owen,
                                        Cockeram, Sgt. Moses

91. 7 Jun 44   Liberator S   Same except   8h day; 2h
                                    Sgt. Plummer   30m night
                                    for F/Sgt. Owen

'Cork' patrol. Five times from Scillies to Brest Peninsula. Sighted and attacked one U-boat at 00.15 hours. Considerable flack, but own front gunnery good. Bombs slight undershoot.

92. 11 Jun 44 Liberator VI K   Same   5h day; 5h
                                                       30m night

'Cork' patrol. Saw one aircraft shot down fifty miles west of Brest.

93. 15 Jun 44 Liberator VA   Same   7h 40m day;
                                                       6h night

'Cork' patrol. Very little seen.

94. 20 Jun 44 Liberator VI K   Same   7h day; 4h night

'Cork' patrol. Flak from Ushant.

95. 24 Jun 44 Liberator VY   Same   7h day; 3h 30m night

'Cork' patrol. Watched survivors of U-boat being picked up by a destroyer.

96. 29 Jun 44 Liberator VI K   Same   7h 10m day

'Cork' patrol. Recalled.

97. 5 Jul 44   Liberator K   Same except   5h day;
                                    F/Sgt. Evans   6h night
                                    for F/O Andrews

'Cork' (G) patrol.

98. 10 Jul 44 Liberator K   Same   8h 45m day
                                                       2h night

'Cork' (G) patrol.

99. 4 Aug 44   Liberator M   Same except   8h day;
                                    F/O Andrews   2h 10m night
                                    for F/Sgt. Evans

Escort.

100. 8 Aug 44   Liberator X   Same   6h 25m day;
                                                       4h 35m night

Patrol off Bordeaux.

101. 18 Aug 44 Liberator O   Same   2h 55m day;
                                                       7h 30m night

Anti-sub patrol.

102. 18 Sep 44 Liberator [ ]   Same   2h 30m day;
                                                       8h night

Patrol off Trondheim. Shot up by U-boat. Returned early because of damage to aircraft.

103. 20 Sep 44 Liberator Q   Same   1h 30m day;
                                                       8h night

Patrol (Stattlandet). Shocking weather.

104. 24 Sep 44 Liberator Q   Same   1h 30m day;
                                                       8h 10m night

Anti-sub patrol: Stattlandet.

105. 30 Sep 44 Liberator D   Same   6h 30m day;
                                                       6h 30m night

Anti-sub patrol off Norway.

106. 21 Oct 44 Liberator B   Same   2h day;
                                                       11h 5m night

Anti-sub ops, east Faeroes.

107.	28 Oct 44	Liberator B	Same	2h day; 11h night

Anti-sub ops, Norway.

108.	31 Oct 44	Liberator L	Same	3h day; 9h 30m night

Anti-sub ops, Norway.

109.	9 Nov 44	Liberator R	Same	1h day; 7h 10m night

Anti-sub ops, Skagerrak.

110.	14 Nov 44	Liberator T	Same	9h day; 3h 20m night

Anti-sub ops, off Norway.

111.	26 Nov 44	Liberator R	Same	8h day; 2h 15m night

Anti-sub ops, north Faeroes.

112.	9 Jan 45	Liberator V	Same except Wg.Cdr. McComb for F/O Andrews	4h day; 3h 50m night

Anti-sub patrol, Shetlands, Faeroes.

113.	12 Feb 45	Liberator T	Same except F/Lt Storey for Wg.Cdr. McComb	2h day; 8h 10m night

Patrol between Denmark and Sweden. Weather awful. Diverted to Middleton St. George.

114.	5 May 45	Liberator T	F/Os Hind, Smith & crew	8h 30m day

Daylight over Denmark. Attacked and sank one of four U-boats north of Zealand.

MAP ONE
THE SOUTH ISLAND OF NEW ZEALAND, 1922-1941

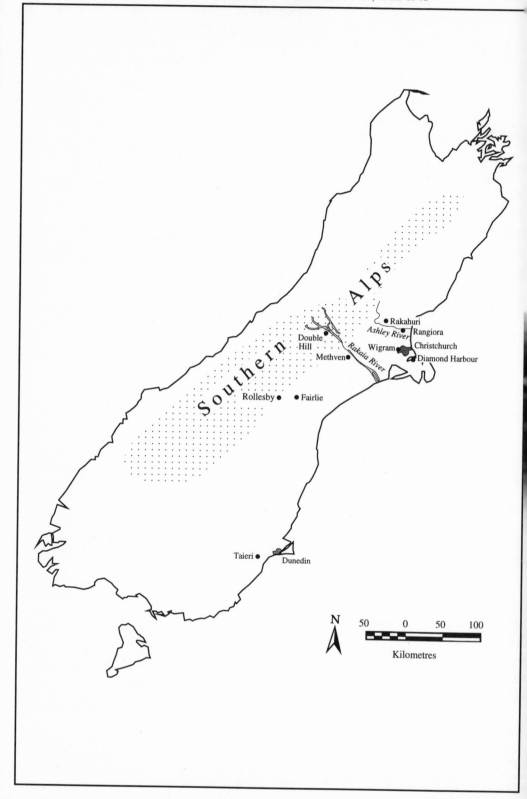

Southern Alps

• Rakahuri
Ashley River
Rangiora
Double Hill
Wigram ● Christchurch
Methven ● *Rakaia River* ● Diamond Harbour

Rollesby ● ● Fairlie

Taieri ● ● Dunedin

N

50   0   50   100

Kilometres

MAP TWO
PLACES WHERE MICK ENSOR SERVED 1941-1945

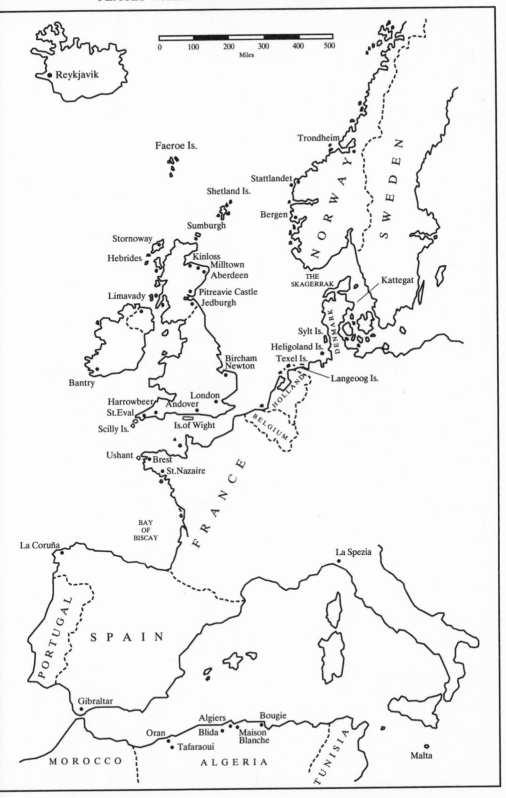

MAP THREE
THE BERLIN AIRLIFT, 1948-1949

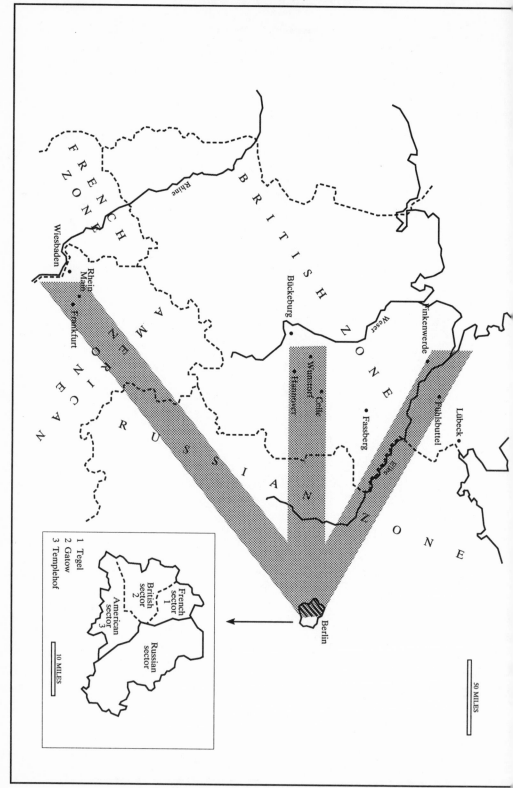

1 Tegel
2 Gatow
3 Templehof

French sector 1
British sector 2
American sector 3
Russian sector

10 MILES

50 MILES

FRENCH ZONE

BRITISH ZONE

AMERICAN ZONE

RUSSIAN ZONE

Rhine

Weser

Wiesbaden

Rhein
Main

Frankfurt

Bückeburg

Wunstorf

Celle

Hannover

Finkenwerde

Fassberg

Fuhlsbuttel

Lübeck

Berlin

Elbe

MAP FOUR
THE NORTH PACIFIC, 1949-1951

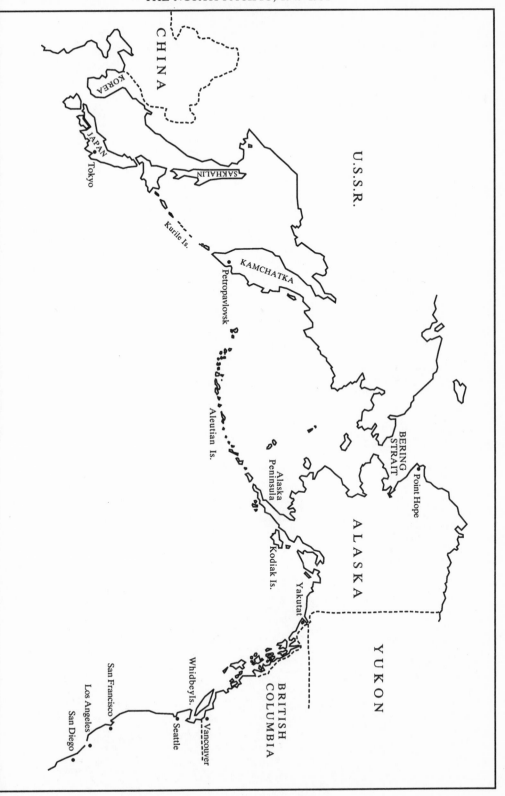

CHINA

KOREA

JAPAN

Tokyo

SAKHALIN

U.S.S.R.

Kurile Is.

KAMCHATKA

Petropavlovsk

Aleutian Is.

BERING STRAIT

Point Hope

Alaska Peninsula

Kodiak Is.

Yakutat

ALASKA

YUKON

San Francisco

Los Angeles

San Diego

Whidbey Is.

Seattle

Vancouver

BRITISH COLUMBIA